A PRINCESS FOUND

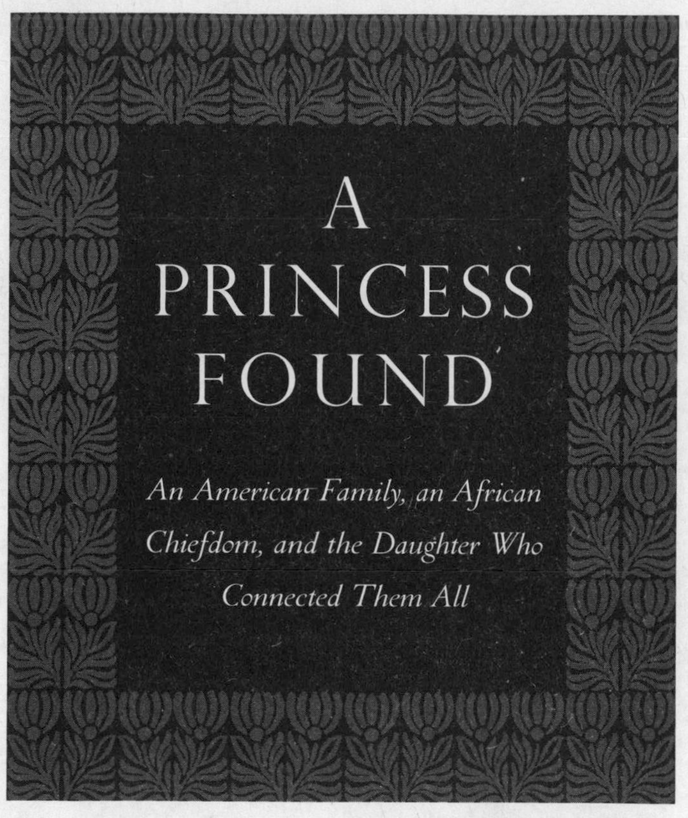

A PRINCESS FOUND

An American Family, an African Chiefdom, and the Daughter Who Connected Them All

SARAH CULBERSON

AND TRACY TRIVAS

 ST. MARTIN'S GRIFFIN NEW YORK

Printed in the United States of America. For information, address St. Martin's Press, 175 Fifth Avenue, New York, N.Y. 10010.

www.stmartins.com

Book design by Claire Naylon Vacoans

The Library of Congress has cataloged the hardcover edition as follows:

Culberson, Sarah.
A princess found / Sarah Culberson and Tracy Trivas. — 1st ed.
p. cm.
ISBN 978-0-312-37879-0
1. Culberson, Sarah. 2. Adopted children—United States—Biography. 3. Racially mixed people—United States—Biography. I. Trivas, Tracy. II. Title.
HV874.82.C85 2009
362.734092—dc22
[B] 2008046212

ISBN 978-0-312-62839-0 (trade paperback)

3 5 7 9 10 8 6 4 2

To my families in West Virginia
and West Africa

S.C.

To the women and children
of Sierra Leone

T.T.

Acknowledgments

My first thank-you goes to my friend and writing partner, Tracy Trivas, whose brilliance, persistence, and professionalism were essential to the creation of this book. Tracy's thought-provoking questions and insatiable curiosity captured the spirit of Bumpe's people and helped to make our journey together a remarkable one. Thank you to Tracy's husband, Alexander, and their family, for their guidance and support as we embarked on the birth of this book.

A book as personal as this one depends on incredible assistance from the people closest to me. I am deeply grateful to my mom and dad, Jim and Judy Culberson, for being my angels. Their wings of love always surround me. My sisters Lynne and Laura and their families—Mike, Jonathan, Austin, Spencer, Mackenzie, and Bryan—inspire me along with my large extended family. I am grateful to my boyfriend, Von, and his daughter, Hana, for their love, patience, and encouragement throughout the process of writing this book. Thanks to Aunt Fran, Uncle Paul, and my late Grandma Sarah, who cared lovingly for my late mother, Penny, and who opened their hearts to me. Thank you to my late birth mother, Penny, for her strength and love. You will always be in my heart.

This book would not have been written, nor would I be who I am today, without the special communities in my life. The first of these is my hometown of Morgantown, West Virginia. The community of my childhood—the schools, Wesley United Methodist Church, West Virginia University—was filled with loving friends, mentors, and teachers. I am grateful for the opportunities I have had to learn from so many dedicated teachers and professors in Morgantown as well as at the American Conservatory Theatre in San Francisco. I also want to thank the extraordinary fellow teachers, families, and students at Brentwood Middle School for their friendship and support. Thank you to Landmark Education for the programs that have opened my eyes to a new world of possibilities that I never imagined.

The entire story came to life because my birth father, Joseph Konia Kposowa, welcomed me into his world. I am deeply grateful to him and to all of my Leonean family. My father also connected me with new friends in Sierra Leone and with the students of Bumpe High School. He and many exceptional people in Sierra Leone, even after losing so much to a horrendous war, were able to convey their gracious spirit and affection to a long-lost daughter.

A special thanks to my Uncle Tibbie Kposowa, for his knowledge, of Sierran Leonean customs, exacting Mende translation, and boundless encouragement. Thank you to my uncles—Dr. Joe Francis Kposowa, for his help with photos and family history, and Dr. Augustine Kposowa, for his knowledge of Leonean history. I want to thank the many relatives and family friends who introduced me to Sierra Leonean customs and made me feel welcomed.

I would like to thank my agent, Mel Berger, for answering all of our many questions and for providing constant support and guidance. Thank you to our creative editor, Monique Patterson, for her interest in this story and for giving us the opportunity to write it. My sincere thanks to everyone at St. Martin's Press.

I want to thank the members of the Kposowa Foundation Board for several years of unceasing effort in service to the foundation's work in Bumpe.

I am especially grateful to John Woehrle, co-founder, for his tireless work in creating the Kposowa Foundation and for his friendship. Thank you to everyone who has supported the foundation. You are helping to make a difference in Sierra Leone and in the world.

Sarah Culberson

Greatest thanks to Sarah who unzipped her heart in hundreds of hours of interviews and had the courage to begin the journey. By confronting an unknown part of herself she journeyed to another continent emotionally and physically—and wildly expanded not just her own life, but also the lives of so many others. Thanks to Jim and Judy Culberson, who graciously allowed me access to their family letters, albums, and journals, and who greeted me with warmth whenever I called them—day or night—to answer the largest or smallest of questions. An extraordinary thanks to Joe Kposowa, who walked miles to the lone hill outside Bumpe with phone reception to take my calls. Standing in the darkness on his cell phone for hours, he answered my questions about his escape to Bo with honesty and dignity. Thanks to Dr. Tibbie Kposowa, Joe's brother and our Mende translator, who translated questions into both Mende and Krio, and who possesses an insider's knowledge of the cultural nuances and customs of the country. Thanks to Mel Berger at William Morris, and to Monique Patterson, our astute editor, who believed in the story from the start. Thank you to everyone at St. Martin's Press. Thanks to my friends who read the manuscript offering notes, especially to Kimberlee Ward, Todd, and Elaine. Thanks to John Woehrle for his profound insights about Sierra Leone. Thanks to Sarah's friends and family, who granted unlimited interviews. A posthumous thanks to Sarah's birth mother, Penny, who revealed her courage, sorrow, and grace through her written records. A giant thanks to my parents, Peter and Carol, and to my in-laws, Sam and Stephanie. A special thanks to Merly for all her help while I camped out in my office. For her constant love, humor, and inspiration, I am deeply grateful to Hadley. Most of all thanks to my husband, Alexander, for just about everything.

Tracy Trivas

Part One

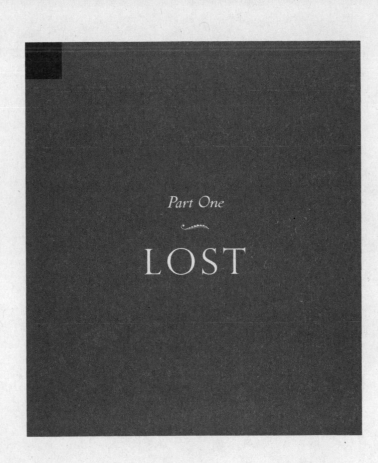

LOST

CHAPTER ONE

Bumpe, Sierra Leone
1994

Before the rebels attacked Joseph's village, they first sent in child spies. That was the way it was done—boys, ages 10–14, pretended to be lost, refugees, or orphans, but they were child soldiers with nicknames like "Commander Cut Hands," "Crazy Jungle," or "Captain Bloodie." For simple scout missions, their adult commanders did not waste precious drugs on the children, hallucinogens which revved them into fearless and brutal machines. Only later in the afternoon, when the rebels ordered the child soldiers to kill did they carve slits into the boys' young temples, pierce holes into their tender veins, and rub cocaine and "brown-brown" heroin into their raw wounds. Tape slapped across the incisions pressed the drugs deeper into their bloodstreams.

The child spies penetrated Bumpe, Joseph's village, at 1:30 P.M., right before lunchtime, acting only like boys. First they asked a passing villager, an African woman with a tin bucket on her head, for water.

"Mama, gi me wata," they said in Krio, the common language melded from the centuries of contact between the colonial British, freed slaves, and Africans.

"Ya de wata," she said, pouring water from her vessel.

"Tenki," they said.

Spying Joseph's well-used soccer ball in the yard, they even began a spontaneous game in the red dirt close to his home. A few boys wrestled. But soon the older boys trickled off, no longer soccer players but now morphed into moles, casing available supplies: sacks of rice, drums of water, mangoes, yams, dried fish, palm oil, and cassava leaves ready to be plucked from backyard patches. Next the population needed to be assessed: How many women? How many young girls ripe for sexual slavery—their ebony legs to be roped together at the ankles and gang-raped? How many new child soldiers could be "adopted and drafted" with the help of machetes, AK-47s, handheld RPGs (rocket-propelled grenades), and G3 automatic rifles?

On December 31, 1994, Joseph Konia Kposowa, forty-one-years old, a member of a ruling Mende family and the son of a great Paramount Chief, traveled to the neighboring village of Taninahun with his two children, five-year-old Hindogbae, and ten-year-old, Jeneba, for a holiday visit with his mother, Musu.

Although his full Christian name was Joseph, everyone in his village called him Joe, which was most fitting as he was a powerful man, worthy of a swift, one syllable name. Although not tall in stature, his presence was unmistakable as a leader in his village. Everyone in Bumpe considered Joe a "big man," a term villagers spoke in hushed tones about important people. Joe ran the prestigious Bumpe High School and took in seven children, besides his own son and daughter, to support and send to school.

The civil war that ravaged the country had not yet touched Joe's village or impacted his students. Although he and the village elders held meetings about the rebels, listening in silence around Joe's portable radio for war updates, no one believed the rebels could be so close—not yet.

When Joe, in his Toyota Hilux truck, left his wife and in-laws behind to continue the simple rituals of everyday life—weaving country cloth, preparing a lunch of rice, okra, and maybe even peanut soup—he had no particular worries. It was a simple day, a day off from teaching at the boarding school where he was the principal, a day not consulting or advising his brother who was campaigning for the position of Paramount Chief. Only royal family members could run for Paramount Chief, a position his grandfather held and his father, Francis Kposowa, held for thirty years, governing thirty-six thousand people.

But it was that afternoon the rebels chose for the first attack.

Joe's wife, Mary, busy working at home with her mother and younger sister, heard the heavy footsteps of men. A mass of soldiers marched forty feet from her window. Assuming the men were government soldiers, Mary dashed outside to thank them and offer them something to drink.

"Come to my house to drink water," she offered, beckoning with her hand.

The soldiers ignored her and kept on walking.

She returned to the house.

"Man's work," she assumed.

"Moiyatu!" she called to her beautiful, doe-eyed thirteen-year-old sister. "Run and tell Reverend Morlai the good news. Army men have come to help!"

Moiyatu ran off to the Reverend Morlai's house to deliver the message.

Minutes later two hundred rebels descended upon Bumpe. Joe's pet monkey, Little, screeched a shrill alarm. Mary heard the popping gunfire and ghastly screams of the villagers and darted straight out the backdoor into the bush. She left everything behind, including a simmering pot of rice on the fire. She sprinted into the forests; her mother, Kadie, trailed behind her.

Only now, as Mary pushed deeper and deeper into the bush, begging her elderly mother to move faster, did she realize the men she believed to be government soldiers were rebels.

Mary prayed for thirteen-year-old Moiyatu.

Running side-by-side along a bush path, Mary and her mother tore through elephant grasses and overgrown weeds. Snarled vegetation flanked the maze of dirt tributaries that linked many villages. Together they traveled eight miles until they reached the village of Balahun where they split up. Mary's mother refused to go any farther. Her feet, swollen and bruised from the sharp grasses needed rest. Mary kissed her mother good-bye. Until she reached her two children, Hindogbae and Jeneba, and her husband, she would not stop moving. Alone now with darkness falling, Mary continued the remaining seven miles to Taninahun. Blisters bubbled on her feet and splinters lodged under her toenails.

Breathless, shaking, unsteady from creeping low in the sun-beaten grasses, Mary reached Taninahun at midnight. Bursting through the door of Musu's home, she collapsed into Joe's arms. Covered in dust, sliced from the razor-edged weeds, Mary could not stop crying.

Back in Bumpe two hundred rebels looted homes, probing for new "recruits" and young girls to add to their junta as "rebel wives." The fifteen miles between Joe's family and the rebels left only a single night to make a decision—if even that much time remained. In Grandmother Musu's dark mud-brick home, plastered with cement and roofed with sheets of zinc, Joseph huddled with Mary and Musu as the children slept.

Mary begged her husband to go back to the village of Balahun for her mother, Kadie. When the sun rose, he promised he would jump into his truck, drive back to Balahun, and search for Kadie. As for Mary's younger sister, Moiyatu, there was nothing he could do. Driving to Bumpe under a rebel attack would be suicide. Joe stepped outside onto Musu's front porch. In the deep African night, listening for gunfire, he swore he could smell Bumpe burning in the distance.

Everyone knew the rebels carried kerosene in gallon cans or even in glass Coca-Cola bottles. That night, in Bumpe, they doused random homes with kerosene. Matches were struck against the houses, which soon blazed in a rapid ring of flames. Burning thatch crackled off the roofs. Forty-seven homes burned to the ground that night.

Joe's house was one of them.

Across the Atlantic, a lifetime away, Sarah Jane Culberson lay in her white canopy bed in West Virginia, staring up at the metal slats in the frame. Like most people living in America, she did not know about the rebels and their atrocities. In 1994, when she was eighteen years old she did not know her father was fighting to live through the night.

In fact, Sarah did not know her father.

CHAPTER TWO

Morgantown, West Virginia
1993–1994

Years ago, as a middle-school birthday present I received a mobile—a yellow satin moon with a bear sleeping on a cloud. Slowly it twirled above my head tied to the canopy frame. I never bothered to take it down. "Pleasant Dreams" was embroidered on the cloud. It seemed I should have been having sweet dreams; there would be no reason not to.

After all, it was homecoming weekend.

In Morgantown, a community of around thirty thousand people, homecoming was a town celebration. Parents bundled their children in bulky wool sweaters, twisted on knit scarves, and filled thermoses with hot chocolate—necessary endurance against the falling thirty-degree temperature. The vans, cars, and pickup trucks pulled into the parking lot behind the huge football stadium, and cars lined the neighboring streets as families raced toward the stands.

During University High's big game against Liberty High School, I shuffled into the high school football stadium with the ten other senior girls who had been elected to the homecoming court. Escorted to center field during halftime, decked in velvet and brocade skirt-suits, one of us would be crowned queen. We all should have been wrapped in jackets that evening, but we braved the weather for the ceremony, our outfits too pretty to cover.

With the cold blasting through our flimsy panty hose, gusts threatening to teeter us from the points of our high heels, we shivered. I was supposed to be wearing my leg brace, having shredded my knee in a varsity basketball scrimmage two months earlier, ripping my ligament in half, but my doctor gave me permission to take it off only for the ceremony.

Finally the band stopped playing. The principal stepped up to the microphone. "The second runner-up is . . . ," "The first runner-up is . . . ," boomed the loudspeaker, "and the new Homecoming Queen is . . . Sarah Culberson!"

My mouth hung open.

The flashbulbs exploded, hundreds of lights blinking from the stands. Friends and family waved, stamping the bleachers; a photographer from the local newspaper, *The Dominion Post*, bolted onto the field to take pictures.

With a giant bouquet placed in my hands, I hobbled off the field. My white, adoptive parents, Jim and Judy Culberson, rushed to congratulate me with hugs and kisses. Little girls in miniature homecoming dresses slid up to me wanting to have a photograph taken with me. Shocked that I had won instead of the girl who had been expected to win, I smiled at my friends, neighbors, and basketball teammates. Maybe all those years of reaching out and being friendly to my classmates counted for something.

I always made an effort to be kind to everybody because I knew how bad it felt when people were insensitive. Through the applause I scanned the bleachers, waving at my teachers, waving at my classmates, even waving at the woman who refused to let her son go out with me because I was half black. A girl with an unknown black father, a girl with an unknown white mother, adopted by a lovely, respected white family, *but still.*

In elementary school, I played house with some of my white friends at recess. Ellie wanted to be the mom; Hannah, the sister; Liz, the baby.

"I'll be Hannah's twin sister!" I said.

"No," they all replied in unison, "you can't."

"Why?" I asked confused.

"You don't match."

"Oh," I said and stopped playing.

In eighth grade, a friend of mine pushed me in front of a boy and said, "Hey, Greg, what did you say about voting for Sarah? Why wouldn't you vote for her?" Greg, stone-faced, refused to repeat to my face what he said to his friends: "I'm not voting for a black girl for student council president." Thankfully most of the rest of my class was color-blind. But in spite of the majority of friends, family, and community members who accepted me, color kept coming up.

Even as a one-year-old, the day I left foster care and arrived at my new home, a neighborhood child asked my older sister: "Is she black or does she just have a really good tan?"

Instead of black or white I felt like the brown girl who didn't match. But, I did everything I could to blend in and look like everyone else. My hairdresser spent hours trying to tame my Afro by slopping heavy, thick goops of cream onto my hair to straighten it. If she waited too long to wash the cream out, my scalp would burn. But when she finished, I had straight flowing hair—just like my older sisters and all my other friends. To me, my kinky hair was shameful and ugly.

Most of the time in my classes, I was the only non–white student. Never wanting to disappoint my adopted family, I somehow came to the conclusion that I must be the representative of all biracial and black people in my predominately white town.

Somewhere in another back pocket of memory, or still tingling in my cells from foster care, I knew how good I had it with my adopted family. Whatever happened, I wanted to be good enough so that the Culbersons with their two, older, biological daughters, would never send me back. Make them proud. Prove on the basketball court, on the stage, that I was worth adopting.

When I shared this with my mom, she laughed, hugged me, and said, "Honey, where is *back*?"

I buried myself in her arms and said, "I don't know. But I don't want to go there."

Adopted two days after my first birthday, it might seem strange this fear of *going back*. How can a one-year-old remember anything, much less the memories of an infant before her first birthday? And maybe children don't remember things, only feelings—a sensation of safety, or one of dread and abandonment.

I was convinced that people would judge the entire black race and every biracial child based on my behavior. I vowed to be unfailingly excellent and unfailingly likeable. Despite being elected junior class and student body president, I wasn't unfailingly likeable.

Sophomore year, one of the few black students at my high school spewed to my friends, "Sarah doesn't even know if she's black or white."

My anger at his comment only confirmed he was right. I didn't know.

CHAPTER THREE

Taninahun

Panic pummeled the village of Taninahun. People raced to gather belongings and supplies as the news spread: rebel soldiers were advancing toward Taninahun. Some villagers refused to pack, refused to leave; too many rebel rumors sparked false alarms. They would take their chances. Not Joe. He had heard too much.

One of the few men to own a portable radio in Bumpe, Joe would listen in the early morning to KISS-FM 104 and the BBC "Focus on Africa" reports of the war. Other villagers came over to gather around, listen, and share what they knew. Stories circulated of a farmer shot point-blank in his eardrums, his body found slumped over with a dead child still clutching his hand. Rebel soldiers skinned a man alive, flaying the skin off his forehead.

Joe had just returned from the ten-minute drive to Balahun where he found Mary's mother, Kadie. When Kadie heard the truck's motor, she ran to Joe's truck. Together they returned to Taninahun where the family waited to escape to the village of Matagelema.

But traps could be set along the unpaved roads. Snipers attacked daily. Ambushed by lurking rebels, many people were stopped at gunpoint, wrenched from their cars, and butchered. Teenage soldiers high on marijuana (*jambaa*) mixed with gunpowder residue, bursting with impunity behind their AK-47s, would force men to choose between life and raping their own sister or mother. Rebel soldiers commanded old men to dance, shooting at their legs like firecrackers until the elderly citizens dropped dead.

Led by Foday Sankoh, a former television cameraman and wedding photographer, the rebels called themselves the Revolutionary United Front, or the infamous RUF and sang out their battle cry:

RUF is fighting to save Sierra Leone
RUF is fighting to save our people
RUF is fighting to save our country
RUF is fighting to save Sierra Leone

Chorus: Go and tell the President, Sierra Leone is my home
Go and tell my parents, they may see me no more
When fighting in the battlefield I'm fighting forever
Every Sierra Leonean is fighting for his land

Where are our diamonds, Mr. President?
Where is our gold, NPRC?
RUF is hungry to know where they are
RUF is fighting to save Sierra Leone . . .

Our people are suffering without means of survival
All our minerals have gone to foreign lands
RUF is hungry to know where they are
RUF is fighting to save Sierra Leone . . .

Sierra Leone is ready to utilize her own
All our minerals will be accounted for
The people will enjoy in their land
RUF is the savior we need right now . . .

Despite the claims of saving Sierra Leone, the RUF movement soon warped into a barbaric campaign worse than any the country had previously endured.

Sierra Leone gained independence from the United Kingdom in 1961, with Sir Milton Margai as its prime minister. He led the nation until his death in 1964; his brother Sir Albert Margai then continued as the prime minister until 1967. From 1967 onward a series of coups destabilized the nation further until Shiaka Stevens emerged to hold power. His stewardship from 1968–1985 plunged the fledgling nation into an abyss of corruption, nepotism, tribalism, sectionalism, and subsequent instability. Steven's successor in the 1986 "election" was Joseph Saidu Momah. He further depleted the country with extravagant spending for elite party members; he undermined the regular army and police force by creating his own Internal Security Unit and impoverished a nation flush with mineral wealth and natural resources.

During Momah's tenure, the country continued in a rapid economic plunge, which created a perfect opportunity for depraved rebel bands to form. It also invited outside despots to fan civil unrest further and ignite rebel insurrections for their personal benefit. Civil war erupted in 1991.

In 1992, with firm support from the people, twenty-five-year-old Captain Valentine Strasser led his men in a successful coup to wrest control of the government until he, too, was ousted by another coup, which later helped Ahmed Tejan Kabbah win the 1996 popular election.

Charles Taylor, the President of Liberia, became the main outside "sponsor" of the RUF. In exchange for a share of Sierra Leone's diamond profits, he provided weapons, mercenaries, and drugs. The RUF did not have a clear political ideology, nor did they seem to truly desire a new government, only control of the mineral and diamond mines, which supplied much of their arms revenue.

One of the most prominent RUF military leaders was General Sam "Mosquito" Bockarie. A former nightclub dancer and beautician, he now transmorgrofied into a field commander. His Small Boys Unit, comprised of child soldiers, was one of the RUF's most brutal.

Along with seizing the country's diamond mines, the RUF vowed to punish the people of Sierra Leone for supporting Ahmed Kabbah, and voting for him in 1996. Chopping villagers' hands off to bloody stumps promoted terror and later served as the rebels' sinister response to the government's voting campaign slogan: "The future is in your hands."

Attempting to annihilate future voter turnout, the rebels simply amputated the offending limbs that dared to cast a vote. With an axe or machete poised, rebels would ask villagers if they wanted a *long sleeve* (amputated at the wrist) or *short sleeve* (chopped at the elbow or shoulder). Often rebels used the amputated hand to slap the victim. Human Rights Watch reported that after rebels hacked off a forty-year-old man's arms they said, "You go to Pa Kabbah and ask him for a new set of arms."

RUF soldiers could ascend in rank by presenting freshly severed hands, arms, or various body parts—lips, ears, and female and male genitalia—to their superiors. The sight of a bloody rice bag filled with hands was not uncommon. Many captured children, brainwashed into becoming these merciless mutilators, were themselves first strapped to boards as commanders carved the initials RUF into their skinny brown chests with filthy razors. Burning lime was rubbed into the wound to set the scar. Then if the child soldiers attempted to flee the RUF, the government soldiers who found the children would kill them for being traitors.

Joe slammed the door of his truck and made a pivotal decision. It was too dangerous to drive. Instead, the family had to walk. Joe led his mother, Musu; his wife, Mary; Mary's mother, Kadie; and Hindogbae and Jeneba, three-and-a-half miles on foot toward the tiny village of Matagelema, which sat closer to the bush. With only forty huts and small farms, maybe Matagelema would not be a seductive attraction to the hungry rebels. To protect his truck, Joe bid a driver he hired to hide his Toyota Hilux in the village of Ngiyeibgoiya, camouflaged behind the house of the village chief. When he gave the word, the driver would retrieve the vehicle.

Grandmother Musu carried five-year-old Hindogbae on her back.

Joe, afraid to reveal his fear, did not talk much along the path, only uttering comforting phrases like: "God will protect us" and "No hardship endures forever." If Joe and his family could reach Matagelema, they could add a few miles of life, a few miles of safety from the drugged soldiers. That morning he prayed that Baby Jenneh, his niece, was still alive and living in Matagelema. Although an adult, she possessed a quality of innocence that never left her face even at the age of thirty-two. She lived with her husband, Moriesana. They could have abandoned the village for the city of Bo, or they might still live in Matagelema and provide a safe house to keep Joe's family hidden.

As Joe trekked across the bush to Baby Jenneh's house, he prayed to God for protection. Bowing his head he also invoked the guidance of the *kekeni*—the ancestors in recent memory. Next he summoned the *ndeblaa*—the brave spirits of his forefathers, believed to be intermediaries between the living and God.

CHAPTER FOUR

Morgantown

Senior year of high school I wished to walk again. The single snap of my ACL, anterior cruciate ligament, back in early September had reduced me from a dribbler, a defender, and a dasher to a hobbler. In my immobilizer brace, my knee was cemented straight. A giant gash, cut down the center of my leg, revealed where doctors farmed part of my patellar tendon to replace my destroyed ligament. Overnight I became a brace wearer, a physical therapy–goer. Benched for the entire year. Without my golden knee ligament, I wasn't sure who I was exactly. The staple inside my knee ground against my connecting bones, making even a trip to the bathroom monumental. In physical therapy I'd submerge my entire leg into a pool of ice water to reduce the grapefruit swelling of my kneecap. Every time I dipped my leg, I swore my skin froze off and floated away in the water. Each time my brace was temporarily removed by nurses, my leg looked like a twelve-year-old's limb, shriveled grotesquely from lack of use.

It didn't strike me then to be grateful to my disobedient knee, a knee that had refused to move forward while the rest of my body chose a different direction. But my knee demanded I stop flying through the air, moving on for the next achievement, the next record, the next award. I wondered who I was without those titles.

Coincidence plucked that moment of my senior year for my humanities teacher, Mrs. Hammersmith, to screen a video on adoption. Watching the tape in class after homecoming was the second time that year I was laid flat, sprawled out, a mess.

The school elevator closed with a thud behind me. I fumbled for my two crutches, set them tight under my arms, ready for the long stretch of corridor before me. I shrugged my backpack evenly on both shoulders. My giant crutches seemed like broken oars, paddling through an endless corridor.

"Hey, Sarah," said a friend in the hall. "Congratulations on homecoming!"

"Thanks," I said forcing a smile as I shifted my backpack.

I passed three classroom doors, seven more to go until I reached my next class. The slick linoleum floor reflected like a black racetrack in front of me, polished smooth. A flat hundred meters. I would not go to the state track meet this year with my knee blown out or play in a single basketball game. My picture in *TEEN Magazine's* "Sportsgirl of the Year" section seemed like a joke. The second bell rang. The imaginary racetrack in front of me vanished and the hall was ugly cold linoleum again. Only four more doors until I would reach my humanities classroom. I took a deep breath and thought of my former teammates riding the big yellow school bus before a basketball game. Already I had missed months of dancing in the aisle of the bus while music blasted. We'd cheer how we'd fight to win the game. Now I could only hear the sad ring of elevator keys jingling in my pocket, syncopated by my crutches' rubber thuds. Finally, I squeaked into the classroom.

"Sarah, just in time," said Mrs. Hammersmith.

I loved her class and did not want to be late. "Sorry," I said, and tried to take my seat without swatting anyone.

"Today, we're going to watch a special video about adoption and social services in this country," she said.

I quietly placed both crutches on the floor by the side of my desk. Did I just hear Mrs. Hammersmith right? I thought.

I leaned forward to get a few inches closer to the screen.

Lights dimmed and soap opera music blasted from the television. The camera panned to a ragged white woman clutching her daughter; the tiny girl held tightly to a rag doll.

The camera stopped on a door sign: SOCIAL SERVICES. The trembling mom sobbed to the social worker, "I have no money to take care of my daughter."

Next a social worker appeared on screen. Leaning over his messy desk stacked with bursting manila files, he whispered to the mom, "We can only take your daughter if she is abandoned."

Moments later the mother and daughter walked through a park. Happy children squealed on swings in the distance. "Stay here, honey. I'll be right back, I promise," said the mother to her four-year-old, leaving her under a large oak tree. When the daughter looked away, the mother darted behind another tree. That same social worker jumped out of his car and scooped up the child.

"Okay, sweetie, you're coming with me," he said.

Kicking and screaming, the terrified child yelled, "My mommy is coming back! My mommy is coming back!"

My stomach compressed into a tight pit. I gripped my desk and waited for the mother to jump out from behind the tree and shout, "Don't take her!" Instead the mom bawled behind the trunk watching her daughter's face contort into a red, hysterical mess.

Then the little girl dropped her rag doll.

Her mother stood behind the tree weeping. Through her tears, in a whisper the mother pleaded, "Please, pick her doll up, please pick her doll up!"

A memory smashed into my brain so quickly, I had to hold my forehead. Suddenly, I remembered a teddy bear that came with me when I was adopted.

The child's doll sunk in a mud puddle.

At the last second, the muddy doll was lifted from the puddle by the social worker and placed into the hands of the shaking girl.

The school bell rang.

I couldn't move from my seat. Was this what happened to me? Did my mother want me to have a teddy bear to remember her? I, too, came to my new family with a toy, a tattered teddy bear. No one knows from where.

I felt physically ill for this woman who had to give up her child. Rapid-fire questions shot though my mind: Where was the father in the video? Where was *my* biological father? Why couldn't the father in the movie help? Did my father ever help my mother? Did my father want to stay with my mother? Why didn't my birth parents want me?

I bent over my crutches, glad to look down at the floor and not meet anyone's eyes. For the past few months there had been so much I didn't want people to see.

Since my injury, a rock of depression hit. Unbeknownst to any of my friends, shared only with my parents and my boyfriend, my mom would drive me to therapy once a week to untangle my feelings of helplessness and maybe even worthlessness without my body working. During those Thursday afternoon rides to the center of town, I'd slide down in the front seat hoping no one from my school would see me driving in the direction of the medical center. I'd make my mom hover right outside the front door of the clinic until all people cleared and I could make a straight hobble inside the double doors. When the young secretary at check-in turned out to be a recent graduate from my high school, I prayed she wouldn't recognize me and reveal that I was in weekly therapy with my world and my knee bashed open.

Worse than her reporting me was the possibility of bumping into any of my dad's medical students. Almost every doctor at the medical center knew my dad. Until I was locked safely behind the therapist's door for my appointment, I hid. Waiting in the hall until I was called was a fierce game of dodgeball; I'd swing my crutches, ducking into the bathroom, slinking behind the soda machine, reaching down for an imaginary magazine—anything to keep from running into someone who might know my dad.

What shame I thought I'd thrust upon him. I couldn't have asked for a better dad and I thought I had repaid him with embarrassment at his place of work: Dr. Jim Culberson's daughter, the star athlete, the adopted child, the homecoming queen, was in need of therapy.

I forced myself up from my seat in class. The teacher flicked on the fluorescent lights and said, "We will discuss the movie and social services tomorrow." Students trickled out of the classroom.

"Hey, Sarah, how does it feel to be *queen*? Congrats!" said a football player, stacking his books for the next class.

I smiled, mumbling, "Thanks." But all I could do was wonder if I, too, was left under a tree.

CHAPTER FIVE

Matagelema

When the village of Matagelema came into view, Joe blinked back tears. The huts still stood. Twenty-five houses topped with zinc roofs glinted in the sun. The other round huts composed of sticks and white clay, with their roofs covered in palm fronds, rose from the soil with a simple dignity. A warm breeze scented with mangoes drifted through the trees. Homes were not charred and leveled to the ground by rebel fire. Villagers milled outside doing daily tasks: sweeping doorways with brooms made from palm fibers, and carrying buckets of water from the well. Groups of men wove large hemp nets for hunting.

When Baby Jenneh saw Joe and his family coming off the bush path, she hurried toward them. The family embraced her. On that day the hugs were longer than ever before. Moriesana, Baby Jenneh's husband, emerged out of the house to welcome Joe and his family. Moriesana's mother and his first wife also gathered around to welcome them and hear the rebel reports.

Baby Jenneh hurried back into the house to cook a big meal for the family. The meal prepared for guests the first night in a village is called *hotamehei*. Custom dictates that the chief of the village host a traveling guest for his first night, and then provide the traveler a host family for his remaining stay in the village. However, because Joe was related to Baby Jenneh, she became the designated host.

The women congregated to help Baby Jenneh chop yams, pound the rice in mortars, and fry plantains. Joe's children, Hindogbae and Jeneba, played with the village kids, who were fascinated by them. To the village children of Matagelema, Hindogbae and Jeneba were "city kids"—draped in fine city clothes and *shoes*. Most of the village children went barefoot.

To impress Hindogbae and Jeneba, the village children taught them how to make slingshots out of Y-shaped sticks, palm fiber, and strips of rubber cut from the inner tube of an abandoned tire. The village girls included Jeneba in their pretend games of preparing food. With empty tomato paste cans, they imitated adult women cooking rice and sauce. Pretending to eat, the children put imaginary food under their chins and sighed with satisfaction. The village children cooked and ate imaginary food all the time.

Behind the house, Joe and Moriesana talked quietly about the attack on Bumpe and tried to predict where the rebels would strike next. Moriesana believed the rebels would not bother with Matagelema. It was too small. Joe warned him to never underestimate the rebels. Like a brigade of African driver ants—fierce, biting, swarming insects—the soldiers know nothing but obliteration. With no logic in their attacks, destruction was based on mood, personal vengeance, or drug-induced fury. Moriesana sighed, shrugged his hands to the sky—to God, and offered Joe and his family refuge in his home as long as was necessary.

But first they needed permission.

Moriesana took Joe to the village chief to be introduced and to give a shake hand fee, known as a *kola* or in Mende a *tolo*. Named after a valuable nut, the *tolo* was a kola nut—the seed of a kola tree that grows wild in Sierra Leone. Rich in caffeine, the chestnut-shaped nut with an aroma of nutmeg was chewed by both adults and children. Extremely bitter, chewing it can thwart hunger. In times long past, a visiting guest would present the nut as a type of payment or tithing to a chief. Now it had a new social meaning. Money, given to a chief, was the new shake hand fee. As *tolo*, a sign of respect, Joe gave some money to the chief of Matagelema.

The chief then gave cups of rice to Joe. This rice would help Moriesana and Baby Jenneh take care of the family the first night in the village. The chief asked how long Joe planned to stay. He did not have an answer.

Grateful to Moriesana and Baby Jenneh for their generous offer to let his family share their home, Joe beelined to the village center where he purchased lamb and sacks of rice to share with Baby Jenneh's family. Word quickly spread through the village that Joe had escaped from rebels in Bumpe.

Many Matagelema villagers were not happy with Joe staying in their village. A man with fine clothes, money, shoes, and a radio was a great liability in their eyes; with his possessions, he could attract rebels. When Joe turned on his radio listening for rebel movement, the villagers pounced—demanding he turn it off. They feared that rebels, overhearing war updates on the radio, would descend on their village.

Certain citizens clamored for Joe and his family to be thrown out of the village. Joe thought of Jonah in the Old Testament. Jonah, thrown overboard by other passengers, was blamed for the raging storm. The difference, thought Joe, "I have not disobeyed God."

Crammed into Baby Jenneh's house, the family anxiously endured the next three weeks until news arrived: rebels marched along the main road headed straight to Matagelema. Joe sent his driver for his truck.

Before leaving Matagelema, while the village slept, Joe, together with a few trusted men, dug a hole in the back of Baby Jenneh's home in the middle of the night. For two hours, using a kerosene lamp to supply light, they buried plates and cooking utensils and "wearings," their clothes—all to hide from the rebels. Filling the hole with dirt, they flattened the site, and spread leaves and palm fronds over it for extra cover.

In the morning, at a frantic pace, Joe and his family packed the Toyota again, adding rice, cassava, and cooking utensils. Baby Jenneh and her husband, Joe's family, a driver, and a cousin, Mamie Kanneh smushed into the truck. Two neighbors, Mr. and Mrs. Henry Vincent Jabba, asked to be picked up at the next stop.

Thirteen-year-old Moiyatu survived the attack on Bumpe and managed to travel to Matagelema.

Back in Bumpe, Moiyatu had also heard the rebels' gunshots and screaming before reaching Reverend Morlai. She ran back to her home, but Mary and Kadie had already taken off into the bush. Left alone, Moiyatu burrowed deep into the forest where she spent the night hiding. In a few days she found the Reverend also hiding in the bush. He helped her reunite with the family. Moiyatu slid into the backseat to travel to Bo with everybody.

As they loaded canisters of groundnuts, sun-ripened guavas, and tins of water in the truck, they heard the gruesome details of the rebels' attacks. Rebels corralled people, burned them alive in their homes, and mutilated the elderly and pregnant women who could not run away. Eyewitness accounts reported pregnant women pleading for their lives. A common episode during the war included soldiers making a bet:

"A bet you; de baby na gal."

"No, na boy."

"A bet you one cigarette packet."

"A gree."

"Den le we open de woman in belleh."

The rebel slashed open her belly.

"You see, na baby girl. You don loss," they laughed.

CHAPTER SIX

Morgantown

When I returned home after school, fresh from watching the adoption video in my senior humanities class, I stormed through the living room, dropping my backpack like a bomb. "Mom!" I yelled.

Coming out of the kitchen, my mom wiped her hands on a dish towel, having just finished chopping the lettuce, cucumbers, and tomatoes for the salad. The tears I sucked back in the school corridor, zipped behind a tight smile, sprung free. By the time I crossed the living room, I was hysterical. "What about the teddy bear? Who abandoned me?" I blurted through tears.

I heaved another question. "Was I left under a tree?"

"You know, let's sit down and have some tea," said my mom, lulling me into the kitchen, her voice steady. My mom placed the Sleepytime cinnamon and chamomile tea on the kitchen table in my favorite mug. Hot tea with honey was a balm in our home, making homework easier and coming inside from shooting hoops tolerable.

I sank into the kitchen chair, terrified that the video was based on my life. My mom moved and hugged me. Dinner simmered in the oven, wafting its reassuring smell through the house.

Calmly she sat down across from me and said, "Sarah, you were not left under a tree."

I stared straight ahead.

She said, "From what I know, you lived with your biological mother, Penny, for nine months and then were put in foster care for three months until we adopted you.

"The day we picked you up we had to wait an extra three hours at the agency in Fairmont, West Virginia. The foster parent ran late, insisting she bathe you one more time, feed you one more bottle. She wrote a detailed list of likes and dislikes for food and nap times. I never found out who gave you the teddy bear, though," said my mom.

My mom went into her closet and brought back the letter from the foster parent. It was dated April 18, 1977.

Esther can eat most table foods. I buy some baby food (junior food) for her when she doesn't eat our food.

She takes Similac with iron in her bottles (one can Similac and one can water). Her doctor wanted her to be on this for her first year. I tried to get her to drink some homogenized milk at the table but she wouldn't drink it.

I was told not to give Esther orange juice. I don't know why. She loves apple juice, apple grape, apple cherry.

Esther is very bad about putting things in her mouth. She is very active.

Esther had an ear infection in March. The infection is gone, but she still has some fluid to clear up. She is supposed to take this Purple Magic four times a day for the fluid. She has a doctor's appointment May 2 with Dr. Crittenden at the Fairmont Clinic for check up about the ears.

I couldn't move. Esther. My name was once Esther.

"Esther?" I asked aloud, looking at my mom.

"Your name was Esther Elizabeth, but we loved the name Sarah Jane," said my mom, smiling.

"Wow," I said, taking in the new information.

"When your dad comes home, we will try to answer more of your questions, okay?" she said, and moved to finish preparing a salad on the kitchen island.

I stirred the tea around and around as if I could read futures and pasts in my own cup. "Mom, why did you adopt me?" I asked.

She sprinkled olives on top of the lettuce.

"Why?" my mom repeated.

I asked her how, growing up in the homogenous farming town of Litchfield, Illinois, population 8,000, she came to adopt me, a biracial daughter.

"Well, when I came back from my last service trip, your dad and I spoke seriously about adoption." My mom traveled all over the world in 1974 on a child development team with Church Women United. In Barbados, Dominican Republic, and British Guyana, Florida, South Carolina, and Washington D.C., she met with struggling women and children. When my mom returned from the volunteer service tour, nightly talks with my dad began about adopting a child who needed a home. Good friends of my mom and dad also adopted biracial children. These children thrived in their new families.

"You know, it may also have had something to do with that bookcase and ice cream truck, too," she said laughing, her beautiful amber-brown eyes crinkling up.

"What?" I said.

"Back in Illinois, my elementary school was a one-room schoolhouse, grades 1–8. Behind the larger schoolroom, a tiny room housed a special bookcase filled with books. Because the teacher noticed how much I gravitated to the bookcase, she gave me a quarter each week to dust the books and the bookcase.

"One book I remember very well was a story about George Washington Carver, who was taught to read and went on to study at Tuskegee Institute to become a famous scientist. I read this book so many times it probably still has my fingerprints all over it." My mom laughed and sliced radishes to add to the salad.

"I marveled that all he needed was access to an education to become a famous scientist. The lessons of his life must have had a profound impact very early in my life about giving a child the chance to learn and be loved."

I smiled at my soft-spoken mom. Tiny hands, shoulder-length hair neatly combed, she was a huge advocate for every child on this planet to be loved and given opportunities. "What about the ice cream truck?" I asked.

She stood still in the kitchen, as if motion might distract her memory.

"In the summer when I was twelve, I would ride with my father in his ice cream delivery truck into the black neighborhoods an hour-and-a-half away in East Saint Louis, Illinois. Sitting high on the vinyl seat next to my dad, I would stare out the open windows watching the neighborhoods roll by. When the creamery truck stopped to make a delivery at a drugstore or soda fountain, I would lean out the large windows seeing a world very different from my dad's farm. It was a world of brilliant color and beauty.

"My dad's duty was delivering large gallons of ice cream to stores for the Litchfield Creamery, but sometimes he would stop to give a little kid a scoop of ice cream. I remember leaning out the window and exchanging a smile with a black child."

I plunged my spoon back in my mug.

My mom checked the oven. She cooked pot roast, with peeled potatoes and tender carrots, melt-in-the-mouth perfect. Suddenly it seemed the heat from the oven thawed another memory for her.

"You know, Sarah, New Orleans made a big impression, too."

She explained that when she and my dad moved to New Orleans for my dad's Ph.D. work in Anatomy at Tulane University, long before children biological or adopted arrived, they took the Melpomene Avenue bus through the black neighborhoods to work downtown. One of their mutual pleasures was riding back and forth on the long bus rides home, meandering through the ethnic neighborhoods full of new smells and the rhythms of jazz in the

French Quarter not seen or heard in the small Midwestern farming town of their childhood.

"I still remember those beautiful mothers," she said. "The way they brushed their children's hair." On the outskirts of New Orleans, black mothers would sit on front stoops braiding their daughters' hair in neat cornrows or combing their children's hair steady and slow on hot summer days. "Even today, if I close my eyes I can still hear those women in the summertime, humming songs to their children on cement steps."

Still sitting at the oval kitchen table, I glanced down at the pretty country-style place mat with hummingbirds. Guilt crept up my spine. Maybe these questions about my biological parents hurt my mom? Why should I care or wonder about my biological parents when I have my mom and my dad and my two older sisters?

My mother opened the oven, removing the succulent roast, her back turned from me. Placing the roast in a warm casserole pan, she drained some of the excess liquid to thicken with cornstarch for a gravy. Gently she simmered and stirred the sauce on the front burner.

Maybe *she* is simmering inside, thinking: "Why does Sarah care? She was only one year old. Isn't it the rest of the time, the other sixteen years with us that count?"

Staring down at the kitchen table, I flashed back to myself as a little girl in this same chair, same position, head resting on the kitchen table as my mom braided my hair before breakfast. Resting my tiny head on my hands in front of me, I would turn my face to one side as my mom wove a perfect French braid, crossing my thick hair over and under, over and under. When she came to the end of the braid, she'd tie a ribbon on the end. Other times she would fasten my hair back in a heart-shaped barrette with red, yellow, and blue satin ribbon streaming down. I'd protect my pretty collection of ribbons in a tin I kept under the bathroom counter. On Saturdays, my mom and I would hold hands and go to the ribbon store for new plaid, polka-dot, and striped bows.

"I'm home," called my dad, back from teaching medical students neuroanatomy at West Virginia University. The scent of the juicy roast beckoned him into the warm kitchen, but immediately he sensed something was wrong.

"Sarah wants to ask us some questions about her biological parents," said my mom with remarkable calm.

My dad bent his six-foot two-inch frame and eased into the kitchen chair across the table. I couldn't help smile at all his pens lined up in his breast pocket. Always grading medical students' papers, he carried a ready supply of red, black, or green felt-tip pens in his pocket.

I stared at my dad's blue eyes, made brighter by his soft brown hair. "Why do these questions even matter?" I asked myself. Again I looked down at the kitchen table, the center of so many happy dinners, a place my dad would help me with geometry and English papers. In fifth grade I had an assignment to build an animal using only glue and toothpicks. My dad and I worked for days, night after night stacking toothpicks, carefully gluing them under the hanging kitchen light. Together we built a twelve-inch giraffe. To this day he keeps it in his study by his desk, a reminder of the time we shared.

"Will they think I don't love them enough when I ask these questions?"

I leaned my elbows on the table, covered my face with both hands, and surrounded my eyes in darkness. More memories flooded in. So many birthdays around this table. My favorite, even after all these years, was the morning of my seventh birthday when my non–junk food mother, knowing how much I loved the popular Strawberry Short Cake doll, treated me to a strawberry Pop-Tart with bright sprinkles frosting the top. "I thought the colorful sprinkles on top of the white frosting looked like confetti. Perfect for your birthday," said my mom.

I exhaled loudly.

"You know, it doesn't really matter," I heard myself saying. "I just wanted to make sure that after watching the adoption video that I wasn't left under a tree, that's all."

"These are perfectly normal questions," said my dad.

"Do you know anything more about my biological mother and father?" I asked.

My dad looked at my mom.

My parents made a swift and protective choice in the kitchen that evening.

Nearly hysterical from watching that adoption video, wearing a knee brace, and removed from my usual social support system, my world somersaulted. My parents did not think this was the right time to begin an all-out investigation for my biological parents. Spending my afternoons searching for my birth parents—when I was dangerously behind on college tests and applications because of my knee injury and surgeries—was not how they wanted me to spend the next crucial months.

Once before, at age twelve, I began asking questions about my birth parents. When my mom parked the car at the end of our driveway after school, she thought this might be the moment to share the details of what she knew. She turned to me in the front seat and said, "Sarah, I can give you some information if you want to hear it."

She remembered how I grabbed my schoolbags, jumped out of the car, and said, "I don't want to hear it!"

Alone in the car, my mom sat staring at the wooded backyard beyond the driveway. She decided not to push it.

Now I was asking again.

"Well," said my mom. "I believe your father was from Sierra Leone, Africa, and a student studying in West Virginia, from an important family named *Capasowa* or something. I remember the social worker told us your biological father had the most dignified presence and your mother was from West Virginia, living near the university. But you know, she might not be alive. She was a lot older than him I believe. We might have a little more info written somewhere, but that's pretty much it."

Suddenly I imagined my father and his "dignified presence." In my mind he rose six feet four inches tall and elegant. Why would a man from an important family *have to* or even *want to* give me up?

CHAPTER SEVEN

Road to Sierra Rutile and Bumpe

Joe held his head in his hands. Hindogbae and Jeneba barraged him with questions from the backseat of the truck.

"Daddi, do yaa le we go back to Bumpe."

"Daddi, do yaa."

The countryside crawled with rebels, booby traps, and ambushes; choosing where to seek refuge was a life-or-death decision. The truck idled under the beating Sierra Leone sun waiting for direction, but Hindogbae and Jeneba again pressed their father about their pet monkey, Little.

Little was left behind in their village.

Joe's wife, Mary, had no choice but to bolt out of the backdoor for her life, leaving Little. During a rebel attack, a family member dared not return to a village for a relative, not even for his own child—much less a pet monkey. RUF soldiers would often round up citizens and force them to conduct a welcoming ceremony; they shot citizens who did not demonstrate enough enthusiasm. Children, stabbed with machetes were forced to lie on their dying parents, their blood draining lifelessly together. Needing more light for night raids, the RUF was known to lock families in their homes, set the house on fire, creating human torches. Names of the RUF units took on gruesome foreshadowing: the KILL MAN NO BLOOD unit that beat its victims to death slowly without drawing blood, the BORN NAKED SQUAD that stripped civilians before their murder.

But now that the family, forced to leave Baby Jenneh's house and the village of Matagelema was back in the truck, Hindogbae and Jeneba begged their father to go back to Bumpe and rescue Little.

"Daddi, we don forget Little," said Hindogbae. *"A wan le we go get tan."*

Jeneba joined in, *"If we nor get tan ee go die."*

"De rebel dem go killam!" said Hindogbae.

"Do yaa Daddi le we go back for Little," pleaded Jeneba.

Joe could not allow himself to think of their monkey with the countryside a fiendish checkerboard of rebels, feral teenagers with machine guns in open trucks zigzagging the roads. He believed the next safest town for shelter would be Sierra Rutile. Heavily fortified by the military, government soldiers were sent there to protect the rutile mines owned by wealthy American and European companies. With so many armed soldiers prepared to defend the mine against the rebels, Joe assumed staying on the outskirts of town would be best.

When they arrived in Sierra Rutile they heard the news: the neighboring village of Mokanji had just been attacked by rebels. Refugees, some barefoot, others bare-chested, who escaped from the assault on Mokanji warned that Sierra Rutile was next:

"De rebel den de cam!"

"Rebels den de cam poil dis ton!"

"Ee nor safe ya oh."

A barbaric standoff at the mine was imminent. Soon, the mine would be stripped. The town would be looted and the mine a raging inferno.

Joe swerved the truck, spinning a crazy-eight in the dirt.

Once he heard the news, he did not stay a minute longer—Sierra Rutile was a death trap. He sped back toward Matagelema with a new plan. Maybe going back to Bumpe would be safe enough. A collective rebel force, massing in large groups, prepared for the assault on Sierra Rutile. While rebel factions gathered closer to the mining town, it would leave a small window of time when the rebels would desert the village of Bumpe. This was Joe's only chance: he could sneak back to his own house, look for his pet monkey, and gather some belongings for his family who left Bumpe with nothing but the clothes on their backs. Maybe the family could salvage a camera, textbooks, a television, and furniture. In the ceiling Joe had hidden a one-barreled hunting gun given to him by a United Brethren in Christ female missionary.

Dust coated the car like a fine layer of sawdust on the path to Bumpe. Abandoned villages, charred, eerily silent, were passed quickly. In a few months on that very road, refugees would limp toward help. Their bandages covering the bloody stumps of missing hands and missing arms. People with missing lips and severed limbs would appear like ghoulish apparitions stumbling out of pillaged villages. Mothers would scream along the road, insane for their lost children.

Joe focused on his monkey who loved to sit on his lap and throw his arms around his neck. Joe prayed that Little had hidden from the rebels. But Little was too gentle, too sweet, too trusting.

Little came to him as an orphan. The monkey's mother and Little huddled in a tree when they were first spotted by village hunting dogs. The two monkeys were safe in the tree, but according to legend, monkeys descend from trees when attacked. Common among the Mende people is the proverb: "There is nowhere to proceed in the sky like birds, but the ground is endless."

The barking terrified the two trembling monkeys; panicking, they fell out of the tree and punched the ground with a thump. The hunting dogs first pounced on Little's mother and ate her alive.

As the mother was shredded among the dogs, passing villagers scooped up the two-week-old baby monkey to sell to Joe. Little was small and dark with a white nose; in Mende his breed is called *hokpakulei*. The villagers demanded the price of 1000 leones for Little, about $1.00, which Joe paid.

The afternoon Little came to him, the baby monkey couldn't stop shaking. For two months Joe cradled him and fed him powdered milk from a baby's bottle. When Little was older, he was allowed to wander around Joe's compound, but he returned for lunch and dinner. He ate rice, but combed the bush by himself for wild fruits. He never ran away because, again, according to legend, "Once a wild animal tastes salt in his diet, he will never return to the wild."

Little was best friends with Joe's dog, a mutt, whose head and mouth looked like a small German Shepherd. The dog was called *Kolumbahun,* meaning *iron in the mouth.* Before the dog died, Little would sit for hours with the dog diligently picking fleas from the dog's fur.

Joe's truck, covered in red dirt, streaked like blood, finally pulled into Bumpe. Everything was silent. Desolate. Most villagers had fled or were still hiding farther out in the bush. Parking the truck far behind his compound, the family stayed in the truck as Joe crept toward his property. Just as he feared, his house was burned. Blackened and destroyed. Joe refused to cry. He kept walking, softly calling, "Little! Little!"

With wild joyful noises, Little emerged from the bush, jumping from tree to tree, and vaulted into Joe's arms. Little would not let go, clinging to his neck like a lost child. Joe raced with Little back to his family waiting in the truck.

Immediately, everybody fed Little his favorite foods: groundnuts and bananas. Joe cradled Little as he ate. Around Little's neck dangled a piece of a rebel camouflage fatigue shirt. Joe ripped it off. Usually rebels would eat a monkey, but because the village was flush with food, they feasted on other sources. Investigating his compound, Joe understood the unnatural silence. The rebels had devoured his twenty pigs.

After feeding Little, the family did not dare stay the night in Bumpe. Together, and in silence, the family scoured their compound. When Mary saw her scorched home she wept.

Little piled into the Toyota with the family, and they set off for the big city of Bo, a highly fortified town, the headquarters of the Southern Province, and Joe's last hope for his family. Already they heard Bo had flooded with thousands and thousands of refugees. By tomorrow, if they made the sixteen-mile journey, the city of Bo would swell with one more carload of refugees and a monkey named Little.

CHAPTER EIGHT

Morgantown

A few days after that pot roast dinner with my parents, although satisfied with their answers, I couldn't let go of the image of the little girl abandoned in the park with her mother watching behind a tree. Thoughts sprung into my head that maybe my biological mother had seen me before. Maybe she was watching me? Maybe she saw my picture in the paper for homecoming? Maybe she came to a basketball game?

Maybe I even knew her.

Resting in my bed, I reached for the phone and called my beautiful, older sister Lynne, whom I worshiped.

"Hey, Lynne, I was just thinking, wouldn't it have been weird if my biological mother ever saw me? Bumped into us, or something? Wouldn't that be freaky?"

"It happened," she said.

"What!" I said, snapping up straight in bed.

"Yeah, when I was around fifteen and you were five," she said.

My sister was famous in our family for her steel-trap memory.

"You, me, Laura, and Mom were out shopping for shoes downtown. This lady came up to us, bent down, stared at you, and said, 'Oh, I have a little girl like that.' "

Goose bumps instantly speckled my arms.

"Mom smiled and stiffened. I think she just knew it was your biological mother. The social worker warned her that your birth mother lived in the area. Then the lady asked, 'When is her birthday?' and she reached over and touched your hair."

"What did Mom do?" I asked, holding my breath.

"She just smiled and began walking away," said Lynne. "The lady knew she shouldn't have touched your head. She kept repeating, 'I'm sorry. I'm so sorry.' "

My whole body shook. "Then what?" I whispered.

"We kept walking into the music store, but I knew Mom was a bit shaken."

"What was the other lady like? My . . . *mother*?" the word sounded strange coming out of my mouth. "Was she pretty?"

"I guess," said my sister. "Mostly, I remember she had a price tag on her sweater, dangling in front. She forgot to cut it off or something—she was a little weird."

All air deflated from my lungs. My older sister thought my biological mother was weird. I wondered if I ever went to school with a tag still inside my shirt, or stuck inside my pants irritating my waist.

"Sarah, you still there?" she said.

"Yeah," I said, trying to breathe.

"Anyway, it only happened once. You're part of our family. We have a great mom."

"Yeah," I said. "You know, my knee is throbbing. Can I call you back?"

"Sure," she said. "Love you."

"Love you," I mumbled and hung up the phone.

My biological mother was not a beautiful lady, elegant and tall; she wore price tags on her clothes, which she had forgotten to remove. My mind spun in dizzy circles.

My birth father was supposed to be a stately African man and my birth mother a blond beauty. Suddenly the picture of this tag spun out of control, out of context. In my mind my birth mother, who forgot a silly, tiny label, twisted into a homeless woman with stringy hair like a street Medusa.

I did not want to know any more about my birth parents—ever. That evening I yelled down the hall, told my parents I had a horrible stomachache, and couldn't eat dinner. I lay in the dark under my canopy.

CHAPTER NINE

Fogbo Junction

The flat tire pierced the air with a pop, then exhaled in a long slow howl. The truck cried, apologizing for its rubber wound. The Toyota Hilux flopped and clunked a few more revolutions along the dirt road. Everyone in the truck tensed still, silent. Each thump of the dying Dunlap tire a pronouncement: a flat tire along the unpaved roads poxed with potholes—some so vast a truck could fall in and tip over—was not unusual. But during the civil war a flat tire was a death sentence. The roads, unrepaired since the war began in 1991, were pitted with an obstacle course of rocks, potholes, and gulleys from the rainy seasons. All passengers knew covering the sixteen miles from Bumpe to Bo would take all day, but no one imagined they would have traversed only two miles before this—a flat tire. It seemed the protective family ancestors—the *ndeblaa,* the brave spirits of the forefathers—slept. At any moment, a passing pickup packed with rebels, wearing Tupac shirts and oversized sunglasses, might materialize out of the tall elephant grasses and start firing.

"OUT OF THE TRUCK! OUT OF THE TRUCK!" shouted Joe.

His family jumped out.

Wet estuaries of sweat trickled down Joe's ebony face, mapping new roads. The rebels had already destroyed his home and his land, and set fire to his village. Joe's jaw tightened, sweat diverting over a cheekbone. They would not steal his truck, they would not take his daughter's virginity, they would not defile his wife, and they would not capture and conscript his son.

"INTO THE BUSH! WAIT AT DASAMU," he yelled, ordering his family and the women to walk along a dusty bush path three miles to Dasamu.

No one protested. Fogbo Junction, a rebel crossroads, was the center of a devil's bull's-eye.

"HURRY!" he yelled.

Carrying food, and a few possessions, Mary and the others began the hour-and-a-half trek to the next village.

Joe bid his driver and Mr. Jabba to stay at Fogbo Junction by the truck guarding their last shot for safety.

Alone, Joe walked two miles back to Bumpe village and found his eighteen-year-old nephew, Noha.

Reaching into his pocket, Joe took out 6000 leones ($2.00) and handed it to Noha. Brave, fast, and lithe—able to dart into the bush in seconds—Noha became the group's final hope.

"Roll the tire to Bo," Joe said.

Noha, a miniature Sisyphus, needed to roll the single flat tire fourteen miles—*one way*—along the unpaved dirt road to Bo and have it inflated. The spare tire in the truck had deflated from the weight of the bags and stores of food.

"When it is fixed, roll the tire back to us. We will wait for you at Fogbo Junction," said Joe.

Joe trudged back to the junction, stood by his truck with the two men, and prayed.

CHAPTER TEN

West Virginia University, Morgantown

I couldn't stall anymore. I clutched my orange cafeteria tray tighter. The food court of West Virginia University loomed before me. Twenty thousand students a day passed through the food court grabbing pizza slices, piping hot muffins, and any other food imaginable.

Senior year of high school I auditioned for the College of Creative Arts, Division of Theatre, and was awarded a full scholarship to college. Sports, after my ACL knee injury, were replaced with the arts—singing, dancing, and acting—a different type of stage. I was thrilled to go to WVU in Morgantown. Since I was four years old, I attended football games with my dad who taught there. Both my sisters and my mom also graduated from WVU. Finally I could claim the alma mater. I planned to live at home and take classes the first few years.

However, standing in the food court on the first day of classes, I did not know what to do. The cafeteria buzzed, people flitting to different food lines; the Mountainlair food court spun like a kaleidoscope of color and movement. In front of the muffin store sat a large group of black students next to some white students I knew.

My palms slipped on the sides of the cafeteria tray. The noise of silverware and voices echoed in the massive room. I scanned the faces again. "Where to sit on the first day of classes? Who to sit with?"

Whispers had started at the summer orientation for minority students. During that mixer, students of color met in the gray-carpeted, community meeting rooms in one of the campus dorms.

So many nights in high school, I wished there were people like me, a familiar brown face in a sea of white—and here was my chance. Even though I felt I should go, I wasn't sure I wanted to attend the mixer. I was uncomfortable feeling uncomfortable. Hadn't I wanted to meet more people like myself, biracial students and black students—meet black people outside of the lone bus driver who drove my elementary school bus and my friends at the black beauty salon who tried to tame my Afro?

At the meet and greet we broke into discussion groups where I challenged a black track star's opinion. Later I was informed by a friend on the track team that this student told the entire team in the locker room, "Forget about asking her out, she doesn't like black guys."

Taco smells in the food court were making me ill, cinnamon buns too sweet; the odor of greasy hamburgers and oily fries hung heavy in the air. Where to sit? Already the track team believed I didn't like black men. If I sat with my white friends would that rumor ring true? But I did know many of the white students from my high school who also chose to attend WVU. I didn't know any of the black students. They were all sitting together and they seemed to know each other.

Lunch was more than choosing the salad bar or pizza. In my mind a new or old identity was at stake. WVU is very diverse but in that moment, for me, all I saw was an invisible line stretched across the cafeteria: *black or white*. I looked more like the black students but I knew and felt more comfortable with my white friends from high school. "Just sit somewhere," I said to myself. In my imagination a group of black students watched and wondered, "Is she whitewashed and going to go with the white people or is she going to come sit with us?"

My heart raced. "Why did I have to choose?" My high school memory of a student saying, "Sarah doesn't know if she's black or white" pounded in my skull. I stood there frozen with anxiety.

Suddenly I saw Mia Gonzales, a biracial friend, alone at a table—not white, not black. I stepped forward, my cafeteria tray now a magnet honing toward her. "Hey, Mia," I called, with my palms sweaty. I sat down in the hazy middle.

CHAPTER ELEVEN

Road to Bo

At first Noha rolled the tire down the center of the dirt road—less chance of popping. Already it had struck a rusty nail. Staying on the main motor road allowed him to see a far distance. Unobscured by the bush, he might be able to detect danger faster. Unfortunately, others could spot him too, a black figure against the sun, an inverse shadow as he rolled the tire. But it was a risk he had to take. Joe had embraced Noha, his nephew, taken him into his home, and supported him with food, clothing, and shelter. In return Noha helped care for Joe's livestock.

Noha thought of little Hindogbae, who loved to watch him feed the pigs. Noha remembered Mary's kindness, her heaping bowls of rice set out for him. Noha did not want to let Joe down, so many lives now depended on him.

With flip-flops on his feet, black shorts, and a soaked short-sleeved T-shirt, wet from the heat, tied around his waist, Noha rolled the tire.

The throbbing pain in his back didn't start right away. He set off at 10:00 A.M. that morning, strong and able.

At first, Noha believed rolling the tire out of Fogbo Junction would be a manageable task, but the bumpy inclines and declines of the dirt roads made his job difficult. When moving downhill, Noha was forced to run as the tire sped away from him, each revolution picking up speed. When moving uphill, the stubborn tire rolled backward, which increased the strokes Noha needed to use. His palms blistered. Carrying the tire on his back for a few miles, Noha allowed his cramping hands a brief rest.

At first, Noha only saw birds swooping along the dirt road. Weaver birds, finchlike birds, darted among the trees along his journey. Then in the distance, Noha spotted small groups of people walking toward him. Adrenaline released in torrents inside his veins. Rebels often dressed in both government camouflage and civilian clothes—confusing victims.

Thankfully, only citizens passed him, emerging from destroyed villages. Refugees reported they'd encountered no rebels along the road so far. Relieved, Noha paused at a stream, cupped water in his hands and drank. For the fourteen-mile trek ahead of him, he carried no food or water.

Pressing against his sweaty skin, money filled Noha's pockets. Joe gave him 4000 leones for transport—in case he could buy a ride to Bo from a passing truck, 1000 leones for food and 1000 leones for the tire repair.

When the road smoothed into a steady red haze, a glittering mirage in the sun, Noha's mind rolled over his own thoughts. Vowing he would not lose the tire, he prayed for a clear road, no ambushes. If he were to die, riddled by bullets or captured as another RUF recruit, what would happen to the tire?

In the scuffle the tire would be ignored, forgotten, wobbling a few paces to the grassy edge of the motor road to collapse. Later, rebels would whiz by in one of their trucks and ignore the discarded tire denting the grasses with weeds snarled in its center. No one would know it represented a rubber grave marker, the deflated hope of Mary and Jeneba, Moiyatu, Hindogbae, Mrs. Jabba, and the women waiting in Dasamu praying for a truck that never came. Passing travelers would never guess that the weary tire contained a tragedy: the story of three men who paced under the scorching sun, praying by a limp truck for a boy who never showed up.

Noha shook his head. That story must never happen. He would not let the family down.

He kept running.

CHAPTER TWELVE

West Virginia University, Morgantown

In 1995, my freshman year of college, Vanessa Williams's hit song "Colors of the Wind" won a Grammy Award. Her beautiful face shone on videos, magazines, and television. White and black girls wanted to look like her. Her light blue eyes, cocoa skin, and perfect proportions subconsciously impacted my concept of what a beautiful black woman should look like. That was the year I got blue contacts. I wanted my hair to be soft, light brown, and smooth like hers as well. But my hair, from years of being doused with chemicals and anti-Afro baths was breaking off in chunks.

As a child, my adopted parents adored my natural hair, admired it, braided it, and marveled at how much hair I had. My dad said as a two-year-old I had enough hair for three people. As his own brown hair thinned, he'd hug me and ask for some of mine. In middle school, my mom, knowing how uncomfortable I was when my hair sprung in every direction, researched beauty salons that specialized in black hair. I was always grateful my mom helped me tame my hair, even if some might think it "enabling," but during those awkward teenage years the last thing I wanted was a 70s-style Afro at school—making me stick out even more.

Sometimes I'd stare in the mirror wondering if my birth father wore his hair in an Afro. Did he have thick, coarse hair? Certain thoughts about my hair I admitted only to myself: Why did I have to get so much African hair?

Couldn't I have gotten more of the white side like I had seen on other biracial kids? Some biracial girls I knew inherited soft curls, "the good hair." Anything seemed better than my hair's wild coiled springs.

In spite of my unhappiness with my father's hair inheritance, my trips to see the hairdresser, Delmon, at her salon conjure up some of my best high school memories. There were so few black people in my community that going to her hair salon was a favorite excursion. Hair immersed me in black culture—or the part of it I could claim.

When friends would call and ask when I'd be back from my hair appointment, I would answer: five hours. They thought I was kidding, but it takes so much time to relax, straighten, or braid my African hair it becomes a major social visit. First Delmon sectioned my hair and added thick hair grease or oil to protect my scalp from burning. Next a white, pungent chemical relaxer coated my hair, paralyzing it into obedience. Hopefully the relaxer would take effect before my scalp burned. Sometimes my hair refused to go straight and the chemical burn on my scalp left little, raised, pus-filled scabs all over my head.

The packed shop included women and men; sometimes men would come into the shop and get a relaxer, a jerry curl, too. With these relaxers I successfully killed off my Afro, ridding the part of me I thought was ugly.

From those years of hair abuse, my hair had become so sickly that cutting it all off, giving it a chance to get healthy was my best option; but starting college, with parched, cropped hair was not ideal. I thought a fake weave over my hair was my only choice. My only cover.

Delmon had since closed her shop, and Julia, beautiful black Julia with her soft, feathered hair and brown tinted glasses, drove to my home to put in a weave. My mom took out a card table and chair in the living room, and Julia, for eight hours, braided what was left of my real hair into tiny braids all over my head. They would serve as anchors for the purchased human and synthetic hair. Next, long, blonde and light-brown hair would be sewn to the tiny braids on top of my head. When Julia finished, I had golden brown hair cascading down my back.

But my African hair refused to be kept down. After a few washings, strapped down into all those tiny braids with the flowy weave on top, my real hair began to swell underneath. Now a growing mountain of hair pushed my fake, golden weave higher and higher on my head. Apparently I hadn't noticed how silly this looked—my hair ballooning on top of sprouting hair.

But one of the WVU black football players did notice.

Disney's movie, *The Lion King*, had recently been released. The baby lion in the movie was named "Simba." When I walked into the student union, The Mountainlair, Tyrone stood a few feet behind me. Out of my sightline he would hold up his hands on either side of his head and mock whisper.

My friend, who saw this over and over again, finally came up to me and said, "Sarah, I just want you to know that Tyrone stands behind you and calls you 'Simba'!"

CHAPTER THIRTEEN

Fogbo Junction

Joe paced in front of the truck. What if Noha did not make it? What if Noha were captured? Then not only would Joe's family be destitute—no working van, no possessions or food supply, no transportation to Bo—but also guilt over Noha's death would plague him. Was it wrong to send a boy on a journey so risky? Not that waiting by the truck was any safer. As the group's leader, Joe had to make decisions for everybody. If Noha did not return by nightfall, and if he himself was not killed by rebels before sunset, Joe would trek to the village of Dasamu, pray his own family arrived earlier that day, and think of a new plan. In his wallet wrapped against his chest, strapped to his body under his clothes, he carried a few thousand leones—all that was left to support his family.

Sweat underneath Joe's gold-plated watchband chafed his skin.

Two o'clock.

Noha had been gone since ten that morning. For four hours, the three men stood tense, eyes darting, ears pricked, alert for any sign of people. If a car or person was spotted in the distance they would need to make a split-second decision to stay by the truck—protect it from looters who might think it abandoned—or to dive into the bush outnumbered and outgunned by rebels.

In the rising afternoon sun, Joe's mind spun circles, more and more scenarios of doom. What if Noha, diving into the bush to dodge a passing truck, encountered a snake? Almost all snakes in Sierra Leone are poisonous: the black tree cobra, the green mamba, and the puff adder—all common, all deadly. The puff adder, with its perfect camouflage of browns and grays, melding seamlessly with the bush grasses, concerned him the most. Noha could easily stomp on a snake in his haste. When stepped on, the puff adder's fangs fold forward, embed into flesh, and inject a deadly venom.

Black spitting cobras are some of the most feared snakes in Sierra Leone. Like an Indian cobra, the black spitting cobra raises its body into a sinewy dance, but when it reaches eye level it spits its poison, a fatal mist so potent it can cause instant blindness and death in one hour. Joe scanned the giant cotton trees and oil palms swaying alongside the red dirt motor road. Black spitting cobras, excellent climbers, often hung from the trees.

If a snake is found in a village hut in Sierra Leone, the entire compound is evacuated until villagers have located and killed it with sticks and stones. Sometimes a snake dancer, a *kaliloigamui,* would be fetched to sprinkle his magic charms, his secret herbs, or spread the pungent bark of a bitter tree, the *danda wulei,* on the floor to fumigate the poisonous viper.

Growing up, Joe once woke in the middle of the night to use the bathroom. When he walked into the living room where his female cousin slept, a five-foot-long black cobra stretched on the bed next to her. Sound asleep, she did not know that four inches away from her a cobra basked in the heat of her body. Slowly Joe tiptoed backwards to his room. He could do nothing. If he startled the girl or the snake, instant death would result. In the morning he walked back into the living room, his cousin was wide-awake and humming. He shared with her what he had seen the night before. She did not believe him. Two days later the cobra was found in the house and killed.

Joe looked down at his feet, his sandals sticky with dust.

He prayed: "Oh, God, please be Noha's guide. Help him return safely. Our ancestors, please pray for him to make it. My father's soul, please protect us and Noha."

What had happened to his country? Muslims and Christians living in peace, a school full of students under his principalship, a bulging piggery supporting his family. He was a successful man, a respected, educated man, the son of a revered Paramount Chief. His father, Paramount Chief Francis Kposowa, had been selected by the British colonial government to visit London in 1953. His father's titles included MBE, Member of the British Empire, JP, Justice of the Peace, and CH, Chief of Honor, a distinction given to outstanding Paramount Chiefs. How, now, was the son of a great Paramount Chief reduced to this: standing on the side of the road, trembling before children with AK-47s?

Children who could have been his students, dressed in their starched white shirts and trim blue shorts, had morphed into a ragtag band of soldiers. At Bumpe Academy, his abandoned school, the uniform, influenced by the old school British colonists, was worn with pride. Before class, a schoolboy ironed his own shirt by heating an old-fashioned flatiron and filling the inside with hot charcoal from the fire pit. To be a schoolboy meant something. Attending school promised a future different than the backbreaking manual labor on a rice farm.

Joe clenched his jaw, ground his teeth. Under his shoe he felt a jagged rock, and another thought jutted into his head: "What if the tire, rolling across the road unearthed a dreaded reddish black scorpion?" With its pinchers it could pierce through Noha's flimsy sandals, a sting as painful as a snakebite, rendering his leg immobile. A scorpion's toxin could swell a limb, make a man dizzy, and provoke a total blackout.

How would Noha make the journey with a numb, swelling leg?

Three o'clock and no Noha.

Joe's stomach growled. Into the bush the three men foraged for cassava roots. One final thought crossed Joe's mind, the darkest thought of all. "What if his family never made it to Dasamu? What if rebels killed his wife, his mother, his neighbors, and his children along the bush path? Or what if he were killed near his truck and his family waited and waited in Dasamu? Who would protect his family? How would his family live? Who would properly bury him or his children? What if he had misjudged Noha? What if Noha did make it to Bo, but decided to abandon the tire and keep the money?"

Four o'clock and no Noha.

CHAPTER FOURTEEN

West Virginia University, Morgantown

I stood alone in the dark WVU theater room before class. The cool darkness, black walls, black curtains, and empty stage inspired me. Possibility and potential rested here. Theater and sports, two physical stages kept calling.

When I was six, my mom started me in classical ballet lessons, which I loved and continued until middle school. The structure, the balance, the movement stirred reservoirs of creativity. After lessons I would come home and turn the living room into my private dance studio. Ballet steps, dance moves—I improvised entire routines by myself in our living room. In 1986 Paul Simon's album *Graceland* had just been released. Even at ten years old, I played the album repeatedly on our record player in the living room. Carefully, with my teeny hands I'd set the record needle on the seventh track to hear my favorite song, "Under African Skies," over and over again:

Joseph's face was black as night
The pale yellow moon shone in his eyes
His path was marked
By the stars in the Southern Hemisphere
And he walked his days
Under African skies
This is the story of how we begin to remember

This is the powerful pulsing of love in the vein
After the dream of falling and calling your name out
These are the roots of rhythm
And the roots of rhythm remain . . .

Twirling around my living room as a little girl humming along to music, I had no idea what led me to this song, and why I loved it so much.

Joseph's face was black as night
. . . And he walked his days under African skies

Over and over I danced to this song, repeating the words, singing to Joseph, calling out to Africa in the empty living room.

My mom, watching my dance from the kitchen, thought my routine so complex that she asked me to show my ballet teacher after class one day. The instructor, who also taught at West Virginia University during the day, chose me from fifty students to play Max in the dance performance of *Where the Wild Things Are*. In my white pajama leotard, I danced solos across the stage for a packed audience.

The seeds of theater sprouted.

However, it was watching a production of *42nd Street* in London with my family over summer vacation that I knew dance was a serious calling. From our balcony seats, I peered my fourth-grade eyes down on the stage below. Rows and rows of hard tap shoes tickling, scuffing, slamming the bare stage, energized me like nothing had before.

From my earliest years I was able to pick up a dance step immediately—able to flip, turn, and move with agility. When I turned sixteen, my parents threw a Sweet Sixteen birthday for me. As a surprise, they sent this letter to friends and neighbors:

> Sarah's sixteenth birthday will be on April 15. We are planning to surprise her with a series of special messages on each of the sixteen

days before her birthday. If you would like to write a favorite memory (a paragraph or so on a note or card) and send it to us by March 25th, we will arrange it on a birthday "advent" calendar. We know she will be surprised and pleased to hear from you. Just address your card to us, and we'll keep it a secret. Thanks a lot, Judy and Jim

After collecting all the memories, they bound them in a book as a present. One of my favorites was from my mom's brother and his wife:

Dear Sarah, Happy Sweet 16! And you are a sweetheart. My first memory of you is when you were rolling, climbing, and balancing all over your dad in your living room. You were one year old. Your dad said, "Sarah's really physical. She's really coordinated." What an understatement! Even then we could tell how much you enjoyed being on the move. Enjoy this special day . . . All our love, Aunt Sandy and Uncle Jim

In dance and theater in middle school, I found expression for my energy, my need to move, and also sense of acceptance. One of the best teachers I ever had, Miss Adducchio, taught us stage makeup, lighting, and body movement. Edgar Allan Poe's, "The Raven," was performed as a staged reading—all students dressed in black, mini ravens lining the stage, crowing warnings.

In theater, skin color was fused, and acceptance was possible. In seventh grade, Miss Adducchio chose me for the lead in our school production of *Snow White and the Seven Dwarfs in the Black Forest,* which we took on tour to three local elementary schools. In a school of white students, I, the brown girl, was chosen to be Snow White.

Theater in college also challenged me—made me question what masks I already wore. One of my African American teachers, during a private drama review conference suddenly asked, "What is your real eye color?"

Blue contacts floated over my irises.

"Brown."

"Why are you wearing those contacts?"

"Why?" I paused. My mind wandered. Should I tell this teacher how once when I went into a 7-Eleven convenience store, I spotted a beautiful blond lady, the kind of lady whom I wished might be my birth mother—my fantasy of where I came from. When another lady in the check-out line noticed my blue eyes, believing them natural, she said, "Oh, your eyes are so beautiful. You are so pretty." I hoped the blond lady overheard in case she was my biological mother.

My teacher stared at me, straight through my flimsy plastic lenses, straight inside me. Could this teacher see the layers of protection I had wrapped myself in? Did my teacher think I was a black woman hiding out under blues and blonds?

"Why do I wear them? Well, I like them," I said, forcing a smile.

"Why don't you just let your brown eyes show?"

I didn't have an answer.

Another time I spoke with an African American woman. She also asked me about my fake blue contacts, but then she added, "You know, I don't understand why all of these black men are with white women."

Heat flamed through my body.

Too stunned and hurt, I did not respond.

"*I am a product of a black man with a white woman*," I thought. "*So what does that make me? A mistake? Was I?*"

CHAPTER FIFTEEN

Fogbo Junction

The Sierra Leonean sky is known to play tricks on travelers. The sun can glare so hot that water slicks appear a few feet in front of one's eyes; sunsets flame in such a profusion of reds and yellows it is as if the sun is dying. In the distance, an ebony, T-shaped figure moved along the horizon. An abstract Picasso, an elongated figure appeared to be moving closer toward Joe's truck.

Joe squinted his eyes. He wondered if he were hallucinating. The three men stood silent watching the figure move closer.

In the distance Noha carried a tire on his head.

Noha had just traveled twenty-eight miles.

Joe cried out, "There's Noha! There's Noha! Thank God for his life!" He rushed to greet him. The men clapped and cheered. Noha put the tire down and rolled it to the driver.

Mr. Jabba said, "Noha, you're a man!"

As the driver worked on the truck, Noha recounted for the men how he had rolled the tire down hills, carried the tire up hills on his head, and zoomed straight into Bo going directly to the BP gas station [British Petroleum] on Dambala Road as Joe commanded.

While the mechanic patched the punctured tire, Noha grabbed some street food, a cheap plate of rice with cassava leaves.

Wasting no time, he began his exodus out of the teeming city, circled around heaps of garbage, stepped over the beggars, and out again along the dangerous unprotected main road, away from the government soldiers who let him pass.

Fifteen minutes later, the tire was back on the axle. The men reversed the truck and dropped Noha off in Bumpe. Joe let him keep the extra money. Noha headed straight to a medicine woman. Tevie needed to be rubbed on his back. Made of clay and secret herbs, Tevie is shaped like an egg and dried in the sun to harden it. When mixed with water it becomes a paste, which allows the medicine to absorb into the body and heal the patient. Noha needed Tevie all over his back, arms, and legs, which were now in spasms.

"Thank you, Noha," Joe said again. The driver spun the car around and they sped to the village of Dasamu.

CHAPTER SIXTEEN

West Virginia University, Morgantown

Sophomore year at WVU, as I was leaving the college ballet studio, I bumped into a football player I kept running into throughout the summer. When I left play rehearsals, he was leaving football practice. We always said hello, had a few mutual friends, but never had a long conversation. Sitting at the snack café by the classrooms, eating alone, he smiled as I walked past him.

"Hey," he called out from his table. "How are you doing?"

"Hey," I smiled. Handsome, black, and six foot three, he was gorgeous but approachable.

I knew he played on WVU's team, and although I loved to go to the games, I couldn't name players or recite game statistics. Game attendance for me was about socializing in the stands with friends and family. But for most West Virginians the WVU Mountaineers are revered and adopted as their pro team. With a sixty-thousand seat stadium, a minimum of one player goes pro every year, and some years as many as five players are drafted into the NFL.

I walked over to his table, sat down, and we talked for over an hour.

"Could you give me a lift to the downtown campus?" he asked.

The sprawling WVU campus was linked by a tram that carried thousands of students every day to classes, but a car ride was a lot faster.

"Sure," I said.

In the ride between campuses we clicked.

"We should really hang out sometime," he said, as I pulled up to the curb to drop him off.

Yeah," I smiled. "I'd like that."

"I'll call you after Saturday's game."

"Great."

When I returned home that night to my parents' house, I glowed. My family was busy cooking in the kitchen.

"Why such a good mood?" asked my mom.

"I just hung out with the nicest guy."

"A student?" asked my mom.

"Yeah, a senior. He's a football player."

"What's his name?" asked my dad, folding up the newspaper, getting ready to eat.

"His name is Lyle? . . . Lovett? . . . Something with an *L*?" I said. "It's an unusual name."

"Lovett Purnell?" said my dad.

"Yeah! That's it!" I said. "Lovett! I hope he calls. He's really nice."

My mom and dad froze.

"Sarah, do you know who he is?" asked my dad.

For over twenty-five years my dad volunteered for the WVU football stadium ticket office. Until the mid-90s he passed out complimentary tickets given by WVU players to family and classmates. He left three hours early on a Saturday to pass out tickets.

"Lovett's a senior, I know that," I said.

"Sarah, he's one of the best tight ends in the country. The best tight end in the Big East! He's the captain of the WVU team. The NFL scouts are already vying for him. He'll probably be drafted by the end of this year."

"Really?" I said. "He said he'd call after tomorrow's game."

That fall Lovett was featured in the *Mountaineer Illustrated* magazine. The article read:

> " 'I just want to thank the fans for their support. There is no other place I'd rather be than right here, and I mean that from my heart.

That's not something to gain anything because I'm a senior and by now people either love me or hate me. It's been a great time here and I really enjoyed it and I just want to go out with a bang. I hope people will say that Lovett Purnell was a class guy.'

They already do. Lovett, they already do."

Saturday morning could not come fast enough. I had never been more excited for a football game. Although my family had season tickets to all the games since my dad became a professor in 1968, the games, for me, were more about family, friends, and traditions: blue and gold scarves, hot chocolate in silver thermoses, sidewalks dappled with golden maple leaves, driving to the game early with my dad, and coming home after a game to a warm dinner that my parents had cooked that morning. A vat of chili might be started early on a Saturday morning, or a huge lasagna prepared for friends and neighbors to share when we all returned home after a game.

But this Saturday I was focused, riveted, and watching number 82. I never enjoyed a game so much.

West Virginia University won the game.

Crawling through post-game football traffic along the winding West Virginia roads, passing the poplar, maple, and wild cherry trees in their autumn glory, my dad and I both couldn't stop smiling. "Amazing game!" said my dad.

I rolled down the window to smell the autumn air. Crisp leaves and hay. Nutmeg and cedar smoke. My dad fiddled with the radio. On WAJR-AM, the post-game commentator happened to be interviewing Lovett.

"Dad! It's Lovett!" I screamed.

Pepperoni rolls, hot with melted cheese and meat rolled into the piping hot dough waited for us back home.

When my family sat down to eat, conversation buzzed around the table.

Lovett's game was recounted step-by-step. Our neighbors joined us for a late afternoon lunch. I shared how Lovett said he'd call after the game.

Chuckles from the guests spun around the table.

Then the telephone rang.

Every fork stopped midair.

My eyes grew huge. Tiptoeing toward the phone I said, "I'll go get that."

Enthusiastic nods circled the table.

"Hello?" I said.

All ears perked up to listen.

I clutched the phone, then peeked my head back into the kitchen to the waiting table. I mouthed, "It's him!"

During that phone conversation, I invited Lovett over the next day to meet my parents.

The next night Lovett stayed for dinner. An upright piano stood in the living room, and after dinner with my parents, he asked if he could play.

"You play?" I said.

"In church," he said, and sat down. Devoutly Christian, he played a church song: *"It must be, it's got to be, the spirit of the Lord calling me, fall over me Lord, fall all over me."*

By Sunday night my entire family was in love with him.

When he left that evening he said, "Now don't you tell any of my boys I play the piano."

He was dead serious.

We began to date, and I didn't say a word about the piano.

CHAPTER SEVENTEEN

Dasamu

Cheers erupted in the village. When Joe's truck came into view at Dasamu, Mary, Jeneba, and Hindogbae ran to the truck, clapping.

"Daddi is here!!"

"How are you, Daddi?"

Hindogbae plopped into Joe's lap.

Traveling three miles earlier that morning, the group of women and children reached Dasamu, a village of twenty huts, around eleven o'clock. Ninety percent of the villagers had already fled to Bo, leaving a few elderly inhabitants. When the group arrived at the village, they knew no relatives, nor could they buy food, which was scarce. Thankfully, the remaining villagers knew Joe. He had often stopped or traveled through their village on previous trips to Bo. One old woman let Mary, Musu, and Mamie borrow pots and her cooking fire, which consisted of three large, flat stones on which the pot rested. Firewood placed between the stones smoldered. Mary had boiled eggplant and rice in anticipation of the men's return.

Now she set a bowl before Joe. Too nervous to eat, Joe ate only a mouthful. Five o'clock and they still had eleven-and-a-half more miles until they reached Bo. Traveling at night was out of the question. Conversation with the villagers about the rebels and their movement within the forest terrified the group further.

Joe watched his family eat, wondering if it would be their last meal. His stomach hurt. Horrible thoughts consumed him. If attacked, he wondered which family member would he ever see again? Who would have the greatest chance to live?

Sweet Jeneba, ten years old, had only begun to learn to cook rice from her mother. Hindogbae, too young for school, loved to build forts from palm fronds.

Would his children survive the war?

Immediately after the meal, the group piled inside the truck to Bo.

No one in the family knew that Joe had given an order to the driver: in the event of a rebel ambush, Joe commanded the driver to keep driving. Any roadblock, rebel blockade, stop-and-search point, or a direct order for the truck to stop, the driver was to disregard. Joe believed that they had a better chance to live if they kept driving. Some of them would certainly be shot, killed upright in their seats, but if they stopped, death, rape, torture, and maiming were certain for all of them.

Joe's mind twisted around two other possibilities that he didn't discuss with anyone.

First, what if the driver was shot? Joe only knew how to drive an automatic. The Toyota Hilux was a stick shift.

Second, what if a large tree blocked the entire road? Government soldiers and rebels alike were known to blockade a road with trunks of giant cotton trees or piles of palms, making an escape impossible.

The truck door slammed. "It was up to God now," thought Joe.

CHAPTER EIGHTEEN

Maryland

At the end of the school year Lovett was invited to the NFL Scouting Combine, where NFL teams audition and interview players. After that, we visited my sister Lynne, who lived in Maryland, where Lovett also met with an agent. Lovett and I waited in her living room, while my sister filled glasses of mint iced tea in the kitchen. When her twin boys, one-and-a–half-years old, toddled into the living room, they spotted Lovett, imposing and huge. Wails erupting, they screamed for their mom. Their older brother, four-year-old Jonathan, ran into the room, assessed his younger brothers' crying and said in his little boy voice, "Oh, they don't like black."

My sister and I gasped at the same time. Air sucked out of both our lungs, and my sister narrowly saved the glasses of ice tea from crashing onto the floor.

Jonathan saw the shocked expression on my face, heard both his mother's and my sharp intakes of air, and blurted out, "SPIDERS! They don't like black spiders!"

Lovett burst into laughter and bent his six-foot, three-inch, 238-pound frame down to the boys' level and introduced himself.

My sister burned red and my entire back shot stiff.

Nap time came before we sat down for tea. Tucking Jonathan into bed, my sister sat on one side of him and I sat on the other.

Gently my sister asked, "Jonathan, do you think black people are different than other people?"

"No," he shook his head, perplexed.

A big football player in anyone's room could be intimidating for anyone, but especially for two one-and-a–half-year-old babies used to being at home alone with their mom.

"Are different-colored people scary?" she asked.

"No."

"What did you mean when you said your brothers don't like black?"

"They got scared because Lovett is big."

"Yes, he is big. Does that have anything to do with black?"

"No," he said.

"No, it doesn't." She kissed him on the head.

"Good night," and I kissed him on the head next.

My sister gently closed the door to his room.

Walking down the stairs, back to Lovett, I realized that sweet little Jonathan was commenting on Lovett being different. Confusing *tall, big,* and *imposing* with a color.

That evening I apologized to Lovett and explained a little boy's confusion.

Lovett laughed again.

"Sarah, I understand," he said. "I'd be scared of me, too, if I were a toddler!"

Meeting Lovett my sophomore year created a powerful shift for me. He was the first person in college that made me feel accepted. He set such high goals, practicing so much personal discipline. Maybe because he was so at peace with himself, he radiated some of that inner balance to me. A month and a half after the Combine, Lovett received a call. The New England Patriots drafted him.

CHAPTER NINETEEN

Road to Bo

With eleven more miles to Bo, everyone in the truck was silent. No radio, no chatter, not even a group prayer. Adrenaline pumped through Joe's body. Every primal fight-or-flight synapse readied as the truck bumped along the road to Bo.

Two miles covered, and no other cars. Refugees walking, yet still no sign of rebels. Joe's eyes scanned the bush, hyperalert for movement or camouflages. Along these final few miles Joe thought of America. He reflected back to his life twenty years earlier in West Virginia where he might have stayed, but chose to return to his home, Sierra Leone. Now, because of that choice, he was sputtering along a stretch of dirt that would determine whether his family would live or die.

But he had wanted to come home—to Africa. He had wanted to teach, to bring back his education to the people of Bumpe village. He wanted to return to a place of constant climates and be relieved of the sudden jarring from hot and dripping West Virginia summers to freezing West Virginia ice storms. He had wanted to come back to a land where life is lived outdoors; the sharing among extended family members constant, and where most everyone is kin; a place where friends and relatives visit frequently and without notice. He missed the masked dancers on Christmas Day and the libation ceremonies with bowls of hot rice set out for ancestors. He missed the wild mangoes and guavas that grew all over the village and the okra sauces and sweet potato leaves cooked in palm oil that his Grandma Abie made. He even missed the taste of powdered beans.

Joe did not understand discrimination in America either. In Sierra Leone, with the exception of the missionaries, everyone was black. Whites in Sierra Leone, like the United Brethren in Christ missionaries who started the high school in Bumpe, were helpful and gracious people. They brought kerosene for hurricane lamps and antivenom medicine to his village.

One of Joe's best friends in America during his five-year stay was a white pastor, Reverend Amos Kipe. When Reverend Amos vacationed in Florida, he asked Joe to house-sit and take care of things while Joe attended school. As promised, Joe began mowing the Reverend's front lawn.

A white male, passing by in his car, stopped and yelled out his window, "You black nigger, what are you doing in this white neighborhood?"

Joe loathed how some people in America claimed to be Christian, but did not like black people. "How could they reject what God has created?" he wondered. Over and over again he asked himself if people would discriminate against him in the next world.

Up ahead on the road, the next world might not be far off. A band of soldiers blockaded the road.

CHAPTER TWENTY

West Virginia University, Morgantown

Shakespeare in the hallway at WVU was common. Acting partners often practiced a scene before class, volleying lines back and forth.

"Thou shalt . . . ," I said, repeating my lines to my class partner, Kristina.

"Thou Shalt . . . NOT!" mocked two black women passing by in the hallway. Exploding into laughter, they kept walking, singing: "Thou shalt NOT!" Their falsetto voices echoed down the hall. They were the same girls who laughed at me in the student union when Tyrone called me "Simba." My acting partner was infuriated by their mocking remarks. She stopped mid-sentence and started to yell down the hall.

"Please don't!" I said. "Anything you say I'll have to deal with later if I am alone."

Kristina looked at me. "Okay, Sarah, okay."

Adrenaline zinged up my spine. If only I could separate rudeness from my racial identity. I wondered if the two women were just rude, or if they viewed me as a light-skinned target? Just the past week when visiting with a white friend I unwittingly was caught in a fight between my friend and her black boyfriend. During the argument, someone called out, "And you—you're just a little white girl!"

His words sounded like: "And, you! You're not black enough!"

I wanted to scream, "Leave me alone!" All of my past anger came up. That night in my diary I wrote:

> What would happen if you woke up one morning and everything was white? Everyone was made of snow. Beautiful white sparkling snow and along came a little ball of fire and wherever she went, people didn't understand her because she was hot and would melt them. She lived in a snow white world and little fire had to learn how to fit in this world. She would see another little fire somewhere but they were confused by her because she looked like fire but acted like snow people. So now little fire didn't know where to go. She didn't look like snow and didn't act like fire . . .

Racial identity questions made me wonder: "What did my biological father look like? Was he the color of dark coffee beans? What were his features like?" Phrases I never heard growing up were: "You have your mom's big toe!" "You have your father's nose!" "Look at that dimple—just like your grandpa!"

Even before more heavy thoughts crossed my mind like—"Why was I given up?"—I just longed to look like someone—anyone. So many times I scanned faces in the crowd, searching for familiar features.

But I did not begin a physical search for my birth parents in college. I was too busy, distracted with plays, academic courses, and classical singing lessons. Although I thought my desire to search for my father had subsided, my subconscious began the search again without me.

I began dating an African.

After Lovett and I amicably broke up when he left for the NFL and I had two more years of college, I started to hang out with a group of African students studying at WVU on student visas. Makana sought me out first.

Five African students from Ethiopia, Ghana, and Nigeria congregated at small house parties. The BBC news blasted on the radio. They debated world politics, American trade policies (they loved President Clinton), and African leadership.

When Makana and I began dating I knew he was from an elite African family. Long and lean, six foot three, with a shaved head, he was so smooth a black skin tone that he looked painted. A statue or an African carving could not be more stunning. Without an ounce of fat, Makana's every muscle was sculpted and visible. He was disciplined and determined and ambitious—focused on an education that he could bring back to his country.

Heaping bowls of spaghetti bubbled on the stove in Makana's apartment. Friday and Saturday nights in the Africans' home were spent talking, eating, and listening to music—especially rap. The Africans loved American rap. They loved the saying "*East Side, West Side!,*" which they appropriated to mean the "East side" of Africa and a playful tease against the "West side"—Ghana. Rap music for the African students revealed a mastery and dexterity with words and rhythm they could not believe. Rappers talked with a command of language the African students coveted—an ability to slide in and out of rhythm, an ease with consonants that took them years to master in school. "The rappers handle the Queen's language so well," they would say, referring to the British-taught English in their countries.

For acting class, one assignment was to master a strange dialect. An Ethiopian accent seemed exotic enough so I asked one of the Ethiopian housemates for lessons, which he gladly gave, but he would not let me tape his voice. In Ethiopia taping a voice or taking a picture is forbidden in many communities. Soul stealing was still believed in, and protecting the vibration and timbre of one's voice was paramount.

Spending time with the Africans, I learned that a few of them came from polygamous communities—their rich fathers had many wives, which enabled the women and children better access to resources. However, for one African student who did not live in the house, the polygamy allowed him to think nothing of cheating on his American girlfriend. As elites in their own country, the five African students bore an incredible responsibility to return home educated—mixed at times with attitudes of entitlement.

As Makana and I continued to date, his treatment of me changed. One afternoon as we were driving, I opened a bag of chips. He turned to me and said, "You really shouldn't eat that. You're getting a little fat."

When I called one evening and said I wasn't feeling well, that I had caught a cold, he said, "Well, don't come over and give it to me."

For three months we dated, and after three weeks I should have known better, but something inside me was twisting, turning, connecting wires that should not have been sparked. I realized I substituted Makana's approval as an African male for symbolic approval from my birth father. "Was my birth father like Makana?" I wondered. "Was an elite African, studying in West Virginia, like my father?"

For three months I stayed, attracted by his bearing, his beautiful accent, his love of the BBC "Focus on Africa" and world affairs; and maybe I stayed because if he turned out to be a good guy, my father was a good guy, too.

CHAPTER TWENTY-ONE

Tikonko Junction

For Mende people, heaven is called *ngolegohun*, the great white sand, and is believed to be a place of abundant food, and hell is a place where one devours one's own body. In Tikonko Junction, six miles after Dasamu, Joe thought of both heaven and hell. Looking through the dust-streaked windshield, he began to tremble. Up ahead a band of soldiers, all armed, stood in the middle of the roadblock. They were not dressed in the green and brown camouflage uniforms of government soldiers.

"Stop the truck!" they commanded. Surrounding the truck, black faces peered into the windows on all sides.

Joe could not stop shaking.

Too many weapons, AK-47s and single barrel guns swung on their backs, aimed, and poised. Any plan to outrun a roadblock or abandon the truck and dart into the bush collapsed.

The driver put the truck in park.

One soldier approached the truck, swept his eyes over Hindogbae and Jeneba. The women, wide-eyed in the back, did not look up.

The soldier assessed the family's belongings. "Kamajors," the soldier said to Joe.

"Kamajors!" repeated Joe and he threw his head back, laughing and tearing at the same time. Reaching his hand out the window, he shook the soldiers' hands one after the other, pumping his hand with theirs with gratitude, respect, reverence.

"Kamajors!" he cried to his family.

"Kamajors!" they all shouted, laughing and clapping.

In Mende *Kamajoi* translates to *hunter,* but not an ordinary hunter. Kamajors not only braved the night to track leopards, but also confronted evil spirits and witches who roamed the forests. A *Kamajoi* was a member of a secret society. This line of great hunter-warriors, adorned with amulets, guided by ancestral spirits, initiated in rituals deep in the bush, and coated with ointments and herbs with magical powers, were believed to be impenetrable to bullets. They were also believed to possess the power of invisibility and divination.

Joe studied the Kamajors' uniforms. Dressed in country cloth *ronkos,* their shirts were covered in talismans of cowry shells, tiny mirrors, and animal horns.

Regardless if one believed the mythic powers of Kamajors, it was undisputed that Kamajors became an unpaid civil defense force, a citizens' militia, a band of great hunters aligned with government forces. They called upon traditional hunting myths to imbue them with the psychological stealth greater than the feared RUF. To counteract the rebels terror, Kamajors reactivated traditional myths in an act of "reverse juju." Soon they coalesced into a guerilla force who petrified rebel soldiers.

"Where are you going?" a Kamajor asked.

"Bo," replied Joe.

One of Joe's former students, now a Kamajor, approached the car window and shook Joe's hand.

Joe jumped out of the truck, unlocked the trunk, and gathered some palm oil, rice, and lima beans to give to the group of Kamajors. Kamajors fought without a salary. It was up to the citizens to support them for their protection.

"Thank you," said the soldier.

It is disputed how Kamajors united into a fighting force against the RUF, but one version reported by a Sierra Leone scholar, Patrick Muana, in his essay, "The Kamajoi Militia: Civil War, Internal Displacement and the Politics of Counter-Insurgency" is as follows:

> Following an RUF attack on a village in the Jong (Jange) Chiefdom, the rebels are reported to have massacred people in the village including a great "Kamajoi" and medicine man called Kposowai. His brother Kundorwai, is said to have been captured by the rebels, forced to carry looted goods, and tied (*tabay*) securely for the night whilst the rebels pitched camp. As he drifted to sleep in spite of his pains, Kundorwai is said to have had a vision of his brother who had been killed the day before. The ropes fell loose and the elder brother invested him with the authority to take the message to all able-bodied Mende men that the defense of their own lives, homes, wives, and children was a sacred duty. To assist them in the task, Kposowai is said to have shown Kundorwai a secret concoction of herbs and instructed that a stringent initiation process should precede the "washing" of the warriors in the herbs. This concoction would make them invisible in battle, impervious to bullets, and endow them with powers of clairvoyance if all taboos were kept. Kundorwai is said to have then slaughtered the RUF rebels, freed the other captives, and trekked several miles to a secret hiding place where he initiated the first set of men.

"Be well, good luck," said the Kamajor.

"Thank you. May God bless you," said Joe.

Seven miles remained until they reached Bo. Joe knew that unlike the Kamajors, they would travel the final miles to Bo with no herbs granting invisibility.

CHAPTER TWENTY-TWO

Chicago

Yale School of Drama, the American Conservatory Theater, New York University, and Purdue all held graduate school group auditions in Chicago during my senior year at WVU. Instead of auditioning for different master's degree programs all over the country, a consortium of schools called URTA, the University/Resident Theatre Association, hosted one weekend of auditions which saved students time and money.

By my senior year of college, I knew I wanted to pursue a master's degree in fine arts.

Plus, I wanted to stay in school.

Diving into Los Angeles or New York at the age of twenty-two terrified me. I knew I needed more training, more professional feedback, more time to grow up and have a better sense of the world and myself.

One rainy weekend, while still a student at WVU, I flew to Chicago to audition for graduate school. The next three years of my life would be determined in a weekend.

After the private acting audition for A.C.T. two interviewers asked me, "What do you like to do best in your free time?"

"Weddings!" I blurted out.

"Weddings?" they said and laughed at the abruptness of my response.

"I love going to weddings!" I said with a smile. "You get to dance, eat cake, and socialize, and everybody is happy."

It must have been an unusual answer, nothing self-serving or coy. I didn't say I love to read plays, write scripts, or make socially conscious documentaries. No, I said the first thing that sprung into my mind.

Weddings.

People dancing, people belonging. Eating food in abundance; a community that believes in the beauty of a partnership.

Was my subconscious erupting or percolating again? Did my birth parents ever marry? Buried beneath, did I want a love story for them? An elopement, a secret wedding between a white woman and black man in a field, in the forest, on a beach, even in a city hall?

But there was nothing.

My birth certificate failed to tell me what I needed to know most. It did not state my biological parents' names. Instead it listed my adopted parents Jim and Judy, both thirty four years old when they adopted me. How did I get here? How did a man from Sierra Leone ever meet my mother, a continent away? How did my father even travel to America? How did a man from an "important" family, as my mom told me back in high school, even bump into my biological mother, a local girl from West Virginia?

I had no answers. However, I did get a reply from A.C.T. a few weeks later. San Francisco would be my new home for the next three years.

CHAPTER TWENTY-THREE

Bo

The city of Bo opened like the city of Oz, except an African version of Oz in the middle of a civil war. The yellow brick road morphed into red dirt gullies jammed with potholes, Kamajors, refugees, and rebels. Government soldiers surrounded the steaming, overcrowded city, bloated with 20,000 refugees and amputees swelling the population to 80,000. Checkpoints and roadblocks radiated outward from the city. All roads into Bo were now fortified with tree trunks, traps, and soldiers.

By late afternoon, Joe's truck made it to the outskirts of the city, near Bo's airport, where he was stopped once again. Government soldiers checked inside for weapons, machetes, and guns; they opened all bags, rustling through their clothes; after climbing into the truck, even searching his pockets for ammunition pellets, they allowed Joe's vehicle to enter the city.

People packed the streets. Horns blared as traffic stalled. Filthy mopeds wove in and out of traffic, wheeling around street umbrella stands. Vendors hawked anything—used shoes, old clothes, rotted fruit—to make money. Joe's truck sputtered along the main drag joining a twilight zone parade. Lost children scanned faces and the hems of dresses for their mothers, amputees wept along the side of the road. People who had lived in the bush for days arrived in the city famished, barefoot, and without any relatives. Men with wheelbarrows besieged the streets. In Krio they shouted for work,

"Job-dae! Job-dae! Job-dae!" Stray dogs roamed Bo. Cholera and typhoid fever assaulted the city as sanitation was nonexistent.

Joe's truck drove up Fenton Road, the main street in Bo, passing Lebanese diamond merchants' boarded-up shops and bars. Star beer, Fanta, Guinness Stout, and Coca-Cola sweated in glass bottles on dirty outdoor tables for the rich. Government soldiers with guns ready, dotted every inch of the city. Babies, tied to their mothers' backs in large pieces of cloth, wailed, adding to the confusion and chaos of the street.

Inside the truck, Little, accustomed to the small village of Bumpe and his favorite trees, went berserk. Inhaling the dust from the packed streets of a Third World African city in the middle of a civil war was enough to make a man or animal insane.

Women in their *lappas* swooshed by on either side of the truck carrying multiple baskets of fabric stacked upon their heads. Hawking pathetic bundles of scrawny wood, little boys roamed the street desperate for a buyer.

Only a year ago, the bustle of women on Fenton Road in their vivid tie-dye *gara* fabric looked like mobiles twirling past—an African tribute to Matisse. But now the bustle on the street knotted into raw survival. Kerosene lamps and wells would need to service eighty thousand people.

Although Joe had a well-to-do cousin, Mrs. Gladys Soya-Bonga, who lived in Bo, he feared her home might already be overcrowded with relatives. She was one of three wives. His cousin's husband, Mr. Foday Soya-Bonga, a pharmacist, owned a compound housing his three wives, which included two large, two-story houses.

Joe's truck pushed through the street toward 21 Fenton Road in the heart of downtown.

Darkness was descending over Bo, and Joe decided they would stay the first night with his cousin Lansana Mansarary and his wife on Beimba Road. Lansana owned a much smaller apartment, but they could reach his home before complete blackness overcame the city. The driver dropped the truck's other passengers off along Fenton Road, as they had plans to stay with their own relatives.

The driver continued on to Beimba Road, where Joe asked him to sleep in the Toyota outside Lansana's apartment for fear it would be stolen. Inside Lansana's home, Mrs. Mansarary served everyone a good meal, but could not offer Joe's family beds—only mats on the floor.

Early the next morning Joe planned to visit the Soya-Bonga compound. He needed to see if there was any space left for his family.

CHAPTER TWENTY-FOUR

San Francisco

Finding housing in San Francisco was almost as bad as finding parking there. People took turns guarding a parking spot along the curvy streets, making sure to save the space until a friend pulled into the plot. Coming from Morgantown, West Virginia, with its sprawling mountains, and a stone's throw from Cheat Lake, a place where even the most modest homes sit upon at least an acre of land, I was unprepared for my new residence in the Haight-Ashbury district. Instead of wild deer, chipmunks, and pileated woodpeckers in the backyards, my surroundings included open cafes lining the streets, incense wafting out of Rastafarian shops, and leaflets littering the street advertising midnight poetry slams.

Walking along Haight Street, acclimating to the steady rhythm of buses crisscrossing the city, I thought back to my A.C.T. audition that brought me here. I shook my head laughing at how I blurted out, "Weddings!" But now in the heat of the city, I was not thinking about weddings or my birth parents, or Africa, or my missing father; instead I missed wide-open spaces and nature. For me, any association with nature made me think of my dad.

As a child I found a turtle in my backyard, and my dad, always the scientist, suggested I paint my initials on its shell in red paint: S.C. Then we let it go, hoping one day we might see it again and discover how far it traveled. Only a week later a neighbor across the street called and asked if we lost a turtle. He found one in his driveway with an S.C. on its back.

An ambulance zoomed past, and I stepped back onto the sidewalk.

No wild turtles walked the streets of the Haight-Ashbury district. Instead, steady sirens, which would have all the neighbors talking back home, blared constantly.

For a few weeks before classes at A.C.T. began, as I searched for permanent housing, I lived with some family friends, sleeping on their couch. I baked chocolate chip cookies with their two young children, Ian and Rose, admired their cool collection of black-and-white photographs lining their cobalt blue bathroom, and tried to learn the city bus system. Strolling through Chinatown, up the hills of crowded shops with hanging skinned chickens, fresh fish, barrels of noodles for sale, and streetlights in the shapes of Chinese lanterns, I maneuvered through pulsating crowds.

No one knew me in San Francisco.

Ethnic people, people of color, an entire Chinese section of town—truly diverse people populated the streets.

I didn't stand out at all.

"I could get lost here," I thought, and that felt like a good thing.

"Are you from Brazil?" someone asked me on the street.

"No," and I smiled.

My back ached after a week of couch sleeping, and in a few days I would know if my application for a studio apartment for students was accepted. Until then, I kept exploring the streets, weaving through racks of vintage clothes positioned on sidewalks, swirling past hippies in long gypsy skirts, peeking into tattoo parlors and body piercing shops, and smiling at lots of brown-skinned girls with Afros who smiled back at me.

CHAPTER TWENTY-FIVE

Bo—Fenton Road

Sleeping bodies lined every square inch of the two houses on 21 Fenton Road. Over one hundred relatives descended on the Soya-Bonga houses, and more relatives, refugees from Bumpe, knocked on the door everyday for shelter. In fact, the Soya-Bonga home had a nickname: "Bumpe Town." On an average day, twenty relatives arrived at Gladys's home, most clutching a single bundle of clothes.

Joe and his family were no exception.

Early that morning Joe and Mary walked down Fenton Road toward the compound. In the distance they spotted Gladys sitting in a chair on the veranda. As they approached the gated compound, which surrounded an inner dirt courtyard, Gladys called out a greeting. *"Bu Waa!"* she said rising from her chair.

"Bu Waa!" Joe and Mary called back.

Gladys was not surprised to see Joe. Many relatives recounted their stories of escape through the bush, trekking thirty miles on foot to seek sanctuary in the government-fortified city of Bo. Gladys did not turn one person away. In fact she cautioned people to stay. When a truckload of her cousins from Yengema and Kpetema decided to venture back to their villages and retrieve their belongings, they never returned. Rebels ambushed them, locked them in their house, splashed kerosene across the outside walls and torched the house. No one escaped.

As long as there was room on the floor or on Gladys's front porch, people were welcome to sleep at her home. Although as a host she would make one token dish to offer guests as Mende hospitality required, guests were responsible for their own food. Sometimes relatives would eat at other homes and come back in the evening to sleep.

The largest room, the living room was used to sleep people packed in rows. At night, women used one of their extra wrappers, a loose African dress, as blankets to sleep on or under. Nursing mothers cradled their babies under their arms, protective wings against the mass of bodies. Thirty-seven people slept on the living room floor. The closeness of the bodies in such a small space gave birth to a sauna—overheated people gasping for air through the long night. Because the room retained so much heat, the windows were propped open for relief.

In swept the mosquitoes.

Malaria soon infected half the people in the house.

Unlike many of the relatives flooding the house, Joe was given a single bedroom instead of floor space. As an educated man, a high school principal, and son of a Paramount Chief, it would be disrespectful and shameful to not give him a private room.

Inside the tiny room Mary and Joe slept on the bed with little Hindogbae between them. Their daughter Jeneba and Mary's sister, Moiyatu, slept four to a bed in another room with two other female cousins. Little, with no trees in the center of the compound for him, was temporarily locked in a detached building in the compound called a kitchen house. This small storage unit held pots, pans, buckets, and wet rice in its ceiling. Inches from the zinc roof, the rice dried from the radiant heat of the hot metal.

Daily necessities such as using the toilet became hour-long undertakings. Starting at four in the morning, different members of the household lined up to use the two latrines in the back of the house. The deep hole in the ground bubbled over with sewage. The next bathroom shift began at five o'clock in the morning; then again at six o'clock. Finally the latrines became so overwhelmed that workers had to be brought in in the middle of the night to empty them. With a city on the brink of starvation, latrine emptiers lined up for the coveted job.

Everyone within the house had only to look outside on the street below to feel blessed. Thousands of homeless refugees on the streets with no family, no income, no savings, made each guest grateful for a sliver of floor space.

CHAPTER TWENTY-SIX

San Francisco

San Francisco's homeless population filled every other nook in the city, contorting into impossibly narrow doorways, their faces appeared as gaunt gargoyles. Mentally ill women pushed shopping carts up steep hills, and an army of homeless flopped on park benches.

Coming from West Virginia, I had never seen so many homeless people in a concentrated place. Back home, the most visible homeless man on the streets of Morgantown was the "yup yup" man. An elderly grandfather-type, a fixture on the downtown street corner, endlessly agreeing with himself.

After a few months in the city, every time I ate out in a restaurant I saved half my meal to hand to a homeless person on the way home; and I was eating out a lot because my new apartment had no kitchen. Finally I found a studio apartment, one tiny room that was affordable—perhaps because of its location on the city's trash and recycle route. Just outside my window, beginning at five o'clock in the morning the recycling truck came to hoist away the street's empty bottles and cans—a jolting crash of thousands and thousands of falling glass bottles and aluminum cans cascading into the truck's metal chamber.

One fall evening, hauling my Riverside Shakespeare, a book as heavy as a cement block, I headed to the corner laundromat. I shoved my clothes in the washer and sat on top of an unused washer to study my lines for class.

Tide liquid, goopy blue, pooled in puddles below me. The late autumn light cast a warm glow through the dirty windows, as I read alone in the Wash-&-Go undisturbed.

Suddenly a man dashed into the laundromat, a white man in his forties, nicely dressed. Frantic, with his head swiveling in all directions, he asked, "Is there a bathroom in here?"

"I don't think so," I said.

"Oh, okay," he said breathlessly.

I resumed reading, legs dangling over the washer, when I realized the man was still in the laundromat. He had propped open a dryer door to disguise his mid-section, a steel apron in front of him.

"Are you masturbating?" I blurted out.

"I'm sorry, so sorry," he said, embarrassed. "It's really great you're not freaking out." He dashed out into the night.

I jumped off the washer, looked out the front door into the crowded city street, and knew he wasn't coming back. Alone again, I wished I was home, far away from masturbating men in laundromats. Looking out the dark city window, I loved my new freedom, a city that burst with shades of brown, black, and every color in between, but I missed singing in the choir at church with my dad. I missed running up to the third floor of the church for practice, people warming up, trilling notes, and dressing in our long burgundy choir robes. I missed the hot chocolate and Danishes the choir director set out for us. I missed singing Christmas carols, holding candles in the dark—"Silent Night" ringing through the church as the heat from the candles lit our faces and the little circular paper protected our hands from the hot dripping wax.

Although my classes from eight in the morning to ten at night covering speech, dance, voice, acting, stage combat, Alexander Technique, diction, and fencing all kept me busy, I had never been so lonely. Spiraling thoughts filled my head. I thought back to my childhood when my parents read me a book about adoption.

It was called *Different & Alike:*

> Because we are not all exactly alike, we say we are different. Being different is only another way of being you. Some differences are

> greater than others. Your skin may be black, white, or yellow—and you notice it is different from someone else's skin . . . And having different people in the world is what makes it an interesting place to live!

Inside the book pictures of cartoon children filled the pages. The one I remembered most was a girl in a wheelchair. At that young age, I did not quite grasp the words of the book—only the pictures. I never shared this with anyone, but I remember concluding as a child that if someone in a wheelchair was different, and my parents were reading me this book, I must be as different as the girl in the wheelchair. At that young age I wondered if I was disabled on the inside.

Homesick, exhausted, and overwhelmed by the city, my pregnant sister Laura came to the rescue. Laura, her husband, Mike, who was a Lieutenant Colonel in the Air Force, and their three-year-old daughter, Mackenzie, were stationed across the bay at Travis Air Force Base. On many weekends I took the ferry across the bay to sink inside a warm, loving home filled with familiar family photos.

One Monday in the middle of dance class at A.C.T., Mike called me with the news: "It's a boy!"

Mike, in his Air Force flight suit from the 21st Airlift Squadron, picked me up at the ferry landing in the city of Vallejo. He dropped me off at the base medical center where I could share some alone time with Laura while he went to pick up Mackenzie staying with friends.

When I walked into Laura's hospital room, Laura looked pale and exhausted in her light blue hospital gown. After having a cesarean section she could hardly move.

"Laura!" I said and kissed her on the cheek.

Beside her lay her son, all 8 pounds 12 ounces of him swaddled in his blanket, asleep inside a plastic hospital bassinet.

"He's beautiful!" I marveled at his perfect pink fingers, his chest billowing up and down. Less than twenty-four-hours old, his head was covered in a tiny blue-and-white-striped hat.

"How are you?" I asked, holding her hand.

"I'm in so much pain. I can't even pick up my baby. It hurts too much."

"What can I do?" I asked.

"I can't even lift my arm to brush my hair. Can you get the hair out of my eyes? Can you brush my hair?" she asked.

"I would love to," I said.

My sister's shoulder-length blondish hair was limp, strands still plastered against her neck from sweat. Slowly I took the plastic-bristle brush and gently combed against her scalp. With each stroke Laura became sleepier and sleepier and my mind began to wander. I thought of my birth mother. "Did she give birth to me all alone in the hospital? Who came to visit her? Did she gaze at me from her bed the way Laura looked at her child—eyes filled with love, exhaustion, and awe?"

I kept stroking Laura's hair until it fell soft and untangled around her lovely face. With a hair barrette, I fastened some strands to keep out of her eyes.

When I was a baby I shared a bedroom with Laura. At one-and-a-half years old I used to throw empty plastic baby bottles at her from my crib trying to get her to change my diapers. In the hospital I finally got a chance to be a big sister back to her.

Mike and Mackenzie returned and joined us in the room. Mackenzie, in her denim jumper and turtleneck with flowers, ran to see her new brother. Her long, brown ringlets bounced behind her. I filmed the family together, watching Mackenzie kissing her baby brother for the first time. She wanted to name the baby *Smitty* or even *Daisy* after her favorite doll. To Mackenzie's chagrin, Laura and Mike decided on *Bryan*.

I flashed back to when I learned my name was once Esther. I wondered how my birth mother came up with my name. Queen Esther in the Bible kept her husband's love. She also saved her people. When my birth mother gazed at me in a hospital bassinet, I wondered what dreams she wished for me.

CHAPTER TWENTY-SEVEN

Bo—Fenton Road

When evening enveloped Bo, a strange beauty arched over the Soya-Bonga compound. As the women inside the gates began to cook the evening meal, each of their fire pits lit a corner of the courtyard. Like bursting fireworks, one fire after another sparked to life. With a passed ember stick, twenty small cooking fires were lit in the outdoor space shared between the two houses. By rotating a single pot or pan between three stone hearths, the women cooked a plate of rice or a bowl of boiled vegetables, and for another day everyone managed to eat.

While the mothers cooked, the children passed a dying soccer ball between the fires, or played games of hide-and-seek. On nights when the full moon emerged, the entire compound rejoiced. Rebels destroyed the electricity supply in Bo, but the iridescent moonlight granted a few illuminated evenings. Children would sing folk songs to the full moon. In their high, sweet voices, the children greeted the moon in the blue-black African night:

Ngawu nini la,
the new moon has appeared
elaa Ngolehu lor
it has appeared in the forest

Mu loong a kpekpeya yawobu gorla huwe
we are standing in appreciation.

The full moon in Africa, a giant orb, sunk low in a silky black sky, became primitive electricity for villagers. Before the war, children played games all night under the celestial illumination. Adults poured into verandas and clearings to tell stories, sing, and recount memories.

With the threat of rebel attack looming daily, relaxed moments like these were rare.

If life inside the compound was unbearable for Joe, outside on the streets was no better; so many people from Bumpe recognized him, that when he walked the streets, relatives begged him for money, and friends trailed him with relentless pleas for help. He struggled to support his own wife and children. Supporting anyone else was not an option.

Joe vowed that in the next few days he would canvas Bo searching for another home for his family. In the meantime, he had his driver park the truck inside the compound tucked away from Fenton Road where it could easily be stolen or stripped of its parts.

The sole redeeming factor about the overcrowded house was its proximity to the largest open air market in the city. Joe, having money in his possession, went to buy rice, fish, greens, and vegetables. Cornmeal, lima beans, and bulgur wheat, given out from relief agencies such as the World Food Program, sustained half the population. Bags stamped: UNITED STATES: NOT TO BE SOLD OR EXCHANGED bulged with grains, weighted like trophies. Vegetables, transported into Bo by desperate farmers who still worked in unprotected villages, fetched an excellent profit. *Bonga* fish, sold both dried and fresh, trickled into the city from seaside towns. *Bonga* fish was so heavily consumed that *Bonga* was synonymous with a *fool* since the fish is stupid enough to be captured so easily. Market people said, *"You tink say me na bonga?"* (Do you think I'm a fool?) Unpolluted swampland, dotting the outskirts of the city of Bo, supported the growth of cassava leaves and okra, which landowners farmed for the famished population.

Some families without money collected firewood from the surrounding bush—a risky endeavor, leaving the soldiers' protection. However, a sale enabled them to buy a few cups of bulgur wheat. Rice was fast becoming a luxury. A live chicken, a trophy during peacetime, was now impossible to buy.

Even a monkey would be delicious.

CHAPTER TWENTY-EIGHT

San Francisco

Five professors perched in chairs behind the review table. The empty student chair sat in the center of the room before them. Final Review, a twenty-minute meeting with all the professors at A.C.T., took place in June right before summer break. During this meeting, each student's dramatic performances, voice, speech, and dance were critiqued. More than a performance review, students were given feedback on how certain personality quirks, pretenses we brought to roles, or masks we hid behind were impeding our ability to develop as actors.

"Sarah Culberson," called one professor. I entered the classroom, which doubled as the Alexander Technique room, posters of spines and vertebrae hanging on the wall.

I smiled at the five professors and sat down in the student chair. Silence filled the room as they filed away notes from the previous student.

I held my breath, sitting straighter.

Finally, the review of my first year began. I am sure they commented on my dance technique, my vocal range, and my acting scenes at length, but I only remembered one sentence. The kindest, most grandfatherly of the five professors looked straight at me and said, "Sarah, you don't have to smile all the time."

Fire hit my solar plexus.

"Yeah, I do," I wanted to say. "That's how I make things okay."

My professors didn't know how my smile saved me in high school history class when a teacher spoke of African History, Malcolm X, or Martin Luther King Jr. and the entire class, a collective group of heads turned to me, the lone biracial student; as if based on my skin color I should be an expert, an authority, a representative on all things black. I smiled back then because I did not know what to say.

"Thank you," I said.

Ironically, my teachers were able to discern more of who I was and what I was hiding through the many masks of acting. I had expected to hear about posture, diaphragm breathing, and stage presence, but not this. But the Final Review was not an exercise in foot rubs and empty compliments. The review was about growth.

I didn't have to smile all the time.

CHAPTER TWENTY-NINE

Bo—Humble Cottage

Money, wired from London to Joe's brother in Bo, enabled an unexpected diversion during the war.

Every day Joe traipsed through Bo in search of housing, rationed his dwindling savings to provide a meal for his family. Most days, his family subsisted on a single serving of food. However, when Tommy Kposowa, his brother, visited the compound on Fenton Road, he shared a secret with Joe. A few extra leones had been sent from his son, Joe-Songu, living in the United Kingdom.

"Joe, do you want to go to a bar?" he asked. "Forget the war for an evening?"

Joe told his family he was going out with his brother. The two of them headed to Humble Cottage, a bar owned by a Sierra Leonean. Inside, pretty young waitresses scribbled drink orders as African music, reggae, rap, and popular songs blared from a speaker on the stage. Dancing in the middle of a civil war seemed unimaginable, but both men smiled, grateful that the dance floor still existed.

Tommy and Joe did not feel like dancing. But they each ordered a Guinness Stout. Then another. And another.

Brother to brother, sharing their fears, they dared to contemplate: If rebels attacked, where should they go? Did they risk a return to Bumpe to rescue some of the school's supplies—the generator, the desks, books? Would their sons ever attend school? Could their families survive if they died of typhoid? In Sierra Leone, it is shameful for a man to cry. Little boys are taught to control their emotions. As the head of the family, the man must provide food and shelter for his family. A Krio saying states: *Bad man bete pas emit os:* a bad man is better than an empty house. Both the women and men suffered from the pressures of gender expectations.

Joe ordered another stout.

The bitter ale began to swirl in his stomach. It had been so long since he drank anything but well water from the compound. When so many relatives drank from the shared well, the well dried up. Swamp water substituted for well water. To insure against cholera or other waterborne diseases, prudent members of the Soya-Bonga house boiled the water. Others could not wait, and recklessly drank water straight from the swamps.

Tommy reminded Joe of their blessings. Bo, a protected city, was the safest place to live. Ringed by government roadblocks on all sides, and Kamajors reinforcing the soldiers, it was the best they could hope for.

After every beer the waitress collected money. During the war asking for a bar tab was laughable. Humble Cottage trusted no customer enough to pay politely upon leaving. After every drink, Tommy dug into his pockets, scooped out a few leones for the waitress. When each cold, sweaty bottle arrived on the table, both men said a silent thank-you to Joe-Songu and toasted to an evening of forgetting.

CHAPTER THIRTY

Morgantown

Clouds clumped outside my airplane window. In the six-hour flight back to the East Coast for the summer, each passing cloud formed a swirl of images—a perfect backdrop for reviewing my first year of graduate school at A.C.T. Lonely was the best way to describe it. New city, new friends, new apartment, new teachers. Incredibly long hours in class—I wondered if I should go back for year two. Maybe after the summer I should stay in Morgantown? Already I had accepted a summer nanny job. For the past year I questioned if I was meant to live alone, or if the city and graduate school was the right fit for me.

After a few weeks working at my summer job back in Morgantown, my family packed up for the beach. Six hours in the car for a five-day family vacation sounded exhausting. I opted to stay home, see my old friends, and relax.

Before my parents left for the beach, we attended Sunday's church service as a family. I loved how our church slogan on the Sunday program always read,

"A Church In The Heart Of The City
With Its Doors Open Wide
To The World."

When the service ended, my parents chatted with neighbors. While I was still in the sanctuary, a church member approached me.

"Sarah, how are you? How is graduate school?"

"Great, thanks," I said and we talked for a while.

"Sarah, I want to tell you something," this church member said. "I've waited until you were twenty-one to share this with you. I think I know who your birth mother was. Many people knew her before her death. She gave birth to a biracial baby girl. Her foster sister's name is Frances Ryan and her name was . . ."

My chest heaved, head spun, every brain circuit lighting up.

"Wow. Okay. Thank you," I said, memorizing both the names and holding back tears. My birth mother was dead.

"How did she die? When did she die?" I asked.

"I'm not sure when, not recently though. I think she died of cancer."

"Oh," I said.

I think this should have devastated me as it was the first time I actually heard of my biological mother's death. But deep down I always considered the possibility that my birth mother was dead. Years ago that seed was planted when my mom gently suggested, "Your mother was older, living near the university. But you know, she might not be alive."

I thanked this person and ducked into the car with this bomb in my lap. My parents slid into the front seats, in high spirits, conversing about the service.

I said nothing.

My parents could not leave fast enough. That evening with my entire family at the beach, and the house quiet and still, questions raced through my mind about my mother: "Who was she? What did she look like? Why was she in a foster home?"

Finally after a few days I confided in my friend, Dave, from home. Should I contact the foster sister? Two weeks of summer remained before classes at A.C.T. began.

"Sarah, this is your chance, just call information," said Dave. "See if the foster sister is listed. You're about to leave town so you better call."

I have never seen a picture of my mother. I needed to know my birth mother.

Two o'clock Sunday afternoon I dialed information. "Kingwood, West Virginia," I said to the operator.

"Name please?" said the operator.

"Frances Ryan." I held my breath.

Contacting my mother's foster family seemed the best place to start. "There are two Frances Ryans," said the operator.

She gave me both numbers.

I picked up the phone and pressed each number slowly.

All my nerves revved on high.

"Hello?" said a woman's voice.

"Hello, I am looking for Frances Ryan, Lillian Pearl Metheny's foster sister?" I said.

"I'm Frances Ryan," said the woman.

"Hi, I am Lillian Pearl's, or Penny's daughter, Sarah. I'm not sure if you know me?"

"What did you say your name was?" she said.

"My name is Sarah, but my birth name was Esther Elizabeth," I said.

A pause as if she were in shock filled the phone line, and then she said, "Why, yes, yes it is! We didn't know if we would ever hear from you!" Suddenly her voice filled with joy, rolled out an exuberant welcome. "Hold on, I want to get Mom!"

Sitting cross-legged on my bed, my heart raced.

I couldn't believe this phone call was really happening.

"Hello, Sarah?" said an older woman. "I am your mother's foster mom. My name is Sarah Lillian. How about that coincidence? *Sarah* like you and *Lillian* like your mother!" She laughed. "But everybody calls me 'Ponky.' "

"Ponky?" I said laughing, tears lighting my eyes.

"What a wonderful surprise hearing from you!" she said in a sweet West Virginian accent.

For many adopted children, the greatest fear is rejection by birth parents. If they didn't want me then, why would they want me now? One of my adopted friends called her birth mother who hung up on her. This served as a warning that it is best not to call a parent directly, but to write first. Instead, this family was passing the phone back and forth welcoming me, thrilled to hear I was alive and well.

Suddenly I blurted out, "I'd really love to meet you."

"Why yes, we would love that," said Sarah Lillian. "Well . . ." and she began to recite her week. "We have something going on . . . now Fran . . . ," and she called her daughter, "what day do we have a hair appointment, Thursday?"

I interrupted her. "I was wondering if I could come over today."

"Oh? All right . . . yes, you could come over, we'll be here all night."

Fran picked up the phone and gave me directions to their home. Grandma Sarah Lillian now lived with her daughter and her daughter's husband, Paul.

"I'll leave in just a few minutes!" I said, and hung up the phone.

Running around the room, I couldn't get dressed fast enough. Clothes in one hand, the phone in the other, I called my friend back who had encouraged me.

"I am going to meet them," I said.

CHAPTER THIRTY-ONE

Bo—Gbendeva Street

For three months Joe pounded the filthy streets of Bo looking for housing. Most apartments and homes commanded exorbitant rents; he could not afford to leave his cousin's compound shared with a hundred other people. However, the constant crowding and unsanitary conditions at Fenton Road propelled Joe through the city, knocking on doors day after day.

Little desperately needed outdoor space. Joe's brother, Tommy Kposowa, also a refugee in Bo, stayed in a relative's compound where a large nut tree rose like a pillar in the center of the large outdoor space. One morning Tommy arrived at the compound with his truck. Tommy, Joe, and Hindogbae transported Little to the larger housing complex with more trees. When Little spotted the nut tree he bounded into the branches. Children from the neighborhood darted outside to see the monkey. Little shimmied up and down the tree, delighting the children.

Tommy promised to feed Little rice, oranges, and of course, bananas.

Now that Little could flourish in a giant tree, Joe intensified his own housing search. No one doubted the rebels would attack Bo, but it was large enough that if attacked, Joe and his family had a chance to move, run to another side of the city. It was on the outskirts that Joe finally found an affordable house to rent. On Gbendeva Street, this house had four bedrooms and modern amenities. Swampland pushed up against the backyard, which could be utilized for food if the landlord would agree to rent it as well. Within the city limits it was close to the Pastoral Centre by Old Gerihun Road and believed to be safer.

But a city full of starving people is never safe.

Bo, besides Freetown, was the most enticing rebel target. In 1999 Freetown would be sacked and destroyed by rebels who used civilians as human shields. Some of the finest neighborhoods full of diamond merchants, government officials, and the educated elite would be the focus of the most brutal killings. Businessmen would be dragged through the streets as spectacles before their arms, legs, and ears were cut off. Captured government soldiers would be sodomized with jagged sticks in the street as entertainment. But that was still a few years away.

Only three weeks had passed in the family's new home on Gbendeva Street, when shouting roused Joe from his sleep. His neighbor screamed.

"Thief! Thief! Thief!" shouted the neighbor.

Adrenaline shot up Joe's spine. He dashed out of bed to the window.

"Thief! Thief!" screamed the neighbor. The prowler darted between the houses, heading toward Joe's home.

Mary and the children woke. Young Hindogbae and Jeneba cried, terrified. "Rebel! Rebel!!" the children shouted, believing the rebels penetrated Bo.

Joe grabbed pots and pans and banged them together with all his might. Trying to scare the thief away from his door, he beat his fists against the wall.

Banging pots slammed through the house. "HEY! HEY! HEY! THIEF! THIEF! THIEF! GO! GO! GO!" boomed from Joe's throat.

Beating the door, a steady thrashing against the wood, Joe kept up the alarm. The pots, excruciating to eardrums, forced little Hindogbae to cover his ears.

Joe's hands, red and swollen kept beating in the darkness, his sole protection against a starving burglar.

CHAPTER THIRTY-TWO

Kingwood, West Virginia

Rain smacked the windshield, blurring my vision along the country roads to Kingwood. I steadied and steered the car past the farms, the well-kept homes, until my car idled in front of the Ryans' house. The windshield wiper swept a final stroke, clearing water droplets from the glass.

I parked my car on the driveway outside the salmon-colored brick with cream-colored siding. Quickly, I tamed my hair in the rearview mirror, and stared at myself. If I couldn't meet my mother in this moment, at least I could meet her foster mother and sister.

Three tiny steps led up to the house. Before I even made it up the walk, a man came down the steps with a big smile on his face.

"Hi," I beamed at him, "I'm Sarah. I'm not sure if you know me."

A huge smile broke over his face. "Of course I know you. I used to carry you on my shoulders. I'm Paul, Fran's husband. I've known you since you were a baby."

Paul held the door for me. Inside I heard someone call, "She's here."

A slim, middle-aged woman with a beautiful smile greeted me first. "Hello, Sarah," said Aunt Fran. I walked up the emerald green carpeted stairs where she gave me a big hug. Taking my hand, she led me to the living room. Elegant drapes framed the windows and statues of angels perched on side tables.

Grandma Sarah sat on the couch, a soft lamp on each side of her. A handmade afghan fell across her lap. An eighty-year-old woman, around ninety pounds, with cotton-white hair smiled at me from the couch. Oversized glasses looked huge on her tiny face. She opened her arms for a hug.

I bent down to embrace her frail frame.

"We didn't know if we'd ever see you again," she said. "Come sit down."

"Would you like some tea, Sarah?" Fran asked.

Rain continued outside. Hot chamomile tea sounded perfect.

"Thank you," I said. A plate of butter cookies waited on the coffee table.

"We all used to hold you," Grandma Sarah said, smiling at me.

"Your mom had such a beautiful voice. She used to sing all the time, sang at many weddings," said Fran.

"She was such a sweet little girl. Her name was Lillian, but everyone called her Penny," said Grandma Sarah. "Would you like to see some pictures?"

Spread before me on the coffee table, photos of my mother lay face up. An attractive woman with light brown hair, a medium build, and pale skin gazed back at me.

"I have the same tooth!" I said. I always hated that crooked tooth, but seeing the same tooth on my birth mother delighted me. I looked like somebody.

More pictures shuffled across the glass coffee table. My birth mother was far from the blonde Barbie doll I fantasized about. I scoured the shape of her eyes, the tilt of her nose, the outline of her lips, but we didn't share any other features.

"What was my mom like?" I asked.

"Oh, she talked with everybody. Very friendly. No one was ever a stranger to her. A beautiful singing voice. Lots of dramatic talent."

My eyes widened.

"She also had her struggles," they said quietly. "Penny suffered from depression," they said. "Probably with today's medication she'd be fine, but back then she had swings of great energy and terrible lows when she cried and cried. She had postpartum depression, too."

Instead of making me sad, relief engulfed me. I, too, dealt with mild depression since my knee injury back in high school. Knowing it might have a genetic component gave me more comfort than any therapy. A confusion had plagued me when depression hit. I wondered how, when I had such an amazing family, could I be sad? When depression surfaced, it came with an element of guilt: Why should I feel this when I'm so blessed? Somehow knowing my birth mother suffered from this confirmed it was okay for me to be how I am.

"Why did she live with you?" I asked Grandma Sarah.

"Her mom died when she was three and her father left the family. Neighbors and relatives took in the children. We lived next door and took in your mother. We never adopted her legally; we believed her father might come back for her, but he never did and she lived with us until she was an adult."

Secrets adopted children do not share are that both a relationship with their parents exists as does an imaginary relationship or story built around their birth parents does, too. Something like: my birth mother didn't want me, something must be wrong with me; or my birth father didn't know about me and will come rescue me. The variation of stories are endless and have a profound effect on the psyche of a child. For the longest time I wondered why my birth mother couldn't get it together enough to keep me. Was I that difficult? It didn't dawn on me to think she might have postpartum depression or feel overwhelmed as a single mother. Very rarely do adopted children have the capacity at a young age to ask, let alone understand what sorrows, circumstances, or shames their parents struggled with that led them to give them up.

Even hearing these little tidbits about my birth mother's life from Fran and Grandma Sarah, alerted me to the abandonment Penny must have felt in her own life—a dead mother, a missing father. I gazed again at my mother's photo.

"We know she really wanted to keep you, Sarah. But she had very little money and she was a single mom. Your father eventually went back to Africa, and Penny began to distance herself from us."

They didn't offer up any more information or seem to know more about my father.

I stared at the rainbow of pictures spread before me. What did my mother go through? I wished at that moment I could have hugged her, told her that a wonderful family adopted me. If I could only whisper, "It turned out okay, Penny. I had a childhood home full of love, a home filled with laughter and music, a home scented with steaming pot roast on snowy nights. I have an amazing dad who never missed one basketball game, a dad who helped me with my homework under a cozy kitchen table light. I have a mom who always drove me to dance classes, taught me to bake cookies, and who loves me."

Evening drifted through the living room windows. I needed to drive back along the poorly lit, curving roads before it was too dark.

Giant hugs spread around the room as we all said our good-byes. Paul and Fran walked me to the front door. Grandma Sarah Lillian stood up from the couch and waved from the window as I drove away.

In the passenger seat of the car, piles of photos and a napkin filled with cookies weighed down a bag Grandma Sarah gave to me. Gifts to take home. But the greatest thing those three did for me that afternoon was give me the gift of courage. If they hadn't met me with such acceptance, love, kindness, and given me a welcome of such sincerity and delight, I never would have had the strength to search for my father. As it was, the next person I contacted wanted nothing to do with me.

CHAPTER THIRTY-THREE

Bo—Gbendeva Street

With fourteen-inch-deep, empty woven baskets on their heads, market women waited on Joe's front porch to buy okra from him. In his backyard that bordered the swampland, he successfully grew vegetables after buying fresh okra seeds in Bo from the Department of Agriculture.

Joe needed money. But as a school principal, it would be shameful for him to farm or sell vegetables in the market. Even his wife, Mary, an educated woman would bring shame on the family if she sold wares in the streets. Instead, behind his house, Joe planted okra seeds, steady rows for a small harvest to sell wholesale. Poking a long stick in the earth, he sprinkled seeds in its imprint. Every three months in between the height of the rainy and dry seasons, a mini okra harvest helped support his family. The green vegetable, shaped like a squash crossed with a chile pepper grew six feet tall behind his home.

Every few days Mary displayed the okra. Competitive market women sprung upon the porch to haggle the moment it was set out. Inside the house, Joe eavesdropped through the window to make sure Mary held her ground.

Listening to the quibbling over a few vegetables, Joe dreamed of America and her supermarkets and convenience stores brimming with food. Drifting back to his Salem College days, he remembered a deer roaming free on the green carpeted campus. Other students passed by the grazing deer with benign smiles on their faces. "Why weren't all the students chasing the deer? Hunting it?" he thought. To spot a deer and not kill it was absurd to him.

In Sierra Leone a deer was a great prize, hunted deep in the forests by Kamajors, who must outwit not only the deer, but also the leopards stalking it, too. Over and over he told the awed villagers of Bumpe: "Americans see a deer and do nothing!"

Mary wrangled an excellent price for the produce.

Soon fried okra would simmer in someone's stew, sizzle on top of rice or meat. Joe prayed it wasn't monkey meat. Tonight he had some difficult news to share with Hindogbae.

CHAPTER THIRTY-FOUR

Pisgah, West Virginia

I did not want to go to the cemetery alone. Instead I asked my friend, Dave, the one who encouraged me to call Aunt Fran, if he would drive me. From Grandma Sarah I learned the location of my birth mother's burial place.

To avoid the high summer heat, we drove to the cemetery early the next morning. Up a slight hill, orderly rows of polished graves glittered under the rising sun. I read the gravestones one by one until I came to my mother's marker. Respectfully, my friend waited in the car. I stooped down in front of a simple granite stone laid into the earth.

LILLIAN P. METHENY
1941—1987

Again I was grateful to Grandma Sarah for showing me a warm, smiling photograph of my mother before I viewed the cold grave marker. Unlike many of the surrounding graves, my birth mother did not have an upright headstone, but a smooth stone placed flat in the ground. It could easily be missed.

I knelt before it, placed pink flowers on top, and read her name again. Only her name appeared on the stone in capital letters. I longed for a saying, a poem, a one-line inscription chiseled in the granite, something to give me clues about my birth mother's life and how she met my father.

Tears streaked my face in the West Virginia sun before my mother's grave. Exiting the car, my friend walked up the hill toward me. "You okay?" he asked.

"Yeah," I said.

"It's pretty up here." He looked around and said, "One day you might want to think about getting your mother a headstone."

For a moment I didn't know what to say. Did a headstone make a life more important? Did a name chiseled in stone create a more powerful record? My birth mother, before she gave me up for adoption, kept records of her own. On the back of my baby photos from Grandma Sarah, my mother wrote in neat cursive:

Esther Elizabeth at eight months
Squeeling[sic] as Mommy shot the picture. 1976

Esther Elizabeth at desk—the lite[sic] secretary—
She also liked to play records 8 mo. Dec.'76.

In the *Children's Health Record and Instructions For Care* manual that came with me from foster care, her handwriting again filled in TABLE 2 *Record of Growth and Development:* "Date of birth: April 15, 1976 Weight: 7lbs 3 oz . . . only breastfeed [*sic*] milk for first 3 mo." Under MILESTONES the lines for *Smiled* and *First Words* were filled in.

Here she wrote I smiled April 15th, the day I was born. Babies are not physically capable of smiling at birth. Next she wrote my first words: *Da Da* and *God*.

I could only wonder if those really were my first words, or were they the two most important words to her? Or all alone with an infant, did Penny wish I had a father to call "Da Da"?

CHAPTER THIRTY-FIVE

Bo—Gbendeva Street

Joe called Hindogbae into his bedroom. A kerosene lamp flickered on the nightstand. Slowly Joe sat down on the bed next to his son, putting an arm around Hindogbae's tiny shoulder. Even as a five-year-old, Hindogbae's eyes, liquid black pools, loomed large and serious.

Earlier that day Joe had received news from his brother in their compound.

"Hindo, Little was stolen."

Hindogbae stiffened, tears rising.

"This is your fault, Daddi!" Hindogbae yelled.

Joe kept his arm around his son.

"Hindogbae, Little is a monkey. Keeping Little locked in the kitchen house was not fair to him."

"If he stayed with us, we would have protected him," said Hindogbae.

"It was the best choice," said Joe. "Maybe someone took him to a place with more room for him to play."

Hindogbae clenched his jaw, stared at his feet, and shook his leg against the bed.

Joe did not want to look his small boy in the eyes.

With the country at war and the population starving, Little in all likelihood was chopped into soup.

"This is your fault, Daddi," said Hindogbae.

Joe rose from the bed and stood before his son.

In Sierra Leone, a father is the head of the home; one does not challenge or talk back to him. But at that moment, with his tender son's lips quivering, eyes holding back tears, Joe remembered when other people raged at him.

When Joe first heard Penny was pregnant, he did not hear it from her.

His older brother Joseph Francis Kposowa, who lived in the same cheap housing on Jones Avenue in Morgantown as Penny Metheny, called him.

The old house, divided into rental rooms, shared a common kitchen. Joseph Francis rented a room while he worked on his master's degree in agriculture at the university. Penny worked in the WVU cafeteria making food. Penny, who was lonely and eager to make friends often baked a pie, prepared turkey, or shared some food in that kitchen.

Joe, on a student visa, stunned by the individualism of American life, alienated and lonely, traveled from Salem College to see his older brother Joseph Francis almost every weekend.

Penny Metheny and Joe Kposowa met in that communal kitchen.

It is no surprise that a woman who showed such openness, racial acceptance, and welcome would be attractive to Joe. New to America, studious, serious, and homesick, Joe was burdened with a great responsibility to bring his education back to Sierra Leone.

Thirty-three years old, lonely, depressed, and struggling, Penny smiled at him without seeing color. Joe sat down to eat with her and noticed the warmth and joy she was known for in her youth. In high school Penny auditioned for and won the position of head majorette. In her farming community during the autumn Preston County Buckwheat Festival of 1958, she won the title of Buckwheat Festival Princess.

At the end of the summer Penny confided in older brother Joseph Francis and his wife, Evelyn, about the child she was carrying.

Joseph Francis, furious at his brother for jeopardizing his studies and his student visa yelled, "What have you done? We are here to study!"

Joe was twenty-three years old.

Before Joe left to study in America, his mother, Musu, the Paramount Chief's wife, gave her son the traditional African blessing; she spat on the front of her son's right hand, which Joe then rested on her forehead. The Paramount Chief's wife reminded him of the good name of the ruling house of Kposowa.

Neither brother informed their family back in Sierra Leone of the pregnancy.

CHAPTER THIRTY-SIX

Morgantown

After my visit to the cemetery, I drove home to an empty house. The stillness and quiet of familiar things soothed me: my mom's antique quilts, my dad's rows and rows of books, knickknacks from trips to Scotland and England from my dad's sabbatical, and my two black Cabbage Patch Kids with adoption papers.

My family would return from vacation tomorrow. Excited to share with them how I met my birth mother's foster family, I was also nervous my news might hurt them.

When my parents returned home from the beach, I detailed my visit with Grandma Sarah, Aunt Fran, and Uncle Paul. My parents were relieved and happy my meeting went so well. Though my mom wished I would have waited to see them when she was home. "What if the meeting was difficult and you needed some support?" she said. I told her it was just something I had to do that moment and couldn't have waited. In the next four days before heading back to California, I asked if they would meet my birth mother's foster family, too.

"Of course!" said my parents. Before we arranged a visit, my mom gave me a simple handwritten letter.

"If you ever choose, as an adult, to search for your birth mother," said my mom, "I wanted to be able to share with you all the information I knew."

Three months after my birth mother's death, my mom wrote a letter, which she sealed for safekeeping.

June 24, 1987

Dear Sarah,

I am writing this letter to tell you that today I had lunch with Mary Jasper, a woman who knew your biological mother very well. Mrs. Jasper is a member of Wesley Church. She first told me about your mother, Lillian Pearl Metheny, a little over a month ago. This was shortly after she died on March 9, 1987, at the age of 45. I believe Mrs. Jasper came to me because she thought I would understand how sad she felt about Penny's death, and I also feel she wanted me to know that Penny had seen you at age 5 on a downtown street. She told Mrs. Jasper about this and said you looked just like the baby girl she remembered. Of course, I remember her stopping us and reaching down to touch your hair and saying she had a little girl who would be five. She asked your name, and then I hurried us on our way. Later Penny saw your picture in the paper and again talked with Mrs. Jasper about you. She said her little girl has a birthmark on her face. Mrs. Jasper told her she would observe you at church. When she found no mark on your face, she told Penny that you couldn't possibly be the same little girl she gave birth to. In fact, you did have some light areas around your temple on the right side. I believe this is what she was referring to. They faded away when you were still very young as birthmarks often do and were gone by the time all this took place. During all of my conversations with Mrs. Jasper, I have known that she was in fact talking about your biological mother. Your father and I had accidentally seen her name on a document when we were processing papers for your adoption. I have never confirmed this with her though, but I have expressed a desire that she write about her friend so that if someday you would learn that

Penny Metheny was your biological mother, you would then have a story written by someone who cared about her and was often a special friend when she had no one else.

As nearly as I can tell, Sarah, your mother had a difficult life. I think Mrs. Jasper was one person who viewed her life with compassion and caring. Each time she has talked to me about Penny, she has cried. I told her today I didn't want her to share if it was too hard to do so. She said that it was hard, but she wanted to talk about her. I hope this story about Mrs. Jasper and your mother will be comforting to you. They shared a special friendship. Love, Mom

My meeting with Penny's foster family went so well that it gave me the courage years later to write to the State of West Virginia Department of Health and Human Resources and request my adoption files. Inside I read that my thirty-four-year-old mother was in love with my father and that the relationship cooled by the time she discovered she was pregnant. My mother wanted, even expected marriage. But my twenty-three-year-old father was noncommittal, which plunged my mother into despair. Her church encouraged her to place me for adoption, but she insisted she would raise me alone and wait for my father. She relayed to the social worker on the case that church elders told her to stand before her congregation with me in her arms and confess her sin. My mother refused.

After my birth by cesarean, my mother—alone, exhausted, and overwhelmed—could not even walk for over a month from the surgery. In January, when I was ten months old my mother told the social worker she hit me and decided to relinquish me because she could no longer care for me alone. Several ladies at her church offered to take my mother into their home after I was placed in foster care to ease the pain of being without me. With my mother's permission, the social worker suggested that a church member should remove my crib, toys, playpen, and any reminder of my mother's missing baby.

Inside the thirty-five-page state document, my mother's emotional pain is evident on every page. The social worker wrote:

> "Penny hopes that one day Esther will realize that Penny is giving to Esther and acting out of love in placing her baby for adoption. Penny believes that God is directing Esther to her new home, a home that Penny hopes will give Esther all the love and advantage possible . . . Financially, she felt she could not give Esther the future she deserved. Penny wants Esther to have the love and security she was denied as a child."

When asked what type of home my mother desired for me she . . .

> "stated no preference of skin color. She said it mattered about the type of family they were—not the color. Penny did want Esther to be told that she was biracial . . . she wanted Esther to be raised with some focus on music. Penny said she always loved music, and she wanted Esther to have this in her life, too."

From an entry dated February 9, 1977 the social worker wrote:

> "Beyond anything else, Penny wants Esther to know that her natural mother loved her very much—a love so great that she sacrificed her own pleasure of rearing her baby, so that the child could be raised by others who could provide the love of both parents and the financial advantages Penny could not offer her. Penny stated that she has great hope that she and Esther will be reunited in heaven for eternity, and because of this, she can accept the separation of the few years of life here on earth."

An entry on February 14, 1977:

"Penny said that it is really difficult to answer questions people ask about Esther. She has not told anyone at work Esther is no longer with her. When they ask, she says, 'Esther is just fine.' She does not plan to leave the area since she has so many close friends. She said she would be really unhappy if she went to a different community. She emphasized the church as her sustenance. Penny also said that she is unable to be near infants. She cannot go into the nursery of the church without feeling pain. When she does see babies, she will go home and cry. When she related this, she began to cry. I tried to assure her of the proper decision and helped her to reflect on the happy times with Esther. When we said good-bye, Penny hugged and kissed me. We mutually told one another to take care."

My mother, even in her grief, abandonment, and sorrow, put my future above her own.

CHAPTER THIRTY-SEVEN

Bo—Gbendeva Street

Joe stared out the dirty, barred window of his living room. Life in Bo droned into a monotonous rhythm: scrounging for food, waiting for World Food Program supplies to reach the city, praying for a good okra harvest. Joe made a decision: trapped in Bo, his family must make the best use of their time as refugees. His wife, Mary, should go to school and earn her teaching certificate. Even if that meant five days a week she would board at Bo Teachers' College. Joe and the children would make that sacrifice. Moiyatu, his wife's sister, would cook for the family.

No one could predict how long the civil war would rage, and Joe refused to let his children grow up illiterate. Whatever infrastructure remained of the government, whatever working cogs still spun, Joe would use to forward his children's education.

After twenty years as principal of Bumpe High School and as the son of a Paramount Chief, Joe was used to making hard decisions. At night he discussed with Mary the importance of earning her teaching certificate, he remembered one of the biggest decisions of his life, long since past—the decision to put a daughter up for adoption.

Twenty years earlier in the college counselor's office of Salem College, Joe met with the international student advisor, a social worker, and a counselor. Penny came from Morgantown with their baby. In that office, Joe gazed at his daughter for the first time, his cocoa-skinned child.

This was the first and only time he held his little girl.

All agreed that adoption was the best decision for both parties. Salem College provided Joe legal representation for free. All agreed to meet one more time in the Clarksburg, West Virginia, courthouse.

In the state file some notes exist about Joe. The social worker wrote on March 31, 1977:

> "Joe expressed a desire that his daughter be placed with a church-oriented family . . . he appeared to be very dedicated to his schooling and returning to work in his own country. I was impressed with his questions about foster care, adoption, and the future of his daughter. He showed a genuine concern about Esther's well-being."

The social worker on the case commented that Joe was one of the most impressive, dignified people she had ever met and that he possessed extraordinary presence.

Cultural expectations played into the adoption as well. In Bumpe, many of the men were polygamous. Joe's father, the Paramount Chief, had more than a hundred wives over the course of his life. He lived to be eighty-seven-years-old. As the Paramount Chief it was expected that he have as many wives as possible. It was a great honor for a village family if a daughter was chosen to marry a chief. Not only did it bring prestige to the family, it also strengthened the community bonds and made for more peaceable living. As relatives, the women and wives raised the offspring together. Aunts, mothers, wives, younger sisters, and grandparents all reared the children collectively.

Joe had no way of comprehending that Penny was truly on her own, that child nurturing in the American nuclear family—with a single mom and dad—differed so radically from the collective child raising in Bumpe.

At the courthouse, Joe risked deportation. On one side of the courthouse Joe stood with his lawyer; Penny stood on the other side, holding their baby. Respectfully they greeted each other. Grateful that Joe did not deny paternity, Penny did not want to interfere with Joe's student visa.

The judge asked Joe, "Is this child yours?"

"Yes."

"Do you wish to put this child up for adoption."

"Yes."

After signing a multitude of legal forms, Joe and his lawyer left the courtroom before Penny. Joe would not see his daughter again for twenty-eight years.

CHAPTER THIRTY-EIGHT

Morgantown

Overjoyed that the visits with my parents and Penny's foster family went so well, I wanted to call everyone in the family—foster and biological. With the warm reception and tears of gratitude Grandma Sarah showered on me, I assumed everyone I contacted would be just as excited.

I called another relative.

"Hello," I said . . . "I'm looking for . . . I am Sarah Culberson, Lillian Pearl Metheny's daughter. She put me up for adoption when I was a baby."

Silence greeted me on the other end of the telephone. Somehow the silence didn't register as a rejection, only the need for more information, a memory boost.

"After talking to my Aunt Fran and Grandma Sarah, I realized I know one of your friends. I can't wait to tell him about our connection!"

Suddenly out of the silence a clipped voice said, "I wouldn't tell him."

"Oh."

More silence from both ends of the phone.

"Oh," I said again. "I just wondered if you ever met me when I was a baby?"

"No, I never met you. I never told anyone about you."

A chill swept through the phone lines. "Okay, I understand," I said. "Thank you."

The phone clicked dead.

All my fears of rejection, of something being wrong with me, of shame came smacking back. I needed a few hours to sit with my feelings. Then I picked up the phone and called Grandma Sarah and Aunt Fran.

Grandma Sarah, with her sweet gentle voice said, "Sarah, we think it's a treasure you found us again. If someone can't see what a gift it is to know you, they don't know what they are missing. As a matter of fact, in church we got up and told the community your story, our story, and everybody clapped. When I sat down, the pastor looked at everybody and said, 'Well, I think that is our true sermon for the day.' "

After my visit, both Grandma Sarah and Aunt Fran sent me this letter:

> *Dear Sarah, yes, we are still telling our story and showing these pictures. I'm sending all of them to you—so maybe you can share them with your parents. . . . Thanks ever so much for finding us. We really enjoyed your parents' visit and think they are wonderful people. Love ya bunches, Fran and Paul.*

Although the kind letter gave me comfort, the rejecting phone call from that other relative hurt. Someone would not want me to utter a word about our connection? Maybe this person was ashamed of me, that I was something *wrong*. I had never felt so small. If this relative could hurt me so much—what if my own father rejected me? It was a risk I could not take. I stopped searching for my father for the next five years.

CHAPTER THIRTY-NINE

Bo

Cholera infected the city of Bo. Contaminated water, malnutrition, and overpopulation created a petri dish in which diseases flourished. Typhoid fever, dysentery, malaria, and yellow fever brewed.

Joe wondered if he was dying. A Mende medicine man lived down the street, a man his neighbors claimed created miracle-potions and herbal tonics that could cure any illness. Garbed in his long African robes and matching cap, amulets draped around his neck, the medicine man embodied powerful Mende beliefs in natural remedies. Already Joe's friends swore they had renewed health thanks to this healer.

With a small amount of money, Joe approached the medicine man and shared his list of aliments: diarrhea, dehydration, upset stomach, then constipation, and sweats. Although Joe earned his bachelor and master's degrees in the United States, and although he had great respect for Western-medicine, he consulted a medicine man before seeking Western drugs. Even Western-trained doctors in Bo often worked in communion with medicine men, asking a patient what herbs or potions he or she consumed before seeking treatment.

The medicine man, using the root *gbangbai,* concocted a secret herb mixture for Joe's condition. "Sip a little and jump up and down after you drink it so it travels through your body," said the medicine man. Telling a person to jump up and down for the medicine to travel was as common as instructions to "shake the bottle well."

Joe did as the medicine man advised. Stranger things had been demanded of patients. Medicine men often directed a client to drink a potion only if he stood outside his front door facing away from his home. Almost always a medicine man required the patient to bend down and pick up the remedy created for him. Handing a patient medicine directly would insure its failure. The patient must reach for the medicine himself.

At first the native herbs seemed to bring relief, so Joe drank more. And more. He even jumped up and down harder. Soon Joe had such a severe bout of diarrhea, he believed he was dying again. Dehydrated, sweat gushing from his body, weak all over, he knew he needed help immediately.

Did the herbs cause this sickness, now more virulent than the first round of symptoms? Or did he drink too much, self-medicating with a potion meant to be consumed in moderation only? This time Joe headed straight to the hospital in Bo, standing in line for Western drugs. Before the war, doctors from relief organizations and missionary doctors were widely accessible. But with the war raging, most all foreign nationals evacuated. A few doctors from Belgium stayed; a scattering of Sierra Leonean doctors trained in Russia remained for the people.

Seeing any doctor required Herculean patience. Joe sat in the waiting room of the hospital until a nurse called him into a room. Fortunately, being a school principal came with a few perks. Many of the nurses knew Joe; out of respect for his position, they made sure he saw a doctor within two hours instead of the usual all-day wait.

Finally a Sierra Leonean doctor reviewed his symptoms. Joe paid the doctor, took the prescription, and headed to the hospital pharmacy for his medication. But with a spate of amputees in the city needing medicine, a man with a severe case of diarrhea paled in comparison to a child with a severed hand.

CHAPTER FORTY

San Francisco

Back in San Francisco for year two of A.C.T., an assignment for students required sharing about ourselves through a project. I chose a dance interpretation of Paul Simon's "Homeless" from his *Graceland* album.

On one side of the stage, I set a sign with "black" written on the left with a lit candle before it. On the other side of the stage I set a second lit candle in front of the word "white" written on a sign. In the center of the stage was an unlit candle. Dancing as if ropes, tied around my wrists, wrested me violently back and forth to each side of the stage, I personified a physical struggle, straddling an invisible schism. The music and my body spoke.

Homeless, homeless
Moonlight sleeping on a midnight lake . . .
We are homeless, we are homeless . . .
Strong wind destroy our home
Many dead, tonight it could be you . . .
And we are homeless, homeless
Moonlight sleeping on a midnight lake
Homeless, homeless . . .

At the end of the song, I picked up both lit candles from either side of the stage and together, from both their flames, I lit the center unity candle. On the back of the "black" card was the word "bi" and on the back of the "white" card was the word, "racial." I blew out the two candles and kept the single candle on the stage in front of my new word, *biracial*. As darkness descended and the song ended, I sang, "Home . . ." and exited the stage.

Before discovering my birth mother's foster family, I would not have wanted to be witnessed in my identity struggles on stage, but now I wanted to begin to share how I felt. As I began to know myself better, I wanted my classmates to know me better, not a mask, or a smile, but the person I was discovering. A new respect for myself and from my classmates was born that day, and the rest of the year was spent peeling away deeper and deeper levels of myself.

During winter break, my parents flew out from West Virginia to visit. When giving them a tour of the school, I spotted an odd expression on a classmate's face. Later that evening I bumped into my friend and said, "You looked so surprised when you saw my family."

"Yeah . . ." he said.

"I was adopted," I said.

"Oh! I thought your mom had an affair with a black man and your dad was cool with it."

I laughed and said, "That is the most creative thing I've ever heard." Instead of bubbling issues of race creating deeper internal chaos from his comment, I loved his story. I realized just as I made up stories about things I don't know—so does everybody else.

While my parents visited my apartment, my dad and I sat on the side of my bed talking. He said, "Sarah, I am so proud of you for going after your dreams."

It hit me how lucky I was for my parents' full support. They never said, "Yeah, try acting, but get a real job soon."

That winter my parents brought me a gift, handmade by my older sister Lynne. With incredible detail, she'd mounted pictures of my birth mother into a beautiful album. With each colored paper cutout, each picture framed, she told me without words how happy she was for me, how much she loved me as a sister. Finding my birth mother showed me a giant chunk of myself, and let me see more clearly how lucky I was to have my mom, dad, and sisters.

Even my professors, the same ones who last summer said I didn't have to smile all the time, came up to me, and asked, "What happened? You're so different this year. What's going on?"

"I found my birth mother," was all I said. I did not need to say she died of cancer, or that I don't think we look anything alike except for our crooked tooth, or that she had some mental health issues, or even that a relative rejected me. No, finding her, knowing even a glimmer of the truth gave me my own story.

As spring semester rolled around, my class began a Nigerian play. I was cast as a Reverend's daughter. Besides learning a Nigerian accent, A.C.T. sent me to a Nigerian hairdresser who could braid my hair into an elite Nigerian style to authenticate the character. My hair needed to be braided into tight, cropped cornrows as a base to hold an elegant crown of synthetic braids high on top.

For over a week, I cruised the streets of San Francisco with this monument of hair on my head in a balancing act that demanded erect posture and a noble gait. The dignity demanded by this tower surprised me. Throughout the time it took to braid it, I became very close with my hairdresser, a stately, Nigerian woman.

As I sat in her hairdressing chair, *Ebony, Essence*, and *JET* magazines strewn around the cramped hair studio, I told her about being adopted.

"I just found my birth mother's family," I said.

"Why don't you find your father now?" she said as she divided my hair in sections, nicking the comb down the center of my skull.

"I'm afraid to find him." I said.

She swiveled the chair, a casual revolution. In her rich Nigerian accent she said, "In Africa, when a child is found, it is a great celebration."

"Oh, you don't understand," I said. "My father gave me up. I wasn't lost."

She stretched and pulled my hair, creating a foundation for the braided crown.

"It doesn't matter when a child is found. It is a celebration."

"A celebration?" I thought. If I ever showed up in my father's life, it would only cause problems. Problems with his family if he had one.

If he didn't want me in the first place, why would he want me now?

CHAPTER FORTY-ONE

Road Back to Bumpe

"Daddi, don't go!" begged Hindogbae to Joe.

"Joe, please," pleaded Mary.

"Daddi, stay with us," cried Jeneba.

But Joe needed to check on his school back in Bumpe for the Ministry of Education. Joe needed to retrieve any and all records for his students. If he didn't, and if the war ever ended, Bumpe High School would have no chance of re-opening in Bumpe. His recordless students might stay in Bo and Joe would have no job and no way to support his family. An eyewitness account on the state of the school was necessary. Joe needed to find out: What was the extent of the rebel damage after two years of fighting? How bad was the looting? Would his students' records filed away in his office be intact? Did the rebels burn the classrooms? Was there anything left?

A group of four other men agreed to meet that morning and walk the sixteen miles to Bumpe together. Kamajors had felled so many large trees as roadblocks along the road that driving was not an option. Walking the sixteen miles was the quickest way back to the village. On his feet Joe wore tennis shoes; on his shoulders, he carried a small bag with a few clothes inside.

Joe did not tell Mary what to do if he were killed. There is no such thing as life insurance in Sierra Leone. Sierra Leoneans can be superstitious; to make a plan for one's death might make it come true. It is best never to speak of it. Instead Joe only said to his wife, "If I do not return in a week, find out what happened to me."

Around ten o'clock in the morning after eating a hearty breakfast, Joe left for Bumpe with the other men. All four had a different reason for embarking on such a risky trip. Some in the group wanted to check on their homes—or what might be left of them. Others hoped to find relatives who remained in the village. Those villagers who elected to stay survived by living in the bush surrounding Bumpe during the day. At night, they returned to their homes. All five men in the group hoped to find food in the village to bring back to their families.

Already Joe knew his home was destroyed, but he prayed the school remained intact or at least the most valuable parts like the generator house, the large boarding dorm facility, or the school kitchen for the boys and girls.

Along the dirt road stretching between the city and the village, the men made a plan: if any suspiciously dressed person was spotted on the road—jump into the bush and run. Every man for himself. No one in Joe's group was armed. Even if the group could somehow attain a weapon illegally, it would be crazy to carry it. If they should run into government soldiers or Kamajors along the road, and a weapon was discovered in their possession, they would be accused of being rebels. Anyone believed to be a rebel was executed on the spot.

As the men began the first mile of their journey, an omen appeared. The *mbala,* a small bird with a long beak, swooped up in the trees. A prophetic bird, its familiar cry rang out: "Kperie! Kperie!" It is believed that through the bird's call the ancestors speak, summoned from the dead. How the bird cries can determine one's fate.

The men froze, their feet planted in the red dirt. If the bird did not finish the final half of its call, it meant the luck was rotten. They would need to turn back.

"Fio! Fio! Kperie! Kperie! Fio! Fio!" the bird cried.

Smiles broke out on the men's faces. If the bird sang the second half of its call, the day would be safe. Joe turned his face to the sky. A silent thanks to God.

In the late afternoon the men approached the village. The bird's cry was indeed fortuitous. Only dust, sun, and silence accompanied their walk. At the outskirts of the village, all agreed to split up and meet in a few days for the return trek. Each man was eager to complete his private journey.

Joe headed directly to Bumpe High School. His heart raced as he walked to the outer rim of the town where his school stood. Founded in 1963 with the help of the United Brethren in Christ missionaries, the highly esteemed boarding school attracted students from as far away as Nigeria, helped countless village children have better lives, and encouraged girls to get an education. Although its buildings were basic, the school boasted a large campus with airy classrooms, a science laboratory, dorm facilities, flush toilets, a power generator, a library, a kitchen, and teacher housing. Even its green center lawn was mowed.

Joe walked along the trodden path to the school. Rising from the overgrown grass, blackened, charred, and roofless buildings greeted him.

Men from Joe's village were conditioned not to weep. Joe clenched his jaw tight. All alone on the dirt path, once pulsing with students streaming between classes, Joe needed to compose himself before he took another look. For thirty years, Bumpe High School symbolized the pride of Bumpe. Now it was crumpled into ruins, destroyed by thugs.

First he stepped inside the library: not a single book remained, each and every volume burned in mass fires or was used for rebel cooking fires. He entered a classroom that was now roofless and stripped, no desks in sight—all used as firewood. Graffiti splattered the inside of another classroom: "RUF," "Superman," and "The Killer" grooved the wall in black charcoal. Bullet holes staccatoed into the walls, patterns of grotesque modern art. A school that once accommodated up to six hundred students was reduced to rubble. Unruly trees, shrubs, and vines wound their way inside the open roofs, tentacles through the broken glass windows. Mattresses and beds in the dorms were all carted away.

Next Joe forced his way into his former office. Glass crunched under his feet. All alone in the desecrated school on the outskirts of town, feeling increasingly uncomfortable, Joe wanted to leave. In the heart of the village, at least he would be in the company of a few men.

His eyes scanned and sifted through the debris on the floor. He stooped over. A student's name on a file peered up at him. Joe gathered whatever remains of his school he could fit in his bag.

Following the students' bush path, he wove his way back to a clump of houses. His friend, Jay Jay Abdulai, offered him food and shelter. Noha had long since left Bumpe to seek shelter in Bo. Only Jay Jay and a few others stayed.

Jay Jay and his wife, Gbiengape, dared to remain in Bumpe. The name Gbiengape was given to the firstborn twin and means *to arrive suddenly*. Twins in Sierra Leone were believed to possess supernatural spiritual power (and two infants *both* surviving a natural birth would indeed seem miraculous). Joe did not know Gbiengape well enough to confirm any special psychic powers, but she was an excellent cook. Having heard that four men arrived in town, Jay Jay spoke with a hunter. "If you can catch some meat, we will pay you," he promised.

Later that evening the hunter arrived with a dead monkey. If a visitor to Sierra Leone passed villagers eating monkey meat, he would know the group consisted of Christians, as Muslims in Sierra Leone never eat monkey or pig. Before the war, a monkey could command 20,000 leones, but in desperate times when no one had anything, the hunter accepted 2000 leones. Joe, as Jay Jay's guest, paid for the meat, which Gbiengape cut into soup served with tomato paste, onions, salt, and pepper.

Although Joe bought the baby monkey, Little, as a pet years ago, eating an adult monkey caused him no distress. In Sierra Leone, where starvation is a daily reality, protein is a valuable commodity. The common belief that God made animals to be eaten prevails.

The men licked their lips. The delicious soup, served with rice and palm wine, coated their empty bellies. Most men never became drunk on palm wine if accompanied with monkey soup because the meat, very similar to cow meat, is so thick, rich in protein, and filling.

Around the fire, Joe discussed the state of his school. Many report cards and student records scattered on the ground had been trampled, but were still intact. Already he brought three rice bags full of papers to Jay Jay's. In the next few days he would attempt to recover as many scattered papers from his school as possible. With the Abdulais' permission, he would store what he found in their home. If Joe did not try to maintain the records of his school, he ran the risk of losing all his students who might remain in Bo to finish school when the war ended. With his personal house burned down two years ago during the first attack on Bumpe, his only option for housing his family would be the government house provided to a principal.

Jay Jay passed around more wine. The hunter returned to the Abdulai home as darkness fell.

"Come join us," offered Jay Jay.

The hunter took a seat around the fire. Jay Jay and Joe finished eating the monkey's brain and the sweetest meat, found beneath the monkey's ears. With its liverlike consistency, and without a single bone to contend with, this delicacy was reserved for a guest or head of the household.

For five days Joe remained in Bumpe salvaging what he could. Mornings he combed through each and every classroom looking for a book to save, a file to pack, anything that might help his beloved school.

He also checked the principal's house, only to discover that house was roofless, nothing left but cinder-block walls and rotted wood doors.

In the afternoon, Jay Jay and Joe walked to a small stream that meandered off the larger Tabe River. Here, Jay Jay erected a fence of palm fronds across the river. In the center of this fence he created a hole where fish could swim into, but instead of freedom beyond the hole, the fish swam straight inside a fish trap, a bamboo cage that allowed fish in, but never out.

After five days of constant work collecting articles from his school, shuttling them back and forth to Jay Jay's house, Joe needed to get back to his family. Two of the original men who journeyed to Bo had already left. Early on the fifth morning, Joe and his two friends began the dangerous walk back to Bo.

CHAPTER FORTY-TWO

Los Angeles

After the American Conservatory Theater class commencement of 2001, the sixteen members of my graduating class negotiated the respective labyrinths of Los Angeles and New York City talent agencies. After all of our extensive classical theater training, a consultant came to A.C.T. to speak with our class about the business side of acting. Agents in Los Angeles and New York differed. In Los Angeles, the consultant said, "You better get sexy." Television and film, a universe away from the stage, put different demands on actors. "Open-toed shoes over clodhopping clogs, and sexy dresses for the women in interviews," suggested the consultant.

With my scruffy clogs dumped in the garbage, and armed with honey-colored Caribbean braids down my back, I prepared for Los Angeles. Our A.C.T. professors matched us with scene partners, pairs that would best highlight the talents of both students. On a designated day at the Tiffany Theater on Sunset Boulevard in Los Angeles, an audience full of agents, managers, and talent scouts viewed our graduating class in short scenes, one after the next. If a talent agent showed interest, each student received a phone call for an interview.

A week after the Los Angeles auditions, we would repeat the auditions in New York City for those actors who hoped to work in the city. Thankfully I received three interviews during the first audition set in Los Angeles.

The first agent asked about the upcoming New York auditions. "Where are they being held in New York?" he said.

I said, "Somewhere in Manhattan."

He snickered, "You *are* from West Virginia."

Fortunately, my second agency interview covered different ground. The agents asked about technique and training. When they concluded the meeting they said, "We'd love to work with you."

Although I auditioned in New York, my heart was already taking root in California. Coming from West Virginia, I craved open spaces again, green things, and immediate access to nature. Los Angeles, in spite of its sprawling city reputation and awful traffic, has amazing access to trails, mountains, and the ocean.

Dismantling my futon, selling my dresser, and unloading anything unnecessary was step one. Then with the help of my incredibly patient and generous boyfriend, Jeff, we loaded my meager belongings and ragged teddy bear from foster care, which always traveled with me, into a rental truck. Using an online search service, Westside Rentals, I found a roommate and a two-bedroom apartment near Beverly Hills. After a seven-hour drive, with Jeff following behind mc in a U-Haul, we rolled down the I-5 into Los Angeles with all my worldly possessions.

CHAPTER FORTY-THREE

Road to Kawaya

When Joe finally returned to Bo, blue-lined, loose-leaf paper littered the city streets. On them a dire warning was written in English: rebels planned an imminent attack on Bo.

Joe dashed inside his home to greet his family. Little Hindogbae came running to hug him. Mary, relieved at the sight of her husband, missing for five days, wrapped her arms around him.

Together Mary and Joe sat in the living room as Joe recounted what he witnessed in Bumpe—the rebel graffiti, the bullet holes, the missing roofs.

But there was no time to share the details. Joe held a sheet of paper in his hands. Part terror tactic, part calling card, rebels used these types of "warnings" to incite panic. Spies who infiltrated the city dropped hundreds of papers on the streets. A final stronghold, a taunting jewel, Bo would never go unmolested by the rebels. On the outskirts of the western side of the city, rebel soldiers already massed.

If the Kamajors and government soldiers failed, Bo would not stand a chance. Nowhere in the city would be a safe haven. Rebels did not even respect medical neutrality. They sacked hospitals, dragged patients from beds and hacked doctors to death for not saving a rebel leader's life. It was too risky to remain in the city.

One of Joe's brothers, Samuel Kposowa, lived in the village of Kawaya, far into the bush, only accessible across a river. Samuel made the five-hour journey to Bo a few times to purchase provisions for his family that were impossible to acquire in his tiny village. Powdered soap, salad, Maggi cubes (bouillon cubes) were all hoarded. Samuel and Joe made a pact: If Bo became too dangerous, Joe and his family would trek to Kawaya and seek shelter with Samuel's family. Joe hoped he would never need to take his brother up on his gracious offer, but the day had arrived. With an immediate attack looming, the population of Bo panicked.

Leaving for Kawaya on foot in the morning was the best option. But first Joe needed to decide how to protect his belongings. Should he attempt to carry some along the narrow bush path to Kawaya? Or was storing them a wiser choice?

Joe flashed back to a riddle commonly asked of children to test their thinking skills. "How is it best to carry things?"

Riddle: If a man stands on the bank of a river and is given a boat to take cassava leaves, a goat, and a leopard to market, how will he do it in only two trips?

If he puts the goat and the cassava leaves in the boat, leaving the leopard on the bank, the goat will eat the cassava leaves, and he will lose money at the market. If he takes the cassava leaves across the river first, the leopard left on the bank will eat the goat. But if he takes the leopard and the cassava leaves, and then returns to fetch the goat, he will triumph.

The answer came to him. Although he did not need to decide between a goat or a leopard, he decided to divide up his possessions. Rounding up his most expensive items purchased in Bo, Joe packed his television, extra clothes, camera, fan, pots and pans into his truck. In the Pastoral Centre, inside a church compound, rooms could be rented. In one of these locked and guarded rooms, he stashed his worldly goods.

The next morning Mary, Jeneba, Hindogbae, his wife's young sister, Moiyatu, Joe, and two porters, whom he paid 3000 leones each—about \$1.00, left on foot for Kawaya. The family members carried what they could on their backs in straw bags. Not knowing how long they would take shelter in the remote village, they brought salt, bouillon, tomato paste, tea, toiletries, a kerosene lamp, and a foam mattress, which Joe carried on his head for the five-and-a-half-hour trek. No one brought water. When the rainy season descended upon Sierra Leone, the flush rivers provided more than enough.

Joe led the way along the winding bush path. The children, Hindogbae, Jeneba, and Moiyatu sandwiched between Mary and him. The porters trailed behind the family. After four-and-a-half hours of walking, the family reached the Tabe River, engorged with rapid currents from the rains. On the other side of the river, the village of Kawaya beckoned. Snug and secure behind its river moat, the moving water posed as a huge deterrent to rebels, many of whom had never learned to swim.

At the edge of the gushing riverbank, Joe called out, "Who! Who!" that echoed across the water: "Who! Who! Who!"

A villager heard the call and ran to fetch Samuel Kposowa, Joe's brother. The communal village canoe, an old six-foot-long dugout, made from a cotton tree, would need to be paddled across the surging water to ferry the family to safety.

While the family waited for Samuel, Joe hoped the canoe still existed. In peacetime no one dared steal the village canoe, as every person's livelihood and safety depended on its fair use. However, in wartime, the entire country had spun out of control, as ancient codes and social mores turned upside down.

In the past, if anyone dared appropriate the canoe for his private possession, the penalty was fierce. The village chief would immediately send for a town crier to announce the theft or desecration of the canoe. "*Alondo . . . ooo! Alondo . . . ooo!*" (Attention everyone!) he would call. He would implore the thief to return the canoe and pay a fine to the chief for redemption. If the thief did not come forward in three days and confess, the chief or a village representative could petition the Paramount Chief to pay a fee and invoke a medicine man to curse the crook.

The tribal medicine or *juju* was then brought in a covered bag or box and placed in the center of the village. The medicine man cursed the thief to death. Anyone who did not come forward to confess or anyone who even talked with this burglar, would also die. After three days, the medicine man, activating the medicine, called on the name of God to inflict disaster on the criminal. He cried out to the entire village, using thunder medicine to curse the thief. Villagers, so petrified of this thunder medicine, or *juju*, rarely stole, and the culprit almost always came forward.

Samuel called across the river bank to Joe. *"Bu Waa!"* he said. Samuel dragged the canoe behind him.

Samuel Kposowa, a village native, now needed to negotiate the running waters with the primitive wooden paddle. Twice.

The family watched his hard, long strokes propel him across the rushing water. Porters loaded the canoe and then left immediately for Bo. If they did not leave right away, the journey back to Bo in the dark could be fatal.

The sounds of the rushing water terrified the children. Only Joe knew how to swim. The shooting water threatened to capsize the canoe. Crocodiles, another danger, petrified the passengers. Although they rarely attacked people, everyone knew they lurked in the rivers. Village dogs, lapping up water along the river's edge, were often crushed in their jaws. The family had to cross the swollen river in spite of the raging currents and the threat of crocodiles. In the canoe, Mary and the children clutched the edge of the boat as Samuel paddled.

CHAPTER FORTY-FOUR

Los Angeles

Magnolia trees bloomed in the front of my new apartment and bougainvillea cascaded over the patio in the backyard. Inside, sunbeams stroked the hardwood floors and illuminated the crown moldings of my 1940s fourplex. With my housing secure in Los Angeles, I needed a flexible day job that would allow me to go on acting auditions.

Before dropping some headshots off at my agents in Century City, I passed a candle shop, *Illuminations.* With candles flickering in the window, soft, dim light inside, silver trays of angelic votives, floating candles bobbing in vases, the entire store glowed like a soothing oasis. I ducked into the warm, scented store, and applied for a job. If auditioning in Los Angeles proved to be stressful, at least my day job could calm me.

I first auditioned for a part on *Frasier.* At twenty-four years old I was sent out to play a 16-year-old. When the casting director saw me he said, "When I need a grandma, I'll call you."

While I waited for other auditions, I got a part in a play. At the Globe Playhouse in West Hollywood, I performed in a choreopoem, a multipart poem-story titled, *"For Colored Girls Who Have Considered Suicide When the Rainbow is Enuf."* The performance won us an NAACP award for best ensemble. A troop of deaf actors, some from the group Deaf West, paired with us as we dove into the language. Characters called lady in red, lady in green, lady in orange, and the ladies of the rainbow held center stage.

Cast as lady in yellow, reading the lines of poetry, I expressed my character's sorrow and hurt on the stage. My partner signed the poetry just as eloquently to the audience:

i've lost it
touch wit reality/ i don't know who's doing it
i thot i waz but i waz so stupid i waz able to be hurt
& that's not real /not anymore/ i shd be immune/ if i'm
still alive & that's what i waz discussin/ how i am still
alive & my dependency on other livin beins for love
i survive on intimacy & tomorrow/ that's all i've got goin
& the music waz like smack & you knew abt that
& still refused my dance waz not enuf/ & it waz all i had
but bein alive & bein a woman & bein colored is a metaphysical
dilemma/ i havent conquered yet/ do you see the point
my spirit is too ancient to understand the separation of
soul & gender/ my love is too delicate to have thrown
back on my face

my love is too delicate to have thrown back on my face

After a day of driving all over Los Angeles for auditions and late nights of performing, I plopped down onto my couch. I stared up at the ceiling, looking at swirls in the old plaster. I did not have a steady relationship with my then-long-distance boyfriend who helped me drive to Los Angeles. In fact, I had had many passing boyfriends, but not one relationship had lasted very long. With the hardwood floors creaking and Santa Ana winds blowing outside, I thought about my birth father.

The tragedy of 9/11 had just struck in New York City and I couldn't stop thinking about my friends in the city. At that moment, like most Americans I kept taking stock of my life and the people in it. I wanted the people in my life to know how much I loved them.

I also wondered if finding my birth father might complete something. Selfishly a part of me wondered, if I found my birth father, could it help me in my relationships with men? I wondered if I feared if I got too close to someone that he might leave. Was there a part of me that believed, in some deep-recessed core, that if my father could give me up, anyone could?

Earlier that week, I casually asked a friend who happened to date a private investigator what it would cost to begin a search.

"Oh, thousands of dollars. Remember, Sarah, most parents who give up a kid don't want to be found."

"Yeah," I shrugged. My father would probably hang up on me.

"My love is too delicate to have thrown back on my face . . ."

CHAPTER FORTY-FIVE

Kawaya

Life across the river in Kawaya spun backward in time. Populated with mostly illiterate farmers, there were no schools, no toilets, and no access to trade. Unlike the large open-air markets in Bo with aid in from the World Food Program, all food in Kawaya needed to be hunted or grown.

Now that Joe's family had successfully crossed the river, safe on the banks of the tiny village, he had no choice but to farm and cultivate a garden. On designated Fridays, Joe joined with the village hunters in search of deer, antelope, and the cutting grass—a cross between a rabbit and a large guinea pig. To gather the hunters, a leader blew on a large deer horn, a musical trumpet that alerted all able and willing men to leave their homes, rice fields, or gardens and join the chase.

Using nets made from nylon ropes purchased in Bo and woven by a village net maker, the band of twenty men pooled their collective nets and set out for the hunt. Leaving around ten o'clock in the morning with the best hunting dogs in the village, the men were careful to feed the dogs very little—they needed the canines hungry and fierce in pursuit of prey. Many of the seasoned hunters invoked *juju*—magic. Inside the caverns of their mouths, the hunters sucked on a sacred stone; some attached pouches on their clothes filled with secret fetishes like shells, animal teeth, dried scorpions, ashes of ancestors, snake heads, or any other potent magic. Before a hunter's father died, he would pass down his own secret medicine for a hunter to use in capturing prey.

Joe and the men waited in the bush. Nets attached to the top of small trees and pegged to the ground created an entrapped fence for unsuspecting animals. Cutting grasses bred in the bush in abundance—easy to capture in big nets. Hunters brought cutting grasses home to their wives, who reserved the heads for their husband. Eating the head of an animal honored the head of the household. Husbands often ate the brain of an animal, which was considered a delicacy and believed to make the consumer smarter. Many villagers believed that an animal fried in palm oil was purified of any diseases.

Even porcupines were hunted. Once roasted over fire, its quills flaked off as easily as fish scales. Some villagers believed the porcupine's bitter intestines prevented malaria.

Deer, the most difficult animal to kill, were the most prized. Only with strong nets, fearless hunters, and luck could a wild deer be captured. Guns were not used to hunt, only nets and machetes. A hunter needed to come close enough to an entangled deer, clobber it with the blunt side of the machete, and refrain from ripping the valuable nets. If a hunter lost courage, frightened the animal, or allowed it to escape, the punishment was group booing and the forced eating of fresh, hot red peppers—peppers so hot that once eaten, a man cried and sweat like a possessed devil.

If a hunter died, which was rare, death was attributed to witchcraft, or a predestined curse. However, if a hunt was successful, the deer would be divided by acts of bravery. The bravest hunter or the owner of the strongest nets would be given the neck, head, skin, and inside of the deer to bring home to his family. Everything would be consumed except the skin, which was used to stretch across drums used in sacred ceremonies, or on the masked dancers.

The masters of the hunting dogs, honored for their contribution to the chase, were given the lower body and backsides of the animal. The general hunters who aided, but did not make great contributions to the hunt, were rewarded with the four limbs. Deer meat, so prized and delicious, was usually consumed right away when the hunters returned to the village.

In the evening Joe, Mary, their children, and one of Samuel's wives, Hawa, sat on the veranda of Samuel's home. On the open porch a hammock hung for the men to sit in and pass around gourds filled with palm wine. As the family told stories and the children played, the African sun dipped lower and lower in the sky. Fireflies swirled their reddish glow next to the river. In Sierra Leone, fireflies have the same name as stars, *dumbekei*. In the Bible three wise men followed a star to find the baby Jesus; fireflies, with their bright, flickering light, are similarly regarded as omens of good luck.

However, tonight no fireflies came close to the veranda. A message from Joe's dear friend Jonathan Daramy back in Bo arrived via villagers who had traveled from Bo. During the rebel attack, soldiers ransacked Bo's Catholic Pastoral Centre. Fleeing thieves took advantage of the panic. Every single item Joe possessed was stolen.

After breaking down the door to the storage room, looters carted away his television, generator, all of the family's cooking pots, every last pair of their shoes, sheets, silverware, cameras, stereo, CDs, trunks, and even their electric fan.

When Mary heard the news she wept. Little Hindogbae, now seven years old and so proud to own a small television, was shaking. Joe paced the veranda and assessed his life: his home and school were destroyed by the rebels in Bumpe; his pigs were slaughtered; all his belongings in Bo were wiped out. Except for the value of his education, he was penniless, possessing only the few clothes and objects his family carried on their backs to Kawaya. Joe had no choice but to start life all over again, as if he were a poor student returning to Sierra Leone. Except now, no family could help him as he rebuilt his life. Most everyone in the country was impoverished, homeless, displaced, and starving from the impact of the civil war.

Darkness descended on the village. In the distance Joe spotted a lone firefly, a flicker of red in the night. Jonathan Daramy did send one glimmer of good news. All of Joe's diplomas and education certificates, which Jonathan hid in the attic of his house, had survived.

CHAPTER FORTY-SIX

Los Angeles

After a year of working in the candle shop, a smattering of audition highs, the pits of rejection, and unsteady income, I needed a schedule, regular income, and a community. It came in the form of Brentwood School. One of the most prestigious private schools in Los Angeles, Brentwood planned to structure a new dance program. Friends in another theater company I joined, the Classical Theater Lab, informed me that Brentwood had an opening for a dance instructor.

My Master of Fine Arts from A.C.T. included dance. I jumped on the opportunity to interview. Driving through the campus, lush and green, I had never seen such a beautiful school. In the interview I explained that I would teach about different cultures through dance. Linking the study of Latin America in a Brentwood history class with salsa dancing in my class would be a great way for students to connect with a country. I planned to teach West African dance, Brazilian capoeira, hip-hop, ballet, Cuban salsa, and Fosse-style jazz. Many of the hip-hop steps students watched on TV stemmed from West African dance. Break dancing, derived from Brazilian capoeira—a martial arts type of dance—was further derived from the Bantu people at Central Africa.

"Students really want to learn the cool dances they see in music videos," I said. "I want them to know where these dances come from, learn the culture, original movement, history, and meaning behind the dances."

At the end of the interview I shared that my commitment was not to make professional dancers out of the students, but to have the students leave my class feeling comfortable in their bodies, confident with movement, and knowledgeable about other cultures.

I left the interview feeling good. About a week later I received a phone call from the headmaster who wanted to hire me. The new performing arts curriculum would include dance, history, and culture. I couldn't wait for the school year to begin.

In late August, Brentwood School made my life come alive. Young faculty, enthusiastic students, and supportive parents helped put the ups and downs of auditions in perspective. While Brentwood provided an amazing structure and foundation for me, I questioned other parts of my life. Where was my career going? Why didn't I have a steady relationship? Some of the auditions I went on were for angry black women or street punks. I wanted a committed relationship, but that eluded me, too.

During an evening acting class, I admired one of my classmates. A successful software engineer, he drove a functioning car and exuded joy, the exact opposite of a struggling actor. His attitude and enthusiasm were contagious. Finally, after class one evening I said, "You always seem so excited about things." He shared with me that he signed up for a weekend class at Landmark Education, called The Landmark Forum, "a course designed for people to have breakthroughs in whatever area of life they are working on." Whatever it was he was doing, it seemed to help his acting and his life.

He invited me to a class where a tall, handsome, confident black man stood up and spoke about "not worrying about what everyone thinks of me all the time." Sitting in the back row, I thought, "I would never think that guy would have a problem like that." Next a woman stood up and shared how she was molested as a child and learned to forgive the person, or at least move forward. Inspired and curious about the program I longed to sign up. But I needed money to take the course.

The very next day, I was approached at school to coach the drill team;

the paycheck was the exact amount needed for the self-expression class. Looking at the coincidence as a gift, I signed up for a class the next weekend.

In the initial class, the teacher asked about our first relationships. Even before we have a relationship with ourselves, our primary relationship is with our parents. Our relationship with our parents informs how we perceive and respond to others. My brow wrinkled. I had an extraordinary relationship with my parents. I could not imagine better models or more supportive guides. But as I listened to people talk about their first relationship, the one with their parents, I had a breakthrough.

My first relationship was not with my parents Jim and Judy, but with my birth parents. I realized that I had created a story that I told myself over and over—*my father abandoned my birth mother and me.* Because I knew my birth mother tried to keep me, knew of her struggles, she became blameless and my birth father, the deserting captain.

I realized for the first time that I was furious.

Not once did I question the story I had created: "He used her, abandoned me, and took off." I realized, deep inside, I resented my birth father and mourned my birth mother. In a journal I wrote long ago:

> . . . Penny kept me for nine months so we were together for a total of eighteen months and then bam she's gone. I never saw my mother's face again.

I did not stop and wonder what my father was going through. Did he have to leave? I also never questioned what would have happened to me if I had lived with my father. Or my mother? Maybe their decision to put me up for adoption saved my life. For the first time in my life I saw that my anger toward my father allowed me to be angry, righteous, and untrusting. I didn't want to have anything to do with him. Underneath all the anger was my great fear. "What if he doesn't like me? What if he rejects me again?" I saw that through my entire life, it was easier to be angry than to deal with my feelings. I had been holding onto this fear for twenty-eight years.

I loved The Landmark Forum and I chose to take other courses. I took the Advanced Course and then I took the Self-Expression and Leadership Program. One of the main assignments in this program, which takes place over a four-month period, was to "Develop a project to take into your community." The objective was to learn support, structure, and how to create something; detach the ego from our creation and then let it go into the world. I created a play week for foster children at Brentwood School where I worked with Brentwood's Community Service Director to pair older students as buddies with foster children in a mini summer camp. T-shirt painting, playtime on a donated moon bounce, and a day trip to Universal Studios filled the week.

During another weekend seminar, the question posed by my teacher was, "Where are you holding back in your life? Tell the person next to you."

I blurted out to my friend, Art, sitting next to me, "I am terrified to find my father. I am terrified of being rejected."

Art looked at me and instead of telling me most parents don't want to be found and how a search would be a waste of time and money, he quietly said, "I know someone who could search for him for no more than a hundred dollars. Your father is going to love you."

As fate would have it, Art's stepmother was helping her adopted children search for their birth parents through a private investigator. The next day Art called me with a phone number.

Sarah's father's Toyota Hilux, used to escape the rebels in 1994. (SARAH CULBERSON)

Little girls dance to welcome the Culbersons and their friends to Bumpe, 2007. (VON RAEES)

John carries a bucket of water for bathing. (SARAH CULBERSON, 2004)

Sarah's grandfather, Paramount Chief Francis Kposowa, 1963. (AUTHOR'S COLLECTION)

Sarah and family dressed for Penny's memorial service in Bumpe, 2004. (HASSAN BAJAN)

Joe Konia Kposowa in his twenties. This was the first photo Sarah saw of her father. (AMED PESSIMA)

Many young girls do not have an opportunity to go to school in Sierra Leone. Here is a sign encouraging parents to send their girls to school. (TARANEH SALKE, 2007)

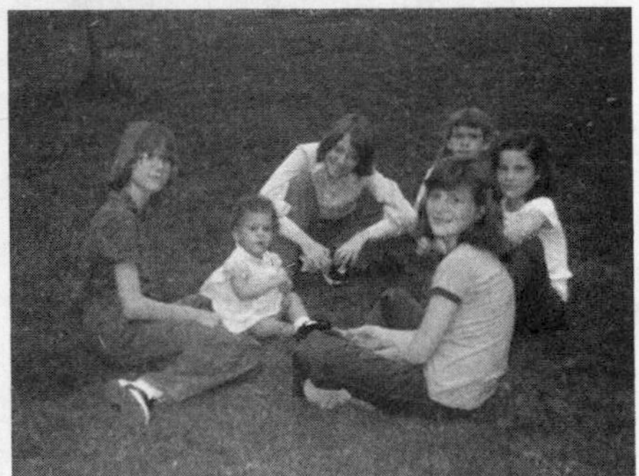

Lynne (far left in denim jumpsuit) introduces Sarah to her friends on Sarah's first day with her new family, the Culbersons, 1977. (JUDY CULBERSON)

Sarah's birth mother, Penny, senior-year photo, 1958. (H. R. KNEE)

Bumpe High School's library was restored by the Kposowa Foundation in 2007, following the Civil War. (Books provided by the LemonAid Fund.) (Von Raees)

Sarah's birth mother Penny (on left) as Buckwheat Festival Princess in 1958. (Grace Morgan)

Aunt Amy and her husband, the Paramount Chief, Tommy Kposowa, who will rule for life. (Sarah Culberson, 2004)

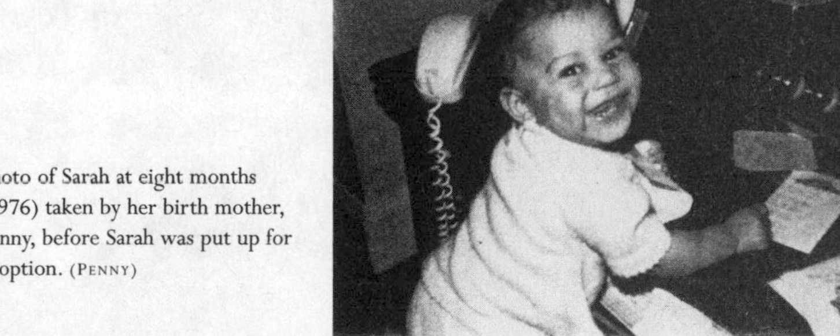

Photo of Sarah at eight months (1976) taken by her birth mother, Penny, before Sarah was put up for adoption. (Penny)

Sarah with her paternal grandmother, Musu, three months before Musu's death in 2004. (HINDO KPOSOWA)

Sarah's adoptive dad, Jim, hugs Sarah's father, Joe, during their first meeting in Bumpe in 2007. (VON RAEES)

Photo of Noha, who rolled the flat tire to Bo and saved the family. (JOE KONIA KPOSOWA)

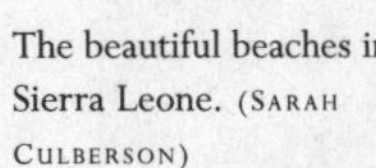

The beautiful beaches in Sierra Leone. (SARAH CULBERSON)

Sarah's last day in Bumpe. Her aunts come to braid her hair. (HASSAN BAJAN)

Sarah talking with Bumpe High School cultural music and dance group in 2007. (JIM CULBERSON)

Typical poda poda – similar to the one in which Sarah and her father took back to Freetown. (VON RAEES)

Sarah with her family, sharing a fun moment with Bumpe's children in 2007. (MARY KPOSOWA)

Street scene from Bo, where Sarah often visited with her father. (Von Raees, 2007)

The photo Sarah sent to her father in Sierra Leone before they met. (Jim Culberson)

Twelve Bumpe High School classrooms were renovated and filled with desks by the Kposowa Foundation. (Von Raees, 2007)

Sarah's father gave her a green dress to wear to her surprise welcome ceremony in Bumpe. Joe wears a shirt made out of the matching fabric. (John Woehrle, 2004)

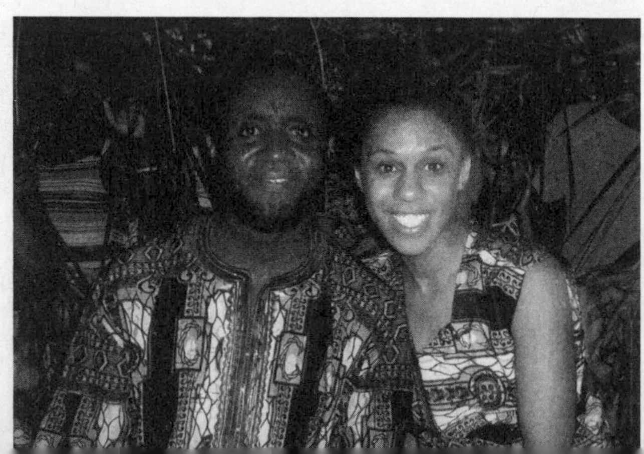

Sarah's adoptive parents, Jim and Judy Culberson, greet the crowd during their first visit to Bumpe, 2007. (VON RAEES)

Typical mud hut common in villages. (VON RAEES, 2007)

The remains of Sarah's grandfather's and great-grandmother's home. It was set on fire during the rebel attacks, 1994-1998. (VON RAEES)

Amputee survivors in the colony next to Bumpe. (SARAH CULBERSON. 2004)

Students in Bumpe cheering for the camera in 2007. (VON RAEES)

Bumpe High school's dining hall destroyed during the rebel attack and rampage from 1994 to 1998. (VON RAEES)

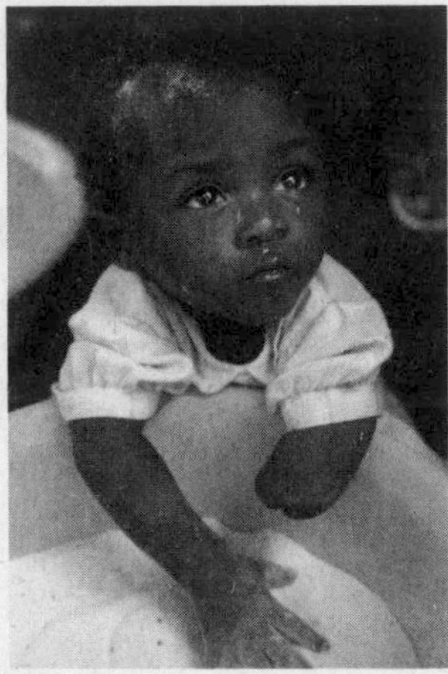

Marie's left arm was intentionally lopped off by rebels around Christmas, 2000. (AP PHOTO/ADAM BUTLER)

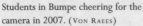

Dale Sparks/The Dominion Post

Homecoming Queen crowned

Sarah Culberson was named University High's queen Friday.

Sarah crowned as University High School's Homecoming Queen her senior year, 1993-1994. (*THE DOMINON POST*)

Sarah's adoptive family: Jonathan, (Sarah), Judy, Jim, Spencer, Lynne, Mackenzie, Austin, Mike Bryan, and Laura. (RICHARD E. LEWIS, 2004)

CHAPTER FORTY-SEVEN

Bo

For six months Joe and his family hid in the village of Kawaya, until they believed it was safe to return to Bo. Bumpe village, still too open and unprotected was not safe, but the imminent threat of a rebel attack on Bo had subsided. Although rebels succeeded in infiltrating the outskirts of the city, the Kamajors and government soldiers had protected the city center. Bo never fell during the eleven-year war.

Back across the river, through the bush, Joe once more led his family to Bo. With his valuables stolen in the rebel scourge, Joe's only hope for supporting his family lay in his education. Even in the middle of a civil war, Sierra Leone's children needed to be educated. As it was, the bulk of the rebels' fighting force consisted of two types of soldiers: uneducated teenage thugs, and drugged, abducted children. Some Sierra Leonean scholars believed if the previous government had invested more in education in the first place, many disenfranchised, illiterate youth would never have succumbed to the lure of the rebel movement.

If and when this war ended, the country's children would need a powerful education to rebuild their battered nation. The next generation could not afford to be illiterate, innocent of world politics, sheltered in villages, and immersed in superstition. The Deputy Director of Education of the Southern Province learned Joe, a refugee, was interested in opening a satellite Bumpe High School in Bo.

"Can you find enough instructors to teach?" asked the Minister of Education.

"Yes," assured Joe. In the streets and markets of Bo, Joe encountered many of his former teachers from Bumpe High School—all desperate for work and longing to teach.

"Would enough children attend?" he asked.

"Yes," Joe said. He knew how badly his former students wanted to learn. Although gathering money for school fees would be difficult for many families, they would find a way to pay the nominal fees—around 20,000 leones or $7.00 a semester. Schoolchildren in Sierra Leone all paid school fees.

A radio announcement blasted over Sierra Leone's KISS 104 station: Bumpe High School planned to re-open in Bo. The refugee school planned to share space at Saint Andrew's Secondary School. In the morning, students from Saint Andrew's would attend classes 9 A.M.–1:30 P.M. In the afternoon, 2 P.M.–6 P.M., Bumpe School would kick into gear.

Twelve male teachers and one female teacher agreed to join the makeshift faculty. Social Studies, Geography, History, Physics, Chemistry, Biology, Religious Knowledge, Integrated Sciences, and Home Economics comprised the curriculum.

The first day of Bumpe High School in Bo kicked off like a celebration. Although malnourished, students burst with excitement to be in school. Thrilled to do something with their energy, grateful to dream of a future, every student showed up on time.

Joe greeted the students in a formal assembly. Seventy-six boys and girls arrived the first day, filing into the large assembly hall. Joe spoke of the gift and responsibility of an education even in the middle of a civil war. Attending school was a privilege. Many young people, even before the war, could not afford the school fees; others were unable to pay for a uniform or shoes. Some were needed by their families to tend rice farms. And many girls, with no access to a proper toilet or sanitary napkins, simply dropped out of school from shame when their menstrual periods began.

In his speech Joe counseled vigilance. They were not in Bumpe anymore. This was Bo, a big city, a fragile oasis in the middle of a war. "Do not walk the streets. Do not leave the city for food. Stay close to home. Go quickly to and from school. If rumor spreads of a rebel attack, stay with your parents." As Joe spoke, he scanned the sea of faces. Recognizing many students from Bumpe, his heart lifted. Many families had escaped the attacks and made it to Bo. At the same time his heart also sank to see so many students missing. The students in attendance looked gaunt, even thinner than usual. He was afraid to ask about some students not present. Later he would learn that some of his pupils were killed or conscripted as soldiers.

His speech continued, "This war is going to be over. There will be change. I want you to trust in the Lord, and changes will come in your life." A few students' eyes wandered, vacant and dazed. Joe understood why the students could not focus. They were starving. Throughout the semester he found himself digging into his pockets, giving a student a few leones to buy a banana at the markets or a handful of groundnuts to keep them awake.

Another student yawned. Again he knew it was not rudeness, but hunger. Students in Sierra Leone were remarkably well behaved in school. All students stood when a teacher entered a classroom and said, "Good morning, Sir," in unison. Schools allowed corporal punishment, and insolence was met with a swift hit on the bottom with a thin cane. Joe's brother Tibbie Kposowa remembered back in his youth when a classmate earned a caning. In anticipation, the boy wore four pairs of shorts to help ease the pain. His ruse was discovered and he was sent home to remove the three extra pairs before receiving his punishment.

Every student knew that education offered the greatest hope for a life outside the rice farms. In spite of the obstacles—an entire classroom sharing a single book and passing it around to read passages, or the lack of pencils and papers—the students diligently applied themselves.

The students were not, however, alone in their struggles. For one week, one of Joe's best teachers did not show up for work. Every morning the other teachers and Joe scrambled to cover his class. Every day Joe grew angrier—no notice, no warning, just a delinquent teacher. The teacher's absence hurt students' studies and their morale. Finally, the following week, the teacher returned to school and slunk into Joe's office.

"Where were you?" asked Joe from behind his desk.

"Sir," the teacher said standing before him. "I left to search for food. My children are starving." With two wives and six children ages 8–14, the teacher had no choice but to risk a journey back to his village in an attempt to gather cassava root, sweet potatoes, fish, and rice.

Joe bowed his head. What could he say? He could not blame a man whose family was starving. He himself grew okra in his backyard to help support his own.

"Your students are waiting for you," said Joe.

"Thank you," said the teacher.

Joe's stomach growled.

CHAPTER FORTY-EIGHT

Los Angeles

" 'Capa-sowa' is turning up nothing. I'm not finding that name anywhere," said the private investigator over the phone. "Maybe it's a different spelling? Can you check the exact spelling of your birth father."

"Okay," I said. I called my dad early Friday morning.

My parents always hinted more adoption information may be available "when I was ready," but I never asked for more. But now I was pushing. I didn't want to be sixty, seventy, eighty years old to begin a search for my father. I needed to know him now. In my mind I knew he could be dead, but in my heart I knew he was alive. I could feel it.

I called my dad.

"Dad, it's finally time for me to find my birth family and I was wondering if you could give me the spelling of my father's last name," I said, taking a gulp of air. "Dad, I know you and Mom have always been supportive about me searching for my birth parents, but I can't do this unless you are okay with it."

My dad said, "Your mom and I are confident in who we are in your life. We understand this is something important to do."

"Okay, I just want to make sure."

"I'm sure," he said. "I'll check with Mom and get the spelling."

"Dad, I would really like to get the spelling by today if that's possible."

"Okay. I'll see what I can do."

That afternoon my dad called me with the correct spelling. My parents stored it in their safe-deposit box at the bank.

I studied the name I wrote on the pad of paper before me: *Joseph Konia Kposowa*.

"Thank you," I said to my dad. "Dad, I just need to try to find him. This has nothing to do with you and Mom not being incredible parents. I just need to know."

"I understand. I just don't know if he would have gone to all those basketball games," he teased.

"Dad, no one takes the place of you."

Did my dad realize my search was about knowing my story and not a reflection of any lack in him? Reading back over one of those Sweet Sixteen letters my mom asked friends to write long ago, one of the neighbors, Janet Frohne, wrote this about my dad:

> *"Memories . . . walking by the park and hearing your dad sing lullabies at the top of his lungs and swinging as high as he could go with a very happy Sarah holding on tightly on his lap when you were two."*

Then I read again what my dad wrote in his letter to me in the Sweet Sixteen book they made for me:

> *. . . Remember how you "loved" cross-country skiing with me, during the years when Mom worked on the weekends? We'd go every time it snowed; you loved to do the long downhills, and then I'd talk you back uphill. I knew it would end when you discovered ski lifts.*
>
> *. . . I recall quietly bursting with pride inside, when you were announced as the winner (track in Ohio), or as a member of the All-Tournament Team (several times!), or as the Outstanding Athlete (CL School), or as Snow White or Max. I don't suppose you realize how good it makes me feel to be your Dad.*

. . . Now remembering the past and seeing you at sixteen, I am mostly amazed at how smoothly and comfortably you have eased from year to year, growing, learning, smiling, continuing all the time to be friends with almost everyone, always showing the people you meet how much good there is in the world. God gives each of us gifts to share; you certainly do a wonderful job with yours! I love you, Squirt. Dad

"I love you, Dad," I said.

"I love you, too, Sarah Jane," he said.

That same evening I dialed the detective.

"I have the spelling," I said.

"Great, I'll see what I can do. Hold tight. I can't do anything until Monday. It might take weeks."

"Okay," I said.

That very weekend I took out my fake hair. It was time to let go of my weave. People get weaves for all kinds of reasons, but mine was to hide. I spent my entire life trying to hide my nappy, kinky hair. I had no idea what my hair really looked like. Straight flowy hair was beautiful to me, hair like my sisters', my mom's and everyone else's hair that I saw on television.

Starting on Friday night, I spent seven hours taking out my fake braids. My head was covered with "undetectables," which were strands of filler hair braided into my natural hair. Three hundred tiny braids snaked all over my head. My friend Kyra came over to help me unravel the braids. When it began to get late she left and I stood in my bathroom with scissors, a garbage can, and a sink filled with fake hair. I stared at myself in the mirror. One side of my head still had tamed flowy fake hair, and on the other side, kinky, wild hair sprung to the ceiling. I was done hiding.

Just as I had never dealt with my natural hair, my African hair, I had never dealt with my African roots. I wasn't quite sure what to do with it all.

Without chemical baths and neat twisted braids, my hair looked disheveled. It had no form. Was I only pretty if I had long flowing "white-looking" hair? I didn't know what I was going to do with my hair, but I knew I had to stop hiding it.

At three in the morning, I finished taking out the weave. A gigantic head of hair shot in every direction. There wasn't enough space to see all of my real hair in the mirror. I pulled my Afro back in a rubber band to get some sleep; it was like having an additional pillow under my head.

Saturday morning, I met a Brentwood student, Lizzy Karp, in the dance studio for rehearsal. Before she arrived I waited alone in the dance room, every sectioned mirror reflecting me. My hair towered on my head. The early morning moisture sprung my Afro to new heights. With all the mirrors, I was forced to look at my hair over and over again. I was teleported back to the age of eight, back to the little girl who wanted to hide her hair but couldn't. This wild untamed mess was shouting, "I'm here, you can't miss me!" I felt ugly. Really ugly. I started to cry. I wasn't sure if it was my hair set free after all these years, or that a private investigator had my father's real name, but I had never felt so vulnerable in my life.

My student pushed open the door, ten minutes early, and caught me crying.

"What's the matter, Culby?" she asked. Some of my students had nicknamed me "Culby" from Culberson.

"Sorry. I'm so embarrassed for you to find me crying," I said to my student. I wiped my tears.

"Why?" she asked, with the innocence of an eighth grader. "Why are you crying?"

"My hair," I said.

"I love your hair. It looks so cool!" she said.

"Thank you," I said. "I'm just getting use to my new 'do. Let's dance."

Monday morning, on a break in the teacher's lounge, my cell phone rang. It was the detective.

"Hello?" I said, wondering if I gave him the wrong spelling again.

"Sarah," he said, "I found your father. A Joseph Kposowa lives in Maryland. He has an unlisted phone number, but here is his address. You might want to write him a letter."

My hands trembled. On yellow-lined paper I wrote down the street address and zip code.

"Maryland?" I said again.

"Was my father in the United States all along? Did he come back?"

"Write to him and see," he said.

"Thank you so much," I said.

"This is why I do this work. Good luck."

"How much do I owe you?" I asked.

"These searches usually take weeks, but this took me three hours. Just send me $25 for the access I paid for certain servers."

"Are you sure?"

"Yes, this is why I do this. I can hear how excited you are. Good luck."

"Thank you!" I said. I stared at that piece of paper for a week. *Maryland?*

CHAPTER FORTY-NINE

Bumpe

After four years in Bo living as a refugee and working as a principal, Joe decided to return to Bumpe. Although the war would not end until 2002, with a peace agreement, international pressure, and amnesty for many of the RUF's war crimes—four long years away—villagers streamed back to Bumpe in droves, eager to rebuild their lives, desperate to farm, longing for ritual and tradition, aching for their family and community to reunite. Rebel attacks still erupted, but largely in the diamond mining areas and in Freetown. Life had to be lived, and living in Bo with the filth, exploding population, and constant struggle for food was no longer worth it.

"We will return to Bumpe," Joe announced.

Cheers of joy sprang from Mary, Hindogbae, and Jeneba. No matter the risks, everyone wanted to return. Jeneba now fourteen years old and Hindogbae now nine years old first needed to understand that their former home did not exist. Joe explained they should not be shocked, that most everything in the village was destroyed.

Joe borrowed a large van from missionaries, the United Brethren in Christ in Bo, to load the belongings he acquired again with his meager principal's salary, and from family help overseas. In the missionaries' van, the family loaded clothes, pots, pans, mattresses, papers, food supplies—as much as they could to rebuild their lives with a single carload of goods.

Already Joe secured a promise from Jay Jay Abdulai that his family could live with him and his wife until Joe rebuilt his own house.

The red clay passage from Bo to Bumpe was engorged with villagers. Peasant farmers carried all their possessions on their heads. Cars passed in both directions; different destinations, but all with the same goal—to return home.

When the truck crossed the Tabe bridge, the river where the regent chief drowned during the first rebel attack in 1994, the strangest sight greeted the family. Pumpkins, bright orange pumpkins sprouted all over the town.

When the rebels burned houses in Bumpe, an odd thing happened. Thousands of pumpkin seeds stored in homes all over the village fell from their storage bags, dumped from their shelves, scattered during the sacking, and tunneled into the scorched earth. Right through the former floorboards, pumpkins grew where the seeds had landed and burrowed into the dirt.

Human bones, picked clean by the birds and bleached in the relentless sun also lay in the bush.

After settling at Jay Jay's home, Joe inspected his housing options. His personal home, burned to the ground, would be too expensive to rebuild from the ground up. The principal's quarters, owned by the government, lacked a roof, the zinc sheets carted off and sold by the rebels. Tentacles of vegetation coiled in every room. But with work and a new roof, the house promised a habitable space.

Every morning at seven o'clock the entire family trudged to the principal's quarters to clean. Inside the gutted house, rats squatted in their nests, gecko lizards roamed the walls, and snakes slithered through the weeds. Bats, believed to be witches, found in or around the quarters were killed. Workers tied palm-frond brooms to long sticks. They beat the bats to death before the shape-shifting witch cast evil curses on the home.

Only Joe and a few workers dared rid the inside of the dwelling of vicious intruders. Outside, in the bright sunlight, Mary and the children used rakes and brooms to clear the bush.

For three months the family worked day in and day out cleaning. Zinc roofing provided by missionaries, and secured by workers, grooved back on top of Joe's home. Inside, Joe and some day laborers painted the walls a vivid yellow. Outside, the laborers sealed the building with a white plaster. Basic furniture brought from Bo and placed in the rooms transformed the space into a home. Mary hung handmade tie-dye curtains. Finally, Joe invited the Reverend Morlai over to bless them.

Inside the living room, the family held hands as the Reverend Morlai asked for peace, love, and safety to inhabit the house.

CHAPTER FIFTY

Los Angeles

Each night after school, I composed a different letter to my father. In draft after draft, I introduced myself. Each night, I crumpled up what I had written. I had no words. Needing a break, I met a good friend, Liat, at Urth Caffé on Melrose Avenue and brought my latest draft with me. After ordering our herbal teas, I pulled out the crinkled blue-lined paper and read to my friend without interruption.

"Dear Joseph . . ." I began.

Once I had finished, my friend stared at me for a few minutes. Then she said, "Honey, are you trying to prove something or be good enough for your father?"

That was not the response I wanted.

I stared down at my letter, floppy on the table. It was true. I had just read a laundry list of my accomplishments, awards, and statistics. I did want to be good enough for my father. Worthy of being wanted in his life.

Loved maybe.

"Just write to him, talk to him, tell the truth," she said.

I crumpled up the letter and tossed it into my bag.

She was right, of course. That evening I lit a candle, sat down at my desk and tried again. "Okay, okay," I repeated to myself. "Stay unattached. If he doesn't want to hear from me, or have anything to do with me, I need to be okay with that. Unattached. Okay."

At the top of the letter I wrote the date, May 3, 2004. Ten years had passed since my high school homecoming: four years of college at West Virginia University, three years in San Francisco, and three more years in Los Angeles. I pressed my pen to the paper:

Joseph,

I've been trying to figure out the best way to compose this letter to you. I wrote one draft and then trashed it, because my friend Liat helped me realize that everything I had written was honest, but I was writing from a space of "please like me," rather than from a space of authenticity. What I've finally discovered at the age of 28 is some people will like me and some people won't and all I can do is be me and go from there, so here it goes. My name is Sarah Culberson and I was born in Morgantown, West Virginia on April 15, 1976. My biological name was Esther Elizabeth and my biological parents were Lillian Pearl Metheny and you. I'm writing because I've finally gotten to a place in my life where I don't want to be forty years old saying, "I wish I had the courage to find him."

I am done wondering "what if" and I've decided to just take a chance and write you. I have so many questions about family history, family hereditary illnesses, do I look like you, what is Sierra Leone like? I am writing because I would love to learn about you, and I would be lying if I said I didn't want to meet you, because one of my dreams has always been to meet my biological parents. Unfortunately, when I looked for Penny five years ago I found out she died of cancer when I would have been ten years old. I did find her family and they are incredible. But I must say it is much easier to find information about someone who is dead because she couldn't reject me. You, on the other hand, are still alive, so my fear to find you was much greater, and I've decided to take that risk. I have so many exciting things I would love to share with you about my life and career. So here is all my information. I would be honored to meet you and I can only pray that you would want to meet me.

Love,

Sarah

A solitary blue mailbox on a Los Angeles street corner was too risky for a letter this precious. Instead I drove to the post office, walked inside clutching the letter, and dropped it into a mail slot.

Peace coursed through my body; I sent a letter, wrote to my father after a twenty-eight-year absence. The rest was in his hands.

Performing a scene from Shakespeare's *The Tempest* with The Classical Theater Lab in Los Angeles distracted me from thinking too much about the thin white envelope crossing the United States. Instead of focusing on the letter, I concentrated on learning my lines for the part of Miranda. I did not choose the character or the scene, but a stranger coincidence could not have been possible. At the very moment I tried to find my father, my character, Miranda, was discovering her father's true identity as a Duke and her own secret identity as a princess.

In the scene between Prospero and his daughter, Miranda, she asks:

Miranda: *Sir, are not you my father?*
Prospero: *Thy mother was a piece of virtue, and*
She said thou wast my daughter; and thy father
Was Duke of Milan; and thou his only heir
And princess no worse issued.

If my father did choose to respond to my letter, it would take months. Of course, before I sent the letter to him, I had to get clear with what I might find. He might be dead. He might be in jail for a horrible crime. I forced myself to imagine the most awful role my birth father could assume: he might be incarcerated as a child molester. He might hang up the phone on me. He might say I didn't want you in the first place, stay out of my life now. He might say I wish we had aborted you. I had to truly own that whatever I discovered about my father does not make me who I am. I needed to prepare—if he even *responded* to my letter—to accept him for who he was and for who he was not.

Whatever happened, I wanted to stop being a victim of "abandonment." It was so much easier to keep a running saga alive about my birth father, the guy who left—it made me a righteous victim. However, I needed to take responsibility for myself and realize the blessings in my life right now.

If he never responded, at least I would know that I tried.

If he never responded, the search would end in Los Angeles with a lost letter.

But it didn't end. It began.

Part Two

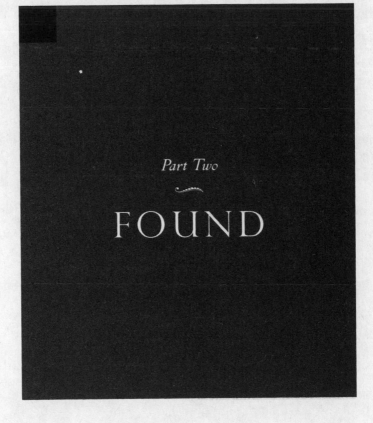

FOUND

CHAPTER FIFTY-ONE

Los Angeles

Four days after mailing the letter, I received a phone call. Late afternoon light filtered through the white cotton curtains in my apartment. A woman with a foreign voice said, "Hello, Sarah, this is Evelyn. How are you?"

I had no idea who was calling. I remembered meeting a Jamaican woman in a coffee shop a few weeks ago. Was this the same woman?

"Do I know you?" I asked.

"I am your auntie, we received your letter," answered Aunt Evelyn.

I froze.

"I was there when you were born. I used to care for you when your mother would go to the grocery store. We are so happy you have found us."

"Thank you so much for calling. I didn't know if . . ." and I couldn't speak through my cracking voice. Tears poured down my face. I had only mailed the letter to the East Coast four days ago. My aunt must have dialed my number the moment she opened my letter.

Aunt Evelyn heard me crying. "I want to get your uncle on the phone."

Uncle Joe picked up the receiver. "Sarah, you mailed the letter to us. I am your father's brother, Joseph Francis Kposowa. Your father is Joseph Konia Kposowa. He lives in Sierra Leone and has been there for twenty-three years. He has survived the civil war, which ended in 2002. I am the eldest brother and was named after my father, your grandfather, Francis

Kposowa. Do you know you are from a royal family? Your great-grandfather was a Paramount Chief of the Mende tribe, your grandfather was a Paramount Chief, and now your uncle is the Paramount Chief. Your father was expected to become the next chief, but he is the principal of Bumpe High School and he chose to rebuild the school after the war instead."

With my mouth agape, I held the phone as if in a dream. Too much information rushed at me at once.

Uncle Joe continued, "Do you know that you are a princess?"

"What?" I said.

"You are the granddaughter of a Paramount Chief in Sierra Leone. As a Kposowa on the paternal side, you could be chief someday."

I trembled. "My father is alive," ricocheted through my head.

"Sarah?" he said.

"Yes," I said.

"Are you there?"

"Yes. I was told about my father coming from an important family, but I never really knew what that meant."

What I would learn later was that in Sierra Leone chiefs ruled individual villages, but all the district chiefs in a vast region reported to one Paramount Chief. In the entire country, only 149 Paramount Chiefs ruled. Before 1896, some Paramount Chiefs used to be called kings. However, when the colonial British administration, under the Protectorate Ordinance of 1896, retitled the rulers Paramount Chiefs, their titles as kings were stripped.

My grandfather, a Paramount Chief, held this title for thirty years, governing thirty-six thousand people. My great-grandfather before him was also a Paramount Chief, and my uncle until his death will be the Paramount Chief. In Sierra Leone, the granddaughter of a Paramount Chief is called a *mahaloi;* the child of a chief with the status of a princess or prince. Only members of a royal family, on the paternal side, can campaign for election against other royal African families to become a Paramount Chief.

"We will contact your father and tell him about you. There are no phones in his village and he must travel to Bo to make a call. We will have someone in Bo go to the village with this message. He is going to be so happy! We are going to let all the family know about you. We will talk soon," said Joe.

I hung up the phone. Elation and fear swirled together inside me. "We are going to let all the family know about you!" I could not have asked for a more loving welcome.

My stomach knotted. I knew they were mistaken. Once my father heard about me, he would ignore me; refuse to see me. I predicted he would be upset I had resurfaced in his life.

The next few hours and days the phone rang off the hook.

A second aunt, Aunt Doreen, called from Washington D.C. "Joe and Evelyn called and told us all about you. We are so excited! I married your father's brother Thomas . . ."

Thomas picked up the line, "We are so happy! So excited you have found us!"

Other relatives called. "Hello, Sarah, I am your Uncle Ali Bundu, your father's uncle, but in Sierra Leone that means that I am your uncle, too. It is so wonderful you have been found! Welcome to the family!"

Family members from all over the United States—from Maryland, Ohio, Washington D.C., and California—called to welcome me to the family.

During the next two weeks, everybody called me except my father.

CHAPTER FIFTY-TWO

Los Angeles

"Doreen, I don't know if he will want to talk to me," I confided to my Aunt Doreen, who called me almost every day. I refused to get my hopes up about my father. I prepared myself for rejection just in case.

"Sarah, he will be so happy to talk with you. It can take weeks to get a message to him in our village. Be patient."

I repeated to myself, "It's not going to happen. Don't get your hopes up. Maybe I wrecked his marriage with my appearance in his life?

"Sarah," said Doreen. "Your family here in Maryland would like you to visit us this summer, meet your father's brothers and sisters. Would you like to come?"

However comforting and exciting it was to plan a visit to meet my new relatives in America, it was a phone call from my father that I wanted more than anything.

Finally, during a break between teaching classes at Brentwood, my cell phone rang. My Aunt Doreen sang on the line. "Sarah! Check your phone messages as soon as you get home!"

Immediately I called my message machine. A deep, rich accented voice, like a rhythmic baritone drum, spoke:

"Hello, Sarah. This is Joseph Konia Kposowa calling from Sierra Leone. I am here in Bo in charge of the census and I heard that you have been found. I am your dad. I am traveling back to Bumpe now, but I will be back in Bo again tonight. I hope you will be there. I want to talk with you."

My hands shook. My entire life I created the story that he would reject me or deny he was my father, and here he was on my message machine. "I am your dad . . . I want to talk with you . . ." The school bell rang.

"I am your dad . . ."

In that moment it was as if two worlds had collided. My head was spinning. I couldn't believe my ears. He said, "I am your dad." I spent my entire life imagining he won't want to have anything to do with me, he'll reject me. Immediately his words began to battle with my two decades' worth of rejection thoughts. Tears rolled down my face. *I* was accepted!

In a daze, I walked to my next class. Twelve eighth-grade girls waited for me inside the dance studio. My eyes could not focus, my heartbeat refused to settle. "Girls, everybody please sit in a circle to start class." The girls gathered in a circle on the hardwood floor.

I searched their faces, twinkling eyes, fresh-faced and eager. "First, I won't be able to teach unless I share this with you. As most of you know I'm adopted. I went in search of my birth parents. First, I discovered my birth mother was dead, but today my birth father just called from Africa. I just heard his voice for the very first time." More tears fell. "I have waited my whole life for this and I want to share it with all of you."

Everyone clapped. Some of the girls came over and hugged me. Another student dug in her backpack for Kleenex for me and her.

After school I went to eat at an outdoor café in Venice, California with my friend, former boyfriend Jeff. Just as the salads arrived my cell phone rang.

"Hello, Sarah, it's Doreen. Your father is on the line, we are so happy! Uncle Thomas is on the line, too."

I cupped my hand around the receiver to block out extra noise, desperate for a quiet place to talk. "Hold on, I am going to move so I can hear . . ." I shouted. The buzz of whizzing bikes and outdoor stereos blasted background noise.

I signaled to Jeff, "I gotta take this!"

"I'll sit right here and wait," he said.

I spun around the café tables and darted into a vintage clothing shop that looked quiet. Mildew and musty scents twirled around me as I pinballed between the racks of clothes. I moved toward the back dressing rooms. I wondered why at this moment, a moment I had waited for my entire life, my aunt and uncle were on the phone, too? What I didn't know was that many Sierra Leoneans have three-way calling. Everybody talks on the phone at once. Welcoming a lost daughter into the family was not a solitary occasion, but a family reunion. I am sure if it were possible, twenty other people would have dialed in as well.

"Hi," I breathed, backing into a clothes rack, the row of metal hangers tilting against me, as if my world had just changed axis.

"Hello, Sarah. How are you?" said my father.

"I'm fine. I'm well. I am just with my friend in a café. I ducked into a shop so I could hear you. It was so noisy outside."

"Okay," he said. "Well, first, I'd like to say to you, I want you to please forgive me."

I inhaled a quick, sharp breath. Silence filled the phone.

"After you were put up for adoption, your name had changed and I didn't know how to find you."

More direct than I could have ever imagined, my father's words hit my heart.

"No," I said, "please, forgive me. I've been making you wrong my whole life to protect myself and I'm not going to do that anymore."

The line became silent.

"Okay," said my father softly.

Later he would share with me that he believed I was asking forgiveness for not searching for him sooner. It was incomprehensible to him that I believed he might hang up on me, reject me, or not call back.

"In Africa, when a child is found, it is a great celebration." The words of my Nigerian hairdresser from San Francisco ran through my head.

We spoke of Penny. My father apologized again.

But I didn't want him to apologize. It was so hard for me to hear. The more he felt he had done something wrong, the more it hurt me.

My father explained the Kposowa family's leadership role in Bumpe. He also explained how I, as his daughter, could become the Paramount Chief of Bumpe chiefdom one day.

"When can I see you? I'd really love to meet you," I said.

"It is difficult for me to get a visa. Why don't you come here?" he said.

My heart flipped. "That's what I wanted to hear!" I said. "I'd love to come this summer."

"Summer is not a good time to come. It's the rainy season. The roads will be very bad, if not impossible. It is better for you to visit in December."

I had no idea how much preparation it takes to host a guest in Bumpe. For a royal daughter's return, the granddaughter of a Paramount Chief, a great celebration must be planned. A celebration would be expensive and take cooperation from the entire village. Extra food must be purchased in Bo. A sturdy car must be rented that could handle the six-hour car ride from the capital of Freetown to Bumpe. An experienced driver who could manage the unpaved roads would need to be hired.

Doreen chimed back in on the line. "Joe, Sarah is visiting us this summer. We will start planning her visit to Bumpe."

What I also did not know at the time was how much was at stake for my father. He had to share with his village that he had an American daughter with a white woman long ago. My visit was a great honor and a great risk for him. As an American choosing to fly halfway across the world, my visit would be a mark of respect to my father. However, if I arrived as a rude, uneducated woman, it would bring him great embarrassment. If I said I was coming and canceled—it would shame my father in front of the entire village.

CHAPTER FIFTY-THREE

Los Angeles

I called my parents. I wanted them to know I spoke with my father and that I wanted to go to Sierra Leone to meet him. I knew they would be thrilled that the conversation went well. All along my mom had been worried a search might end in rejection and that I could be hurt. She also had empathy for my father's family in case they knew nothing about me.

I played my father's message for my parents over the phone. I repeated every word of our conversation.

My mom was delighted that my father was so welcoming and gracious.

My dad also secretly worried that my birth parents' meeting might have been a single-night encounter and that that information might be hurtful to me. Fortunately, Penny and Joe did have a relationship. Already my parents thought highly of my father for immediately accepting me.

"Mom and Dad, I want to make sure you are okay with all of this. My friends keep asking me if you guys are upset or hurt by my search," I said over the phone.

"Sarah, we have been your family for twenty-eight years, and all that time I wasn't worried. You have found your whole truth. This can only add to your being, Sarah," said my mom.

My dad added, "Sarah, I have devoted my life and welfare to you and all of my girls. Remember, I'm a biologist and I understand genetics versus environment. Your mother and I knew that you had special genetic gifts from your family, which didn't come from us, and we also knew how important environment is for a child. The Kposowa family is very fortunate to have you in their family."

I thought my dad was going to say "you are blessed to have this new family." Instead my dad said they are fortunate to have me. That meant so much to me.

Soon after my phone call to my parents, I received a twelve-page letter from my mom. Tucked inside their safe-deposit box, she had been waiting all these years for the right moment to give this letter to me. In my mom's steady cursive, like slow-moving waves, she wrote:

> *On January 12, 1977, we received a phone call from the West Virginia Department of Welfare concerning our application for adoption . . . it was a very cold day. Our car wouldn't start, but we were able to get a ride into town with some neighbors. Following this meeting there were several phone calls and home visits as we were studied . . . on April 14, 1977 Jim was called at school. He actually left in the middle of a lecture to take the call. . . . The social worker wanted to see us right away . . . On Saturday morning, April 16, Jim called the social worker at her home to say that we wanted you as our little girl so we arranged to meet you on Monday afternoon, April 18 at 1:00* P.M. *. . . you arrived in a cute little green dress with a butterfly on the front, we could hardly believe this beautiful little girl was really to be our daughter. . . . You had been sleeping in the car, but you soon woke up and stared, first at one of us and then at the other. Finally, about three minutes later you started crying very hard and kept it up until we left to go home. You finally fell asleep until we arrived. Laura* [sister] *was waiting on the front porch. She had gotten home in record time. Carole Lynne* [sister] *was close behind and from then on through the evening a steady stream of friends and neighbors*

came by to welcome you. We named you Sarah Jane and in those first moments together, you won our hearts and were already part of our family. Love, Mom and Dad

A few days after my parents letter arrived, my father e-mailed a letter to me from Bo, Sierra Leone.

Subject: Letter

Date: Sat, 29 May 2004 16:25:07 +0000

Dear Sarah,

Let me hasten to tell you that it was indeed nice talking to you. It was all like a dream.

I was happy to learn that you have been in close touch with my brothers and other relatives. We have a close family tie. We just love each other and you are now part of this family.

I thought I should tell you a little about myself: I was born in the Kposowa family in 1947. My father was paramount chief Francis Kposowa who was elected in 1942 and ruled until 1972. My mother (Musu) who is still living was one of those early women my father married. My sister who was the elder died in 1986 and I am the only surviving son to my mother, but do have brothers and sisters from the same father.

I have three brothers and a sister in United States: Dr. Joseph Francis Kposowa, Dr. Tibbie Kposowa, Thomas Kposowa, and Jenneh Kposowa. Jenneh is the youngest among those in the United States. I also have uncles and cousins living in the United States.

I attended both primary and secondary school in Bumpe and went to United States in 1974. It was my brother Francis Kposowa who assisted me to travel to the States. On my arrival to the United States, I worked for six months to save money in order to go to college and to also pay for the air ticket my brother bought for me.

It was in January 1975 that I entered Salem College, Salem in West Virginia. It was during this year, that I met your mother, Penny. She shared the same building with my brother. Her own room was just opposite my brother's. By then my brother was doing his master's degree at West Virginia University.

Penny assisted me financially when I was attending college. She did not have a good job and was not earning much, but still helped me in her own little way. It was in April 1976 that she gave birth to you. I am not sure of the actual day but I am sure it was in the month of April.

Because of her low income, she was not able to take care of you. One day I was studying in the college library when three social workers entered and invited me to the foreign student's adviser office. I was asked by one of the social workers whether I knew Penny and whether I know the baby she is having, I said yes. That was the first time I saw you. One of the social workers asked whether I was ready to take care of the baby, I said yes but had no source of income because I was a foreign student. I was then asked to appear in court and sign documents for the child to be adopted and this was done. After this, I never set my eyes on you neither Penny because she already moved from the house where she was living and I was not sure whether she really wanted to see me again.

I continued with my education and graduated in 1979 with a Bachelor of Arts Degree in Psychology and a minor in Religion and Philosophy. I later did my masters degree in Religious Studies. I returned home and started teaching at Bumpe High School, the same high school I attended. I became principal of the school in 1991 up to date.

I am married with two children living in Sierra Leone. My daughter Jeneba is 19 years old and just completed High School, and Hindogbae who is 13 is in eighth grade.

Things are not as good as I expected before I left United States. During the rebel war, I lost almost everything I had. I have to start all over.

Sierra Leone is one of the poorest countries in the world and both salaries and wages are very small and we can hardly make ends meet. Most times, I receive financial assistance from my brothers and sister in United States. Thomas and Jenneh have been assisting.

When I was involved in an accident, It was Thomas and Jenneh who assisted me to pay the hospital bills. If you ask Doreen and Thomas, they will tell you more about Sierra Leone.

We are all expecting you in December. Everybody is looking forward to your visit. Please get in touch as soon as possible now I have opened an e-mail box.

Good luck and take care. With love

Joe Konia Kposowa

CHAPTER FIFTY-FOUR

Maryland

Baltimore Washington International Airport in late June was mercifully uncrowded. It was a good thing because I forgot to tell my Aunt Doreen and Uncle Thomas what I looked like. After talking with my Aunt Doreen on the phone for a month, we forgot to exchange pictures.

Disembarking from a night flight from Los Angeles, I hoped we would be able to find each other at the baggage carousel. I unwrapped the sweater around my waist and put it on. Even though I landed in the full heat of a mid-Atlantic summer, I suddenly became self-conscious. Dressed in comfortable dancer clothes, a lavender tank top with spaghetti straps, I wondered if that would make a good impression on my new relatives. Did I look too casual?

As families milled around the baggage conveyor belt, I spotted two of the blackest faces I had ever seen. Unmistakably African with her hair in towering braids on her head, my Aunt Doreen called, "Sarah! Sarah!"

Walking toward me, arms stretched in a giant hug, Doreen said, "You look just like your father!"

I smiled widely.

Doreen's husband, Uncle Thomas, was dressed in a beige and brown African shirt. "Hello, Sarah," he said hugging me. Although I had only talked with them on the phone, it seemed I knew them my whole life. Thomas grabbed my carry-on for me, and Doreen linked my arm with hers, leading me into the Baltimore night.

In his car waiting just outside the terminal was my Uncle Joe, the eldest brother in the family, the uncle I mistakenly sent my letter to. I slid into the backseat with Aunt Doreen. Thomas joined Joseph up front. Uncle Joe turned around and smiled. "Welcome, Sarah. We will be at my home in thirty minutes."

As we drove through Maryland's suburbs, I wondered if Uncle Joe looked like my father. After dropping off Doreen and Thomas, we arrived at my uncle's home, a divided single-story, two-family home. Inside, a giant vat of West African jollof rice simmered on the stove, scenting the house with African spices. Aunt Evelyn, the very first person I spoke with on the phone, was not at home. At eleven o'clock at night, she was still at work as a nurse on the late shift.

Early the next morning, I opened the bedroom door, tiptoeing to the bathroom in my pajamas. The house was silent. Uncle Joe left early in the morning for one of his three jobs and two of his three children, Musa and Selina, were off at a church youth retreat. I wondered if I was alone in the house when I almost bumped into a fifty-year-old woman sleeping upright in a chair just outside my room. An afghan draped over her knees and a Bible lay open on her lap.

"Sarah?" the woman said, opening her eyes.

"Evelyn?" I said.

"Oh, Sarah! I am your Auntie Evelyn," she said, placing the Bible down and rising from her brown leather La-Z-Boy chair.

"Sarah," she said, "welcome!" She folded me into a warm hug.

"Let me see your hands," she said.

I didn't know if this was a Sierra Leonean tradition—to say hello and instantly ask to see someone's hands?

Gently she took my hands, turned them over, and studied my palms.

I watched her eyes, focused and concerned, survey the crevices in my skin.

"No scars," she whispered.

"What?" I asked, confused.

She took a deep breath. "When you were a little girl," she said, "you touched a furnace at your mother's apartment and burned your palms. I was so afraid you would be scarred for the rest of your life."

Relief shone on her smooth face. She knew Penny well through her husband, my Uncle Joe. Aunt Evelyn shared how kind my birth mother was and how overwhelmed she became caring for me alone. She told me how Penny, while bathing me on a table, in too small a tub, dropped me on the floor. Another time Evelyn said Penny called her hysterically crying. "Esther burned her hand! Esther got burned!"

Although Evelyn was seven months pregnant, she ran over to Penny's apartment to help Penny take me to the hospital.

"No scars," I said. Evelyn held my hand.

CHAPTER FIFTY-FIVE

Maryland

When my Uncle Joe returned that afternoon from his teaching job, he held a bulky envelope in his hands.

"Sarah, do you want to see pictures of your father?"

I had waited almost three decades to see a photo of him.

At that moment euphoria and melancholy converged. Thrilled to finally see him, I was also sad to say farewell to fantasy and imagination that had sustained me all these years. As an adopted child, I fantasized about who my birth parents might be. Of course, most of the time I imagined the worst about my birth father, but on better days he was a hero, a prince.

"Yes, I would like to see some pictures," I said.

Spread before me, an array of old photos fanned the table. The first photo showed my father young and smiling. He wore a green African shirt and an African fez-like hat on his head.

Inches from my face, I studied the photograph. We had the same big eyes and similarly shaped nose. Suddenly I had flashbacks to elementary school when some kids used to call me, "Big honker! Big honker!"

My eyes studied my father's wide nose. We have the same nose. I have an African nose. A beautiful African nose.

I stared at each picture. My father looked elegant, composed, African, and regal. All eyes in the room waited and watched as I picked up the next picture. Another photograph portrayed my father at Joe and Evelyn's wedding in the 1970s. A powder-blue suit with wide lapels transformed my father into a "Saturday Night Fever" dude. I started to laugh.

"I love this one!"

Next they showed me a picture of my grandfather, the Paramount Chief, on a visit to London in the 1950s per the invitation of the British Council.

"That is your grandfather, born in 1890. He was one of 149 Paramount Chiefs governing all of Sierra Leone," Joe said with pride.

"This afternoon you will meet many Sierra Leoneans," said my Aunt Evelyn.

In an hour we would all caravan to an African wedding for distant cousins. Not only was I excited to see and meet Sierra Leoneans, but I also wanted to ask questions to anyone I could talk to about my upcoming trip. My Uncle Thomas and a group of Sierra Leoneans all planned a trip this year in December when the rainy season ended.

At the ceremony, a potluck of Western and African dishes were set out along long tables. Every family member brought a food dish to share. I sampled some of the exotic food and waited for the sugary white wedding cake. From my table, waiting for dessert to be served, I could tell the woman slicing the cake was frazzled. Without thinking I walked up to her and said, "Can I help you?"

"Yes!" she said. "I said I would help, but I'm late for work and will lose my job."

"Go! Go!" I said. "I'll take care of it."

"Thank you!" she said, already halfway out the door.

Suddenly little children started coming up to the table asking for cake. Knowing how much little kids like to help I said, "Yes, you all may have cake, but first I need you all to go on a mission for me!"

More kids gathered around.

"I think this mission might be impossible, maybe way too hard for all of you, maybe too heavy for kids, but if you think you can do it, I need all of you to pass out the slices of cake to the guests as fast as you can."

Every kid in the room darted into action, buzzing through the guests bearing cake. Within ten minutes, a hundred guests held a plate of cake in their hands.

What I didn't know was that the many African guests watched this exchange between the kids and me. Then they called my father.

Later that week my father received a half dozen calls in Sierra Leone: "Joe, she pitched right in, gathered all the children and helped. You will be proud. She is a true African."

CHAPTER FIFTY-SIX

Los Angeles

In the months leading up to my trip my father called me constantly from Sierra Leone. After receiving so many calls from him, something unexpected and strange surged through me: irritation. My entire life I dreamt of my father, prayed for his acceptance, fantasized about his life, and now his daily phone calls annoyed me. Every day at different times, while I was teaching, or driving on Los Angeles's 405 freeway, my phone vibrated.

I did not answer.

Delicately, I tried to explain to my father that if I were teaching I could not leave the classroom and take his call. This was difficult for him to understand. Back in Bumpe, if his phone rang even for local calls (and he was one of the few villagers with a cell phone) he would simply walk out of the classroom. Again, I explained in America this was not allowed; a classroom without a teacher could dissolve into chaos. In Sierra Leone a classroom rarely spins into disorder as students fear a caning in front of their peers.

Again and again my phone buzzed, vibrated, beeped. I began to feel like my father expected me to jump when he called. I had my own life, a very busy life I was trying to manage. After the initial high of connecting, it angered me that after almost three decades of not being in my life, he called me daily. It was too much too soon. "You can't just walk back into my life and be my best friend!" I wanted to shout through the international phone lines. I also learned from my relatives that my father had another daughter, a year older than me, with a woman in Africa.

I was also afraid to get close to my father. I needed time to get used to the idea of having two families. As exciting as meeting so many new relatives was, I put pressure on myself to reassure my adoptive family—Jim, Judy, Laura, and Lynne—that they would never be replaced. When I told one of my sisters I had a half sister, Jeneba, in Africa, she responded with a casual, "Oh." My mom later shared how my sister said in the sweetest tone, "But I'm her sister." Everyone's role in my family needed to shift, to make psychic room for this new family after a twenty-eight-year absence.

My friends, thrilled with the successful detective hunt for my father, wanted to hear all about my upcoming trip to Sierra Leone, but they had no idea of the dissonance dancing in my head. Connecting with my father did not bring the instant peace I naively thought it would. Instead, I feared hurting my dad, Jim. I could not stop thinking about all his years of love and patience, all our cross-country ski trips together, and our hikes through the tall West Virginia grasses bird-watching.

At times, calls to my new father in Africa felt like a betrayal of my family.

Desperate for some space to process everything that was happening, and not communicating what I needed, I avoided my father's calls.

I said I would call him back and never called.

Even as I researched a traveler's visa and set appointments for vaccinations for my trip, I still did not pick up the phone.

Finally my Aunt Doreen called. "Sarah, your father called me and he's a little upset. He feels like you don't want to talk with him."

The phone slipped in my hands. Tears welled in my eyes.

"Sarah?" she said.

"Doreen, I don't know how to do all of this. I want to be there for everyone, but I just need some space and time to think. I know he wants to check in . . ."

What was wrong with me? This was an adopted kid's dream, wasn't it? *A father that calls too much?* But it was too great a shift too fast.

Doreen listened quietly and then said, "I understand. I will talk with your father."

She called my father, shared what was going on in my life, what I was processing, what life was like here in America, and that I couldn't just take his calls at all hours. She reassured him that I cared about him very much, but that I needed time.

Only with Doreen's finesse as an intermediary did the relationship between my father and me move forward and unfold at a pace I was comfortable with.

My father stopped interpreting my unreturned calls personally. He simply called and let me call him back in my own time.

And it took some time.

CHAPTER FIFTY-SEVEN

Los Angeles

- *Crisp, new $100 bills*
- *Toilet paper*
- *Malaria pills*
- *Scarf to protect face against the dust*
- *Flashlight*
- *Towels/washcloths*
- *Imodium AD (for travelers' diarrhea)*

Aunt Doreen sent a long list of things to bring for my trip, now only four months away. Traveler's checks, credit cards, and ATM cards were worthless in Sierra Leone. Cash hidden on the body was best. Money in Sierra Leone was best exchanged on the street. Lebanese store owners in Freetown had the best exchange rates, but they accepted only crisp new $100US bills with no tears to insure against counterfeits. Toilet paper was not readily available in Sierra Leone and sometimes it was like butcher paper, more suitable for wrapping cold cuts in the deli than personal hygiene. Aunt Doreen advised carrying my own. Towels and washcloths were nearly impossible to find.

Still trying to gather funds for my trip, I had not bought my $1,300 ticket to Sierra Leone. I needed to fly from California to Washington D.C., Washington D.C. to Brussels, Brussels to the Ivory Coast, and then on to Lungi Airport. My parents, knowing how much this trip meant to me, offered to pay for my airline ticket but said that I would need to cover my other expenses. With a stroke of luck, I booked a Chevrolet commercial, which provided me the rest of my travel money.

Shots are not covered by medical insurance as traveling is considered "elective." With less than one hundred and sixty days to go, I needed to make sure I was vaccinated.

The Centers for Disease Control and Prevention recommended that people traveling to Sierra Leone take precautions against the following viruses and diseases: Yellow fever, typhoid, hepatitis A and B, rabies, meningococcal meningitis, diphtheria, measles, and polio. They also advised taking antimalaria pills before departure—malaria kills millions of people in Africa.

> Dengue Fever . . . and river blindness are other diseases carried by insects that also occur in West Africa. African Sleeping Sickness has increased in Africa. Protecting yourself against insect bites will help to prevent these diseases.

> A parasitic infection can be contracted in freshwater in this region. Do not swim in fresh water (except in well-chlorinated swimming pools) . . .

> Highly pathogenic avian influenza (H5N1) has been found in poultry populations in several countries in Africa. Avoid all direct contact with birds, including domestic poultry (such as chickens and ducks) and wild birds, and avoid places such as poultry farms and bird markets where live birds are raised or kept.

> Polio outbreaks were reported in several previously polio-free countries in Western Africa beginning in 2003 . . .

To avoid animal bites and serious diseases (including rabies and plague) do not handle or pet animals, especially dogs and cats. If you are bitten or scratched, wash the wound immediately with soap and water and seek medical attention to determine if medication or anti-rabies vaccine is needed.

Blackwater fever, the most severe form of malaria, destroys the red blood cells and turns a patient's urine black.

Most of my friends knew nothing about Sierra Leone's civil war, which ended in 2002, so their excitement for me and my upcoming journey was palpable. But the friends who were aware of the civil war became very worried for my safety.

A high school history teacher at Brentwood approached me: "Sarah, I am very nervous about you going. Please, please, be careful."

As my parents researched more about the brutality of the war crimes, grave thoughts filled them. My mom became terrified that I would be kidnapped or never come back.

Finally I received a call with both my mom and dad on the phone. Together they said, "Sarah, we know how important this trip is to you, and we don't want to stop you, but we are really concerned about this trip."

I knew my mom would be worried, but when both my parents picked up the line I started to become nervous. Back at home my mom was reading articles about Sierra Leone and underlining key words: "Thus when the civil war emerged in 1991, the killing of a human being was not entirely novel; it only took on even more horrific forms under the rebel Revolution United Front."

From a TRAVEL.STATE.GOV printout my mom underlined, "Travelers are urged to exercise caution, especially when traveling outside of the capital. . . . The continued poor state of the economy and the lack of opportunity for many in Sierra Leone have lead many individuals to turn to criminal activity. There has been a moderate increase in armed robberies and residential burglaries. . . .

"Most roads outside Freetown are unpaved and most are passable with a 4-wheel drive vehicle. However, certain stretches of mapped road are often impassable during the rainy season. Public transport (bus or group taxi) is erratic, sometimes unsafe, and generally not recommended." In the margins my mom wrote, *"How will you travel inside the country?"*

I had done very little research about the war. I did not want to know. I only wanted to meet my father. I did not ask my parents or any family member to go with me. I knew if I did I would spend my trip worrying if they were okay. When my parents raised their concerns I shared that as a twenty-eight-year-old woman I was willing to take the risk. "I need you to trust in me. You've always told me to trust in God. That's what I'm doing."

Silence hung on the other end of the line.

My mom spoke, "Okay, Sarah. We love you. We know this is something you must do."

CHAPTER FIFTY-EIGHT

Malibu

I would have a traveling companion after all. For the past few years, I had been involved with a theater group led by an acting teacher named John Woerhle. John, also an alumnus of A.C.T., who graduated nineteen years before me, was an outstanding instructor. Under his guidance, eleven other students and I took lessons and performed in a group called the Black Box Experimental Theater, where we developed ensemble pieces and sketches John and another writer created for each student.

One afternoon after an acting workshop in Malibu, I shared with John that my birth father called and invited me to Sierra Leone to meet him. "Do you want to hear his voice?" I asked. I had saved my father's message on my machine for months.

After calling my answering machine, I handed John the phone. He listened to my father's message.

"Sarah, this is amazing!" he said. "You should get this on film!"

I knew I wanted to take someone with me to film but I didn't know who to ask. If I asked family members, I was afraid I would be worrying about them. I needed to meet my father by myself.

Suddenly an idea sparked in my head and I blurted out, "Wait, do *you* want to go?"

John was my teacher and a good friend. His involvement with theater lent him a great humanity and acceptance of others, and he knew how to film. The reunion with my father could be captured on tape.

"Wow," said John. "That's quite an invitation. Let me think about it."

John discussed the trip with friends and family. His father, a World War II veteran who traveled the world through his work as a first class petty officer in the construction battalion, gave John this advice: "There are challenges and opportunities that come along maybe two or three times in your life and this might be one of them." John's father was so excited about this trip, this African experience unfolding, that he offered to pay for John's airfare. Although having traveled widely, John had never visited Africa. He also had a distant relationship with his elderly father, and the shared excitement for this journey helped forge a stronger connection between them.

In our own ways, Africa was the beginning of a healing process with both of our fathers. A number of John's friends who were familiar with the recent civil war in Sierra Leone advised him over and over again not to go. Finally, John called the American Embassy in Sierra Leone and asked about any travel advisories.

The clerk said now that the civil war was over, the two greatest dangers for visitors were the following:

- *Driving at night—the roads are terrible and the drivers even worse.*
- *Speeches—Sierra Leoneans are known to be such long-winded speakers that a guest may be forced to endure hours of endless speeches even in the smallest public gathering.*

John laughed, believing he could handle a few long speeches, and he would make sure not to travel at night. He agreed to come with me for half the trip, staying only eight days compared to my seventeen days. He began practicing filming with a Panasonic DVX100 and some wireless microphones.

I called my father in Africa to tell him John would be accompanying me for a week to film.

At first my father was very concerned. A second guest would put even more strain on his minimal resources. More food to buy? Would he need to rent a bigger car? Where would John sleep?

I had no idea how much difficulty and expense one extra guest was for my father. Secretly, he was also concerned with what the villagers would think. His unmarried daughter was visiting with an older white man?

"Is John your boyfriend?" he asked.

"No, he is my teacher and my friend," I assured him.

"Then we must all call him professor when he is here," he said.

"Okay," I said.

So the village of Bumpe awaited the arrival of Joseph Konia Kposowa's long lost twenty-eight-year-old biracial daughter and her six foot three, handsome, silver-brown–haired, hazel-eyed professor.

CHAPTER FIFTY-NINE

Los Angeles

Two weeks before my trip I called my father. "I'd like to bring some gifts for you and your family, and for the children in your school. I teach at a wonderful school and could bring some Brentwood T-shirts for your students. Would that be okay? Would your students like that? What do they need?"

"We need desks," he said.

"Desks?" I repeated, embarrassed that I was so ignorant of the basic needs of his students. Bumpe's children didn't need T-shirts, they needed desks, paper, pens, and pencils.

"The rebels destroyed the school. Used all the desks for firewood."

"Oh. How much do desks cost?" I asked.

"Twenty dollars."

"How many do you need?" I asked.

"I will count."

"Could you fax me a letter stating what you need?" I asked.

T-shirts in Sierra Leone did not cut it—unmet basic needs beyond my wildest comprehension awaited me.

A few days later my father faxed this letter to me:

Dear Sarah

A letter of Appeal

Bumpe High School was one of the schools seriously damaged during the rebel war. Most of its structures were destroyed or burnt, furniture and other equipment was destroyed or carried away by the rebels. At the moment, the school is lacking basic furniture for the students. We have up to 582 students in the school. We need furniture for 382 students. A set of furniture will cost Twenty Dollars and the total cost for 382 sets is Seven Thousand Six Hundred and Forty dollars ($7,640). If such a help in terms of furniture is rendered, it will go a long way, as many students will benefit from it for years. No help is ever too small. Whatever is offered will be appreciated. Please contact friends and well-wishers for help. Thank you for any consideration given to this matter.

With lots of love

Joseph Konia Kposowa

I spoke with my parents. What should I do? I couldn't even pay for my own plane ticket, much less a school full of desks. Plus, I was leaving in two weeks. "I'll send an e-mail to friends," I said to my mom.

She said, "Let's share this with friends and family. Maybe we all can help."

That night I typed up this e-mail, which I sent to everyone I knew. Friends forwarded my e-mail to more friends. My parents forwarded the e-mail to all their friends, their church community, and their Rotary Club among others:

Tues, 30 Nov 2004 10:31

Subject: Africa

Hi you guys

As some of you may know I recently found my biological father. He's from Sierra Leone West Africa. I'm so excited to have found him and in two weeks on Dec. 10th, he invited me to come and visit. I'm traveling to meet him and the rest of my huge African family in Sierra Leone, for the first time. I can't wait!!! He's a principal at the high school there, and I asked him if I could bring anything for the students at his school. I thought I would take some T-shirts and he said "We need desks!" I was kind of shocked and then I realized, wow, I have no idea what it is like to go through a war and lose everything. I asked him to send me a fax of what he needed. The fax is below on this e-mail. I'm writing to ask if you would be interested in donating money to buy desks for his school.

Unfortunately I can't take a bunch of American checks to cash in Africa, but I will take any money I receive and put it in a traveler's check and give it to the school on behalf of my friends and family. They and I would really appreciate any amount you can give. If you are interested, you can make the checks out to me Sarah Culberson and mail them to my address. Thank you so much.

Love, Sarah

Next, I called my Aunt Doreen asking what small gifts I should bring for the family. After speaking with my father, she called back and said he would like a briefcase fit for a principal.

My mom and dad searched to find an elegant leather briefcase.

Mary, my new stepmother, was desperate for shoes, since the rebels stole all of hers from the storage locker in Bo.

Jeneba wanted Western blue jeans, and my half brother Hindogbae asked for a watch.

My older sister Lynne, the mother of three boys, offered to buy a sports watch and a soccer ball for Hindogbae.

One of my friends who traveled in Third World countries gave me this warning: "When you travel to Sierra Leone, don't show up being Santa Claus. You have no idea the level of need. Don't arrive looking like a dollar sign."

I didn't believe her at the time.

My father relayed messages through Doreen because calling from Sierra Leone was so expensive. "What does Sarah like to eat?" he asked.

"Rice is great. I love chicken," I said. Chicken was reserved for feast days because it was so time-consuming to raise. Each chick had to be fed and protected until it reached maturity on small farms or in the back of villagers' huts. Asking for chicken was like putting in a request for caviar and prime rib every night. But I did not know that then.

An itinerary of events planned for my trip was e-mailed to me, which I also forwarded to my parents. On December 12, 2004, I would depart the United States and arrive at Lungi Airport, Sierra Leone, on December 13th. My return trip to America was scheduled for December 30th.

My parents and I carefully studied my father's incredibly organized itinerary for my trip. He was methodical by necessity; getting anywhere required hiring drivers weeks in advance, preparing food rations, and buying supplies. With no refrigerator or electricity in the village, food had to be cooked daily and supplies brought in hours away from Bo or Freetown.

With only a week to go before I left, a small miracle happened. Letters and cards with checks started pouring into my mailbox. My e-mail, circulated to friends, had grown exponentially. A few of my seventh-grade students at Brentwood gave checks:

Dear Ms. Culberson, I am sending you a donation to help with your father's school. I hope that this helps a little bit. Have a wonderful trip! Sincerely, Alex.

My church choir director from West Virginia wrote:

Dear Sarah,

Thanks for letting me share in your excitement and joy. I hope the donations you receive multiply like the "loaves and fishes." Much love, Edith Vehse

My friends:

Dear Sarah,

I want to send you a check for the desks . . . in honor of our three grandchildren who will be so important in working for peace and unity with the children of other nations as they grow and mature . . . we are so excited about your adventure in genealogy in real time! Aren't you lucky to meet and talk to those who have formed your heritage . . .

Much love, Nancy

Strangers and friends I hadn't spoken to in twenty years came forward. One of my most sentimental cards was from a woman who once took her daughter and me on a hike in elementary school. I remember her as Cindy, the cinnamon roll lady:

Dear Sarah . . . I don't know if you remember me. When you were about 9 years old I took you and Emily and Rachel and Ashley on a hike through Cooper's Rock. It was a quiet day which I remember with great fondness—we had Pillsbury Cinnamon Rolls afterward at my apartment. Have a wonderful reunion! Love Cindy

In two weeks, thanks to the support of family and friends, we raised $2,500 dollars for the children of Bumpe.

CHAPTER SIXTY

Abidjan, Ivory Coast

"We will be landing and refueling in Abidjan, Ivory Coast, please stay in your seats," said the captain over the intercom. John and I looked at each other, a shot of adrenaline zinged up my spine, a look of concern flashed on his face. Before leaving Brussels, we were told it was too dangerous to even land in Ivory Coast. Only one month ago, the country's ceasefire dissolved, erupting again into a civil war. Already thirty French soldiers had been killed fighting with rebels. Over eight hundred foreigners had just been airlifted out of the country to safety.

I tried to relax in my seat. Looking out the airplane window, the glittering sun played tricks on my eyes, reflecting off the tarmac. I imagined again and again what my father would look like. In my carry-on I brought the photo album my sister Lynne made for me with pictures of Penny. Money, tucked inside a belt wrapped around my waist, dug into my skin. My suitcases bulged with gifts for everyone. Would my father recognize me, see any resemblance? Would he see Penny in my face? Would he think I was pretty? Would he be proud to call me his daughter? My stomach hurt.

I had straightened my hair before the trip. My Uncle Ali assured me that my sister would want to braid it, so I thought I should straighten it because braiding African hair directly from an Afro was very difficult.

However, I shouldn't have bothered straightening my hair because the recirculated airplane air frizzed my hair out into a wild mass, a giant Cocoa Puff grew steadily on top of my head.

I could only imagine the first impression I would make on my father.

My uncles sat a few seats behind me. I met up with them, John, and a group of fifteen Sierra Leoneans in the Dulles International Airport just outside Washington, D.C. Many Sierra Leoneans traveling in the group apologized to me: "Sarah, we are so sorry you are not going to see Sierra Leone before the war. It was such a beautiful country." They described the peaceful villages, the white sand beaches, hundreds of miles of coastline, and the generosity and graciousness of the people. A heartbreaking look washed over their faces as they spoke of their ravaged country.

Before the war began in 1991, Sierra Leone was poor, but relatively peaceful. Journalist Lansana Gberie wrote in a 2002 essay, "War and Peace in Sierra Leone," "It is easy to forget, given Sierra Leone's abysmal and violent state, that before the current troubles started in 1991, there were fewer incidents of violent crimes—robbery, rape and murder—in the whole of this very poor country than in Toronto (Canada), one of the safest large cities in North America."

I checked my watch. Forty-five minutes had passed, and still we had not left the landing strip. Suddenly, the cabin doors opened. I poked my head over the seat in front of me. A steady stream of passengers, mostly Africans, walked down the aisles taking all the empty seats.

"I didn't know we were picking up passengers," I said to John.

"Change of plans I guess."

A stewardess hurried down the aisle of the plane spraying what looked like air freshener; holding it high like a baton as she misted above us.

"What's going on?" I muttered.

A musky and spicy smell filled the plane. Some of the passengers boarding had a strong odor. But it wasn't body odor the stewardess sprayed against. It was bugs, lice, and disease. Potent pesticide released from the flight attendant's can. She trailed a ribbon of poison up and down the aisles.

All passengers would inhale and exhale these chemicals for the next few hours.

Finally after an hour and a half of waiting on the burning tarmac, we received an update. The captain spoke, "In three hours we will land at Lungi International Airport, estimated arrival time is 8:00 P.M."

My father promised he would meet us there.

CHAPTER SIXTY-ONE

Lungi Airport, Sierra Leone

That first blast of heat in Sierra Leone was hard to describe. Even at night, the temperature refused to settle. Only eight degrees north of the equator, Sierra Leone never had a chance to cool down or dry off. Everything was moist. "Africa hot!" was a new type of heat. Wooden doors rotted, books mildewed, and food fermented if not diligently protected from the humidity. The evening I landed, 90 percent humidity wrapped itself around me in greeting. Spigots of sweat sprung up all over my body. My hair was hyper with moisture.

The airport workers wheeled the rickety metal staircase to the cabin door for our exit.

Twenty-eight years I had waited for this.

Exhausted, my stomach in knots, I hadn't nibbled more than a cracker in twenty-four hours from nerves, fatigue, and flying. Following behind me, John readied the camera as my first footstep planted itself on the African continent, a genetic reunion with African earth.

"Put the camera away!" shouted an armed soldier dressed in camouflage and a blue beret.

"Camera AWAY!" said another soldier racing toward John with his AK-47 swinging on his shoulder.

"Okay, okay!" said John, making an exaggerated display of turning off the camera in front of the six soldiers surrounding him. Slowly he put down the camera, now just a benign tourist necklace.

With the end of the war just two years past, the soldiers and police found themselves in the delicate transition between peacetime and wartime behavior. Tensions still ran high.

Would my father recognize me? Suddenly I was so angry with myself. Right before I left, I sent a photo of myself to my father; except I did not send a recent picture with my new Afro hair. I was too afraid. Desperate to make a pretty impression, I sent a picture in front of my sister's Christmas tree where I have a long, synthetic, beautiful weave with highlights.

With my hair expanding like a Chia Pet on my head, I looked nothing like my picture. Now not only would my father not recognize me, he might be disappointed.

Customs passed quickly, and John and I headed for the baggage conveyer belt where an airport official approached us.

"Hello, I am friends with Joe Konia Kposowa. I also attended school in America at the University of Tennessee. Your father is waiting over there."

I froze. I did not want to turn around. "Please tell him we need to get our bags first, and then we will come over." I needed to make sure all my bags arrived. Seventeen days without my supplies and gifts would have been a disaster. When I met him I didn't want to be distracted.

"Sir," added John, "we were told to shut off the camera, but can I film this reunion?"

"Yes," said the airport official. "You have my permission."

When the six soldiers pounced on him to stop filming, John believed he turned off the camera, but the button stuck and it was still running the whole time. Unfortunately, when he went to film the meeting between my father and me, the camera was inadvertently switched from on to off. So the moment of our meeting was never filmed, but the moment in my mind will never be forgotten.

John waited with the bags as I went to the bathroom. Modern toilets filled the stalls. As I smoothed my hair and used my last reserves of bottled water to wash my face, I stared at myself. I was minutes away from meeting my father.

Everything felt surreal. The bathroom spun around me.

John wheeled the baggage cart filled with our suitcases, and I scanned the sea of black faces for my father, searching for the man I had seen in the picture at Uncle Joe's house in Maryland—a face thirty years younger.

Alone, outside the baggage area stood my father. Average height, five feet six inches, with large sensitive eyes set in the deepest ebony face, his round head with receding hairline and trim beard lent him an elegant but approachable look; he wore a silky shirt half white and half black over loose black dress pants. He looked completely vulnerable—frightened even—like I might run away and reject him. It had never occurred to me that he would have any worries about me.

We made eye contact and in that moment I wanted to comfort him. I wanted him to know everything was all right. I hugged him and held on for a moment. I said, "It's good to finally meet you."

He took my hand and looked in my eyes. He said, "It's good to meet you, too." Still holding my hand he led me outside.

CHAPTER SIXTY-TWO

Lungi

Out of the sanctuary of the airport's locked doors, swirling chaos greeted us. In the darkness, porters, and taxi drivers all shouted, competing for passengers.

"NO!" said my father to a porter diving to lift my bags.

"NO!" he said to two other men careening straight for us.

Suddenly a group of eight people surged forward in a circle to greet us.

My Aunt Amy, the Paramount Chief's wife, decked in her purple African gown, elegant glasses perched on her head, and a warm smile lighting up her smooth face, was the first to welcome us. She wrapped me in a giant hug and said, "Let me look at you!" She twirled me around. J. P. Genda, my uncle, the commissioner of labor for the country, was also there to welcome me.

Beyond the airport lights, I had never seen such darkness. I wondered if the capital of Freetown had electricity. Saturated with humidity, the dark night air had a soupy, thick texture.

As the group pushed forward toward the streets, a white 1980 Land Rover, as large as a military tank, pulled up in front of us. My father had rented it for our visit because only a mini tank could handle the potholes and unpaved roads on the six-hour drive back to Bumpe.

"Quick, this is our car," said my father, again not letting go of my hand in the confusion of honking taxis. The driver's assistant carried a long flashlight, aiming it at the trunk and our luggage. I hugged my two uncles goodbye. We would meet them later, as they had separate plans. With John, my father, and me inside, the driver and his assistant tightly sealed the doors to the car and began rolling out into the pitch blackness. My aunt and her driver drove ahead of us.

"We must make the ferry," said my father.

"The ferry?" I said.

The fastest way to travel to Freetown is a one-hour ferry ride. The driver steadied the car through the darkness, moving slowly. Without streetlights, we crawled as if in the most remote outback, not minutes away from an international airport. Only the car's headlights illuminated the road, its lanes filled with people carrying baskets on their heads and children calling out in the darkness. A young girl ran alongside the car hawking oranges in a large, red plastic bowl. My father rolled down his window and bought an orange. People swept by either side of the Land Rover like apparitions floating in the headlights.

As we approached the ferry docks, the car merged into a line of boarding vehicles. Sandwiched between the black sky and rippling water, two giant, Third World ferries, were lit from the dock lights.

"We will get off here on the docks," said my father. Cars were packed so tightly in the hull that opening a door more than a few inches was impossible. At the ticket booth, my father paid for all of us to sit in the VIP section of the boat, up a flight of stairs on the second level.

We entered the VIP section, a square room at the ship's crown with an old wood panel bar with booths, a snack bar, and electricity. I bought a Coke and slid into the booth next to my father. My Aunt Amy and John sat next to each other.

John said, "Sarah, Amy just read my palm and said, 'I'm American, I've traveled a long way, I'm very tired, and I am going to get married someday.' "

We all laughed and joked.

"What do you want me to call you?" John asked Amy as I filmed.

"Amy or Momie." Amy, the Paramount Chief's wife exuded the loving energy of a mother figure, having been a midwife and nurse in London for years.

John smiled. "I'm John," he said.

"John the Baptist," said Amy, smiling.

"Yup," smiled John, and his nickname would stick with him the entire trip.

The boat chugged like an old turtle deep in the night. The ship's whistle sang out, announcing our departure. A few times I left the group to go outside on the open-air deck. The smell of the engine fuel and the ocean swirled together. Freetown was out there somewhere, lit sporadically with the help of generators. On the deck with the brilliant stars in an expanse of sky I pinched myself to make sure this was all real. Around ten o'clock at night the boat docked in Freetown.

We hopped back into the car, now part of the long chain of cars exiting the ferry. It was impossible to believe we were in the capital of a country with sporadic electricity. Finally the Land Rover rolled past large iron gates as we entered into a thick-walled compound. Armed guards, with their AK-47s, stood silently as we unloaded our bags in the parking lot.

More guards were stationed inside the clean hotel lobby. Five round clocks reading different time zones mounted behind the reception desk conveyed a sophisticated ambiance. The hotel was called the *Hotel 5–10,* named in recognition of World Teachers' Day, celebrated annually on October 5. Any dues-paying teacher who belonged to the Sierra Leone Teachers' Union received a discounted rate. Instead of US$25 a night for a room with a modern shower, flush toilet, television, and phone service, a teacher paid only US$7.00 per night. My father paid for three rooms and led us upstairs to our rooms, each of which opened onto a balcony.

At this time I had no idea how many people in the village had pooled their money, sold chickens, and bartered for the car rental, the ferry ride, the hotel, and food to make this happen.

"Good night," said John and he headed to his room.

Exhausted but wired, I asked my father, "Can we stay up so I can talk with you?"

So many questions swirled in my head. With the large group on the ferry it was not the right time to talk. I wanted some private time with my father.

"Yes, come to my room," he said.

CHAPTER SIXTY-THREE

Freetown

"Can I set this up on the television stand to tape our conversation?" I asked as I entered his hotel room. In one hand I held the camera, and in the other I clutched my photo album with Penny's pictures inside. I knew if I didn't tape our conversations I would never remember anything; fatigue, jet lag, and nerves would erase the most important answers.

"Of course," he said. We sat together on the foot of the bed facing the tiny camera. My father had a few burning questions and I let him begin.

First he asked, "How did your parents tell you that you were adopted?"

"Well, I knew because I looked different," I said. "I just knew. I was never meant to feel, 'oh you are not my daughter,' I just felt completely loved and taken care of."

He nodded taking in this information.

I swatted a large mosquito, clapping it flat in my palms. Then I opened the photo album of my birth mother that I tucked safely in my carry-on. I explained my desire to search for my birth parents, first starting with Penny. Together we looked at the pictures.

He shared how proud Penny was to be with a black man, how she was not prejudiced. "She did not discriminate." He continued, "The way you laugh is like Penny."

I took that as a great compliment.

He confided that many villagers did not believe I would actually come. He shared that my visit brought greater respect to the Kposowa family in Bumpe. To have an American travel so far to visit Bumpe honored him and the entire village.

"Really?" I said, stunned. I couldn't believe the village interpreted my visit as an honor, when I was the one who felt so grateful for the invitation. "*I* am honored to be here . . . I have a friend who is adopted and when she called . . . her birth mother, her birth mother wanted nothing to do with her and she's devastated. I called and got the warmest welcome from my biological mother's family, and after writing the letter to you guys, you all could not wait to see me, that is the biggest gift . . ." Out of nowhere, tears came flying ". . . I could ever have."

I started crying, choking on my own words. A reservoir inside unhinged. Embarrassed at the droplets rolling down my face, sitting on the edge of the bed with a father I'd known less than twenty-four hours, I wanted to explain myself from the perspective of a child who was given up by a parent.

". . . for us, being adopted we're scared," and again my voice cracked on my tears. I swiped at my face with my fingers. I hadn't thought to bring tissue.

"We're scared of people saying 'we don't want to have anything to do with you' because we already feel like that kind of happened in the first place even if it wasn't like that; we decided well, they didn't want us."

I inhaled a giant breath, suffocated a few more tears, and continued. "But I have to say to you, I am so thankful that you guys were selfless enough to give me up because I have a family, a life that is incredible. I'm sure my life would be incredible with you, too—you guys made a choice that's got to be hard to give up a child, to say 'I am not ready.' "

When I said the words "not ready" my father did not look me in the eye. He looked down at his feet and repeated in a whisper, "Not ready."

I bowed my head with his, both of us now looking at the ground. "I admire that. I am so thankful. I have the best family in the world and now I have another best family. I have more than I could ever ask for . . . if in anyway I could give you this gift of saying to let your mind rest, 'Oh, I shouldn't have done that, or my brother should have taken her' . . . God has a plan, right? I was supposed to go with this family, that's what was supposed to happen. And I am supposed to come here to see you . . . and I'm here. It's no surprise. It's supposed to be."

My father looked up at me.

CHAPTER SIXTY-FOUR

Freetown

The next morning a knock on my hotel room door woke me. "Sarah, are you up?" asked my father through the door.

"Yes," I said disoriented. We had talked for four hours; until three o'clock in the morning.

"Sarah, come to my room when you are ready," said my father. "I want to give you something."

"Okay," I said and threw on some clothes. Opening my door, sunshine rushed into my room. Outside my second-story balcony I could see the glittering ocean for the first time. Last night Freetown was so poorly lit, that I had no idea that our hotel was overlooking a beach, let alone one with gorgeous white sand, as inviting as a Hawaiian postcard. Pristine aqua water lapped against the wide coast.

To my right, the hills of Freetown arched in lush greens over the city. When Portuguese explorer Pedro da Cintra sailed the West African coast in 1462 and gazed at these very same mountains, he named them, *Lion Mountain*, or *Serra Lyoa*, after the outline of the sleeping lion he imagined under the undulating hills.

My father's door was propped open.

"It is stunning here," I said walking into his room. "The beach looks unbelievable!"

"Yes, it is," he smiled proudly. "Sarah, today we will drive six hours to Bumpe. I want to give this to you." In his hands he held a square of patterned green and black fabric. "We went to Guinea to get the material. Your sister had it made for you. We used her measurements."

As I unfolded the fabric, a beautiful emerald green dress rolled down to the floor. With bright greens and yellows framed in black leaded panels, it resembled a stained glass window. "It is beautiful. Thank you."

"Would you please wear this dress today?" he asked.

"Of course," I said and looked at his shirt. "It's the same fabric as yours."

"Yes," he said.

Immediately I felt honored, flattered to wear matching fabric with my father.

"Here, I will iron it for you," he said. A modern hotel iron lay on the bureau. I watched as my father attempted to press the dress. In Sierra Leone, especially if one is from an important family, it is not appropriate to look sloppy in public. Starched shirts for "big men," important people, must be wrinkle free. Women in Sierra Leone are free to go topless as breasts are for suckling infants, but a woman must not wear shorts as legs are considered erotic.

I could tell my father had not ironed in years; the dress was becoming more wrinkled as he ironed. "You know, I can do it. I love to iron," I said.

"Okay," he said.

"Thank you . . ." I did not know what to call my new father. Calling him *Dad* felt awkward, but I would need to call him something during my seventeen-day visit.

"How do you say *father*?"

"*Kaay Kaay!*" he said.

"Okay. I will meet you downstairs for breakfast," I said. I returned to my room, showered in my last modern shower, and pulled on my new African dress. It fell to my ankles like a gown, but the sleeveless arms and light fabric made it comfortable and elegant.

Downstairs in the hotel breakfast room—a basic cafeteria-style white room glowed with bright sunshine—I met John, my father, and my Aunt Amy. An English breakfast of marmalade, tea, toast, and eggs was set before us, the only guests in the room.

"Kah Kah," I said across the table, sipping more tea.

A strange look crossed my father's face. Did I mix it up? I already tried to memorize good morning: *Bu Waa.* Good-bye: *Ma lor hoi.* Thank you: *Besia.* "How do you say *father*?" I asked again.

"Father?" he said. *"Kaaay Kaaaay"* he made a point of emphasizing the long *A*. "*Kaay Kaaay. Kah Kah* in Krio, you'll have to excuse me," and he bent his head, tried to suppress a laugh, "means *shit*."

I almost spit my tea on the table. We all cracked up. I bulged my eyes looking at him, not believing the first morning with my new father I called him, "Shit shit!"

Suddenly a "Meow" called out from under the table. John and I searched for a stray cat.

"Meow, meow," called out again.

I looked under the table, holding up the white tablecloth.

My father laughed. "Sarah, it is my cell phone."

My father's ringer was set to a "Meow, meow" ring tone. I broke into a huge smile. My father carried himself with great dignity and had a very serious demeanor, but I was beginning to see his playful sense of humor.

"Kaaaay, Kaaaay," I said, deliberately pronouncing the long *A*. "Can I call my parents and tell them I arrived safely?"

"Here, use my phone," he said, and passed it across the table.

CHAPTER SIXTY-FIVE

Freetown

Outside the hotel, our driver loaded our bags into the truck.

"The drive to Bumpe will take six hours, but we must change money here," said my father. If we did not exchange American dollars for leones now, it would be impossible once we journeyed outside the capital.

Piling into the car, we left the safety of the hotel's thick, fortress walls and descended into Freetown. After the war, the capital retained the sagging weight of thousands of extra people who chose not to return to their villages—or who had nothing to return to. A cross between a mob scene, a street carnival, and a back alley, the streets of Freetown swarmed with life. Every square inch of the city burst with an obscene density of people.

Pumping rap and African beats pounded into the fray from street CDs. African women in bursts of colorful fabric wove through the streets. With their long necks erect, the ladies carried loads on their heads that could make a team of horses buckle. Fruits of every shape and color, orange mangoes, golden bananas, diamond-textured pineapples teetered on huge flat platters.

People pounced upon our car selling nuts, sunglasses, rubber flip-flops, and dried fish releasing intense odors. With a city stressed with too many people, it took hours to untangle the street gridlock. Former refugees and amputees begged for money while vendors on the sides of the roads sold papayas, fried plantains, and sliced fruit covered in flies. Small girls maneuvered through the cars and crowds, selling water in tiny plastic Baggies that looked like they should hold goldfish won at a fair. I watched as a man bought a Baggie bubbled at the bottom with water. Over his head, he held the bag, popped a hole in it and let the water gush into his mouth.

Human sweat, humidity, trash, and street food coalesced into heavy city smells. I began to understand why my father said he preferred his quiet village.

Suddenly my father spotted a Mende man with whom he'd arranged a meeting. "We need to get out of the car," said my father. John and I followed him into a Lebanese storefront where the Mende moneyman exchanged our American dollars for leones. Every Sierra Leonean who travels has a relationship with their own "moneyman" or "fixer" who changes leones to dollars or dollars to leones. Street money changers gave the best rates, and people knew from word of mouth and reputation who changed money, who was fair, who could be trusted, and where and when to meet.

John experienced some uncomfortable hostility on the streets. As a tall white male with a camera, many young, angry African men shouted aggressively at him as if John personified the rich West. Through the glass lens of the camera, the men screamed obscenities at the Western world that had turned away as their country spiraled into one of the most brutal civil wars recorded on this planet.

Inside the store, which we ducked into for privacy, the money exchange transpired with incredible fluidity. Part private banking, part furtive dealmaking, I was glad to surrender to my father's expertise in the matter.

Anxious to leave Freetown, we still had one famous tourist sight to see. In the middle of the city, centered in a large roundabout, stood a five-hundred-year-old cotton tree. The Sierra Leone equivalent to the Arc de Triomphe, the cotton tree grew hundreds of feet in the sky, canopying the lanes of traffic orbiting in wild circles at its base. Thrillingly out of place in the middle of the urban sprawl, with a trunk as wide as a car, it was a powerful symbol for Sierra Leoneans. Its leafy branches once shaded a slave market, but in 1787 when British philanthropists and abolitionists bought Freetown Province from a local chief as a resettlement area for former European slaves, the cotton tree's wafting boughs morphed in verdant flags of freedom. Returning Africans were welcomed home by its emerald branches.

Along with its historical role, the tree was infested with giant fruit bats that hung upside down, their black capes glittering in the sun like oil slicks. Many locals believed witches inhabited the tree and that the bats were the souls of the dead. When the rebels sacked Freetown, torched buildings, incinerated human life, and raped children, they did not touch the tree or a single bat. Highly superstitious, even the rebels who had no problem with murder didn't dare mess with the souls of the dead who could haunt them.

Our driver fiddled with the radio.

After forty-five minutes of crawling gridlock, we met up with Aunt Amy and her driver in her Toyota 4Runner outside of the city. In this mini caravan we headed to Bumpe. The white Land Rover lunged into action and the claustrophobia of Freetown soon dissipated. The final vestiges of urban life—the Coca-Cola umbrellas on the side of the roads, the city-limit vendors—faded away, along with the paved roads. Partial pavement now interspersed with dirt roads in a decaying checkerboard of asphalt and grass. A mile up, another fracture of pavement managed to maintain itself until it, too, was overtaken with mud.

We soon left pavement and the city behind, and bumped along gorgeous red clay roads lined with bright green elephant grasses, banana plants with wide leaves, straight and tall *kandi* trees, and leafy cotton trees. The lush landscape, the red clay and wet emerald grasses, and the wide open spaces were a relief—until we hit the potholes.

The Land Rover had no choice but to creep down the side of craters and thrust itself out with a wild burst of gas. Physical stamina was required inside the car, as every new bump shot our heads against the ceiling and back down again. Like a sustained Indiana Jones adventure ride, the bumps did not let up, and now I understood why only four-wheel drives could tackle the roads and potholes the size of small drained ponds. No wonder a hundred-and-thirty-mile distance took six hours—and that was only if we encountered no breakdowns.

I had never before appreciated the well-maintained American roads and highways. Thankfully jet leg came to my rescue. I fell asleep in the vibrating metal chamber lumbering across Sierra Leone's devastated roads. My father rested his flat, black leather pouch on his lap, which I used as a makeshift pillow. I slept for the next four hours with my father's arms resting gently on my back.

CHAPTER SIXTY-SIX

Road to Bumpe

The truck rolled to a halt. Jolted from the lack of movement, I raised my head, disoriented. "Are we here?" I asked my father.

"No. Bathroom stop," he said. I looked around. In the middle of nowhere a farmer's fruit stand hunkered on the edge of the dirt road and a small round thatched hut squatted far behind it.

"Bathroom?" I said.

My father pointed to the hut. I now knew why my Aunt Doreen said to bring toilet paper. As my Aunt Amy perused the fruit display, I ventured back to the hut, branches tied in a circle, with a small opening for a door.

Inside, covered by a piece of thin, flat slate, a deep hole plunged into the earth. The smell could make a person faint and fall into the hole. At night, entering the hut would be dangerous without first checking for snakes. Forgetting to cover the hole, once it was used, could sicken an entire village falling ill. If flies were allowed to travel in and out of the trench, they could carry pieces of excrement, spreading cholera or dysentery.

Back at the car, I used my bottled water to wash my hands, and inhaled deep breaths to refill my lungs from holding my nose in the hut. In Sierra Leone, the right hand was used to greet others and eat and the left hand was reserved for the bathroom; thus eating a plate of rice with the left hand, the "unclean" hand, was taboo.

My father and my Aunt Amy milled around the farmer's table as John filmed their selection of produce. This odd little fruit stand perched on the side of the road displayed baskets of pineapples, potatoes, and cassava leaves. A second table, next to the fruit stand, bore long poles attached to each end that acted as support for a horizontal branch stretched over the table. On the pole dangled seven water bottles with ropes around their necks—a wind chime of plastic water bottles. Each liter bottle, filled with white filmy liquid, swayed in the breeze. Yellow plastic five-gallon gasoline jugs rested below the mobile on the table.

"What's in the bottles and canisters?" asked John.

"Palm wine. Try some, it's all natural," said the farmer.

Cups passed around with liquid swerling inside. Even our driver took hearty gulps from his cup.

"Is there alcohol in this?" asked John.

"No, it comes straight from God," said the farmer.

A cup circulated to me. "No, thank you," I said. My stomach, already too agitated from the bumpy roads, didn't dare ingest much. Although I did buy an orange, believing it would be safe enough to eat underneath its peel.

John and I later learned that pure, undiluted fermented palm wine is "all-natural alcohol"—as potent as potato whisky or vodka.

Aunt Amy inspected yams, potatoes, pineapples, and bananas. Fifteen people from the farmer's family gathered around, wide-eyed and silent as my Aunt Amy shopped. With John filming, the Land Rover idling, and my aunt dressed so regally, the farmer's family must have believed we were a special convoy.

The farmer, behind the table, caught my aunt's eye and pointed to the potatoes. "Buy the white ones," he suggested.

Amy smiled wide, her eyes twinkling, and she said to John who was filming: "Johnny, this man is prejudiced. He is telling me to buy the white potatoes!"

Everybody started laughing.

Amy bought the entire basket of potatoes from the overjoyed farmer, who would be lucky on any other day to see a few vegetables sold if he waited out the entire day.

Back on the road for another hour, traces of all legitimate roads became a distant dream as we headed deeper and deeper into the bush villages. Spectacular pastoral beauty surrounded us. African women, garbed in long graceful *lappas,* occasionally ambled along the red clay, moving rainbows of color against the land. With woven baskets on their heads moving in rhythmic harmony with the grasses underfoot, their timeless presence could have been witnessed centuries earlier by travelers.

Five hours passed, and for the second time the truck came to a stop.

"Are we here? I asked.

"No. This is a junction, a tiny village. We will stop and take a rest." Aunt Amy honked, waved, and passed us as she continued on to Bumpe.

"Amy isn't stopping?"

"No, she will meet us."

At the time, I didn't think anything of it.

We exited the car and John and I were invited to sit on a villager's porch, to rest in the shade. As if a high-pitched alarm bell sounded to everyone except me, over sixty-five villagers stopped what they were doing, poured out of their homes and rice fields and gathered against the railing of the porch to stare at me. A mass of faces gaped at me as if I were a visiting dignitary or alien they might see only once in their lives. Some of the village children asked the driver, who was resting on the veranda, if John was my husband.

"No, her professor," the driver said. One woman reached over the railing and handed me a valuable gift of rice flour in a Baggie.

"Thank you!" I said, accepting the bag.

"Let's walk," said my father. We strolled through the mini village as John filmed. Thirty children jumped up and down all around us. We transformed into the Pied Piper of Sierra Leone, surrounded in a three-foot-deep circle of children. Suddenly, the group of kids started pointing at me, chanting, *"Poo-mui, Poo-mui!"*

"What does that mean?" I asked.

"White person."

"Poo-mui! Poo-mui!" they shouted louder.

White person!

I laughed with the children, but inside I felt dizzy. *White person?* I traveled all the way to Africa, only a few miles from my father's ancestral village where I might finally belong, connect with my African roots, and be relieved of straddling two races—and the children saw me as a white girl.

CHAPTER SIXTY-SEVEN

Bumpe

Six hours passed since we left Freetown.

The brilliant blue sky domed over massive cotton trees, giant sunbeams filtered through the foliage as we pushed deeper into the bush. Occasionally out of nowhere a lone African woman, in a brilliant-colored dress, would flash against the green and red earth, a monument of fruit or mangoes on her head and the whole world seemed in balance, graceful, and strong. John and I believed we were at least an hour away from Bumpe. Our lone white truck began to climb another red clay hill when I heard noise in the distance.

"John, do you hear that?" I asked.

John nodded his head yes. Music or pounding drums, something alive, loud, and rhythmic exploded just beyond the hill.

The truck thrust over the crest of the incline and fifteen, twenty, thirty black-as-night faces flashed in front of the truck.

Row after row of villagers pulsed into the road, singing, chanting, and swaying before the car. High school girls in blue berets, sleeveless white shirts, and raffia skirts swung their hips, calling out welcomes. Schoolboys in crisp white shirts and slacks clapped to African drumbeats.

My heart beat like crazy. "Oh, my gosh!" I said, "oh, my gosh!"

Our driver slowed the truck to a crawl; villagers surged around the truck. The breaking wave of schoolboys and -girls parted to reveal a chorus of forty middle-aged African women, all wearing the same emerald green dress as me, hands in the air, singing: "Pa-da-pa-da-Tang Tang Tang. . . ." In a mass greeting they moved toward the vehicle. Cheers spun in wild ellipses on all sides of the car as a bevy of black palms thumped the car in a vibrating rhythm. The village women seemed to absorb me in their circle; their arms stretched to embrace me, and sing, "You're us, you're here, we're one."

My mouth hung open in disbelief. I later learned that when a family wears the same fabric it is called *ashobi*, and represents solidarity, respect, and an outward expression of love. This tradition is reserved for very special guests to celebrate or commemorate a day so that forever onward if a family member wears that outfit, it is a communal reminder of that ceremony. My father asked a neighbor, Alice, to travel to Guinea to the giant fabric markets where cloth is cheaper, comes in every imaginable color, and can be bought in larger bolts with more yardage. Alice took her passport and the government bus at seven o'clock in the morning, bought six hundred yards of emerald fabric, and returned to Bo that evening. Half the village, including men in custom shirts, women in *lappas,* and children in wraps, all bought yards of the fabric to sew into clothes for my celebration.

"What did I do to deserve this?"

My father's students, dressed in crisp blue and white uniforms and ironed shirts, lined the side of the road like young cadets at attention.

John said, "Sarah, look at that! Did you know you had so many friends?"

"No, I didn't," I said, and tears of happiness poured from my eyes.

I didn't know I had family a continent away who waited for my arrival, thrilled to welcome me. My entire life I planned for rejection, shame, abandonment, and instead a village opened their hearts, clapped their hands, and sang in acceptance.

"In Africa, when a child is found, it is a great celebration," again echoed through my head from the lips of the Nigerian hairdresser.

A masked devil, a huge, costumed creature covered in bushy brown raffia, a cross between "Cousin Itt" and a shaggy Pekinese dog, twirled on the side of the road. Fiber grasses on the masked devil swooshed in front of the truck. Shirtless men with chiseled mahogany chests surrounded the masked devil carrying long sticks, protecting and guiding him. The costumed performer couldn't see well under the heavy weight and texture of the sacred costume. Later I learned that it is a great honor when a masked devil appears at a celebration. This symbolic creature is the sole visual representation of a men's secret society. Besides the five men guiding the creature, not one villager knows the identity of the man underneath the costume. To ask is a great taboo—an abomination.

The Land Rover continued down the large red clay boulevard, now bordered with elementary school children dressed in kelly green and bright blue uniforms, all smiling and waving.

Finally we reached the end of the road, the end of the long parade of well-wishers, when my father asked the driver to please drive us around the empty village.

"Where did everybody go?" I asked.

"You will see," said my father.

The driver looped through the center of the village, full of thatched roofs and open-air verandas. I was too dazed to take in the center of town, too dazed to understand the driver was stalling, circling again around the deserted homes. Only after ten minutes did he drive back into the crowds.

Drums pounded out a rhythm for the people, musical gourds rattled, and the car stopped moving. An even larger group of African women, all cloaked in the same green fabric, circled the truck.

"We are here, please get out," said my father.

Exiting the truck, feet now on the red clay, I stood face-to-face with fifty women swaying and singing: *"Be tang tang tang . . .* (Wait, let me prepare myself to go and see Sarah. Sarah, you have come to your homeland. Welcome home.)"

Overwhelmed, emotions bursting, I did not know what to do. It was one thing to be in a car watching the women—it was another to be enclosed in their powerful circle, rich Mende voices calling out to me, "Welcome home."

I could not speak. In shock, I stood silent in front of them. "What do I do right now? All these women are singing to me?"

Suddenly I found the music . . . my brain, my emotions, my manners—everything failed me except rhythm. *". . . the roots of rhythm remain."* Just as I once danced around my living room as a little girl to Paul Simon's, " . . . *the roots of rhythm remain,*" I did the only thing I knew. I swayed my head and joined their beat. I danced with the women. Cheers exploded from the crowd. Arms stretched upward, the women reached for me, enveloped me in hugs, and hoisted me into the center of the pulsing, moving circle of song, of rhythm, of love. In that moment the universe clicked, Bumpe and America notched into place with music and dance as their bridge.

CHAPTER SIXTY-EIGHT

Bumpe

Walking a quarter mile more, the parade slowly pooled into a large grass clearing. John ran alongside the procession, at times ankle deep in mud, dodging potholes, to capture the village welcome on film.

As large as a high school soccer field, surrounded by old-growth trees, an oblong clearing had bleachers on one end ready for six hundred villagers. Four long tables covered in white tablecloths were set up at the front of the field for visiting dignitaries. The center tables, festooned with magenta flowers were reserved for the Paramount Chief, his wife, Aunt Amy, my father, and me. Single school desks and chairs off to the sides of the head tables were set aside for other relatives who had upgraded from bleacher seating.

A generator purred in the distance, powering a boom box. Four boys dressed as women, in women's dresses and stuffed bras, danced in the center of the green like jesters in a pre-show comedic warm-up. More villagers poured into the clearing, filling every remaining space.

My father's wife came up to the table to introduce herself. A pretty woman, ten years younger than my fifty-one-year-old father, with smooth reddish brown skin, large round eyes, and a gap between her front teeth, carried a red laundry basket filled with glasses and cold sodas.

"Oh, Mary! You're Mary! I was wondering where you were!" I said.

Mary hugged me and set a chilled Coca-Cola down in front of me.

I wondered how my visit affected Mary, if it disturbed her to learn about her husband's past and welcome his child?

While the crowd waited, carnival excitement crackled in the air. A young pretty, thinned-boned woman who looked like Mary caught my eye. With great confidence she glided across the center of the grass heading straight for me.

"Sarah, I am Jeneba, your sister."

"Jeneba!" I said standing up behind the table, reaching over to hold her hand. "I am so happy to meet you."

"Welcome, Sarah," she said.

"Where is your brother?" I asked.

"He is in Bo to finish his final exams."

"Oh, okay. Nice to meet you finally. I've heard so much about you. Beautiful, just like I heard." I reached for her hand again before she floated back into the crowd.

Part school assembly, part town celebration, the Reverend Morlai stepped out into the center of the grass, addressing the audience. Speaking into the microphone, he began the ceremony with a Christian prayer:

> "Our father and our God we want to thank you at this moment even as we are gathered here this evening. We want to thank you for all the blessings we have received from you because you love us so much. In a very special way we want to thank you because of the safe travels you have given to our guests. That this is a very good privilege that we have met them at this time. We know we are going to meet relatives that have parted from us for some time. And we are going to meet new friends. Lord, this is indeed a great privilege that we have tonight. We want your blessing upon this night great Lord that things we do and say here tonight will be said and done in your own glory. That we invite you at this time, even as we begin our program tonight to pray in your worthy name. Amen.
>
> At this time we want to welcome our guests with a song."

Four teenage girls from Bumpe High School, stood in the center of the field, two girls in front and two in back, dressed in white, knee length dresses and blue berets. Singing in rounds, they sang in sweet high-pitched voices:

"People, are you glad for this day?"

The two girls in back answered, "We are glad for this day."

Over and over they asked the village if they were glad for this day. A third chorus sang out, "Sarah, are you glad for this day?"

To everyone's great surprise I sang back, "I am glad for this day!"

The crowd cheered.

"You are glad for this day. That is why we welcome you all. We welcome you all. Sarah, you are welcome . . . we are glad for this day. We welcome you all."

The Reverend Morlai picked up the microphone again . . . "When you know you have a successful man, he is always assisted by a strong wife . . . the Paramount Chief has a very strong helpmate . . ." and the Reverend shared the biography of Aunt Amy's life.

Next the section chief, under the Paramount Chief spoke . . . , "Many months ago, we were called from California for the good news. The news was that we have an elegant, well-educated young lady who has been striving to meet her biological father . . . after twenty-eight years, the long-awaited reunion has been realized. Now we introduce the lady I talked so much about, is no other person but Miss Sarah Culberson. She is a very pleasant lady . . ."

After a brief interlude my father introduced the headmistress and teachers in his school who all came forward on the green to receive applause.

School assembly, cultural performance, town fair, and dry-season festival all rolled into one giant welcome celebration.

Next the Paramount Chief, my Uncle Thomas Kposowa, took the microphone. By now each speech was repeated twice, once in English and once in Mende. The chief proclaimed to the entire population of Bumpe: "Sarah, you are welcome here anytime . . . you can be Paramount Chief here . . ."

I knew my Uncle Joseph said months ago on the phone that because I am a Kposowa on the paternal line I could one day run for chief. However, hearing the Paramount Chief say this out loud to over six hundred villagers gave every word greater significance.

Scanning the sea of faces, I couldn't believe I was the recipient of this ceremony. I kept turning around looking for the real guest of honor. How was it that I didn't need to look pretty, run track, score baskets, or win a vote to merit this? This ceremony honored me just for showing up. When I wasn't quite sure how to handle all of the accolades, my mind started to zone, check out. I needed to will myself to stay focused.

Three hours passed. More speeches rang through the clearing, echoing in Mende, Krio, and English, up to the highest boughs of the trees. I looked at John and smiled. The embassy spoke the truth when they warned John that the things to worry about in Sierra Leone—besides the roads—are the *long speeches*. With no television, movies, or electricity, a town celebration under lights from a power generator was a major event.

A familiar voice echoed over the speakers. My Aunt Amy stood behind the table. The only woman to speak, I cast my full attention on her.

> "I promise, on behalf of the Kposowa family and my husband, I promise, Sarah, we are going to make up for all the years we have missed her . . . we will show the world that you are a Kposowa. And any time that wonderful man, I call him John the Baptist, he is a wonderful man, I hope he will make here a second home. John, you are always welcome and you are part of the family."

A huge smile spread across John's face.

Dusk shimmered, bouncing the final vestiges of light off the grass and clay. The sunset swirled orange and pinks into the night. The power generators blasted full throttle, powering the microphone and illuminating the field. Traditional African women dancers twirled in beautiful *lappas* of every color on the grass stage. Shaking rattles and pounding drums wove sound in and out through the trunks of the surrounding trees. Adolescent girls in raffia, hula-type skirts shook their hips. With no bras under their white sleeveless tops, their unbound breasts swung like yams in and out of their shirts.

Two masked devils appeared again, commanding wild cheers from the crowds. The choir from Bumpe High School sang. Two ten-year-old boys danced; ankle bracelets and rattles on their feet, raffia skirts tied on their slim hips. They danced as if their feet felt fire, moving to an impossible rhythm, almost too quick for sight.

The cradle of civilization birthed right here and it made sense in the music, the drums, and the bodies coming together in expression. With a full black canopy of night overhead, the microphone was finally passed to me. An impromptu speech was required:

> "Hello, everyone! First of all, I want to say God has truly blessed me being in all of your presence right now. I have been traveling here for . . . it's taken about two days to get here from America, in California and every, every, every single moment that it took for me to get here was well worth it. You all are such amazing beautiful people. I am honored to be here with all of you. Thank you for accepting me so openly and beautifully. This is a bigger family that I ever could have expected and when I came in today to see everybody's beautiful smiling faces, you brought a joy inside of me that I can't even explain. I honor, respect, and love all of you. Thank you so much."

> Then I paused.

> "The End!"

> I laughed, punchy from exhaustion and emotion.
> The crowd rolled with laughter.
> "No, it's just the beginning!" I teased the audience.
> John cracked up.
> "Just kidding!"
> More laughter from the hundreds and hundreds of villagers.
> "Thank you all. Thank you."

CHAPTER SIXTY-NINE

Bumpe

After the ceremony, around midnight, we slid back into the Land Rover, our final ride in the truck. In the morning, the driver would return to Freetown—but first we headed outside the center of the village to my father's home. Besides the Paramount Chief's house, the principal's quarters was one of the nicest living spaces in Bumpe. With a generator that could power his DVD player, given to him by relatives in London, or the deep freezer in the corner of the kitchen, my father's home was considered lush with amenities. Still, all of the household cooking was done outside over an open fire on three flat stones. No running water flowed inside.

In the back of the house another room was filled with beds. My father supported and paid school fees for seven additional children whose own parents could not afford to do so. In return the teenage children helped with chores.

For our first night in Bumpe, my father powered his generator at his great expense. Fueled with gasoline at $4.00 a gallon, it was exorbitant to run and thus used sparingly. It also sounded as loud as a lawn mower. Usually, it was only turned on for a few hours at night. However, the night we arrived it illuminated his home, which was much nicer than I imagined. Built with cement blocks painted white and a zinc roof, the house consisted of three bedrooms and a living room boasting a group of fancy, upholstered chairs and a dining table. Outside the front door, a shaded zinc roof hung over two long rows of benches that faced each other. Visitors could drop by at all hours and chat on benches, as was the custom in Bumpe.

John took off his muddy sandals before entering the house and left them outside on the front porch.

Inside, the walls glowed a beautiful ochre, a rich mustard yellow that made the cement blocks less heavy and softened the interior. Festive tie-dye curtains in deep lapis and purple billowed from each window. On the wall a picture of a white Jesus hung over the kitchen table.

Mary and my father gave up their room to me, and Hindogbae gave up his to John. Inside my father's room, a large mosquito net draped over a double bed like a sheer canopy.

When I poked my head into John's room, painted a neon turquoise, something moved on the wall. Chills shot up my spine. A gigantic spider as large as a salad plate, with long, furry brown legs hovered on the walls. Feather-legged baboon spiders are common in Sierra Leone, and most likely the species I spotted, but spiders are not individually distinguished like a black widow in America. Simply called *kasaliui,* by villagers, they were as common as mosquitoes.

"Uhhh! Hello! Everybody! Help!" I yelled. My father rushed into the room.

"There's a humongous spider in there!"

Looking into the room, my father said, "Oh, that's nothing. Spiders are like pets here."

I grew up in West Virginia's countryside. I picked up daddy long legs with my bare hands, but this was a cast member from *Arachnophobia,* an exaggerated Halloween prop—except that it moved its furry tentacle legs in slow motion up the wall.

I started to hyperventilate. "What if it fell on my face while I slept? What if it crawled across my body at night?" Goose bumps erupted over every inch of my skin.

Quickly my father grabbed a spray bottle of Sheltox, a mosquito spray that was effective on most pests. When he let loose the toxic spray, paralyzing the spider, it slid down the wall in a giant thud on the floor. I darted into my own room until my father scooped up the dead beast.

"Good night, everyone," I said with my heart still racing. I needed to check my room for giant baboon spiders, poison snakes, and black scorpions. I ducked under the bed, around my bags, squinted my eyes behind the bureau, removed the pillows and sheets, dug into the mattress crevices, but all seemed clear. I crawled into the double bed, folded myself inside the mosquito net, and stared at the zinc ceiling. Suddenly I heard a pitter-patter. My entire body tensed. Little legs raced across the zinc. What creatures could be making those noises? More spiders, mice, rats, or fruit bats?

Only exhaustion saved me and I fell fast asleep.

CHAPTER SEVENTY

Bumpe

A rooster's "cock-a-doodle-do" vibrated my father's roof. A group of competing chickens clucked directly under my window. Light pounded into the room. I pulled a pillow across my face for a few more hours of sleep until my father called through the door: "Sarah, people are here to see you. Are you up? A lady brought you a chicken."

"A chicken?" I said. I harvested the mosquito netting in a bundle, roped my hair in a rubber band, threw on some clothes, and walked into the living room. A thin African woman presented me with a live chicken.

"Thank you. Thank you so much," I said still dazed from the spider, the roosters, and now a chicken.

Apparently I was supposed to hold the chicken to my breast, clutch it tightly as a sign of gratitude, but I did not know then that was the custom. Instead I stared at the flapping bird in her arms.

"Thank you," I said again.

"Here, take it from her," said my father.

"Oh, okay," I said confused. But I held out my hands to the bird. I had never handled a chicken in my life and didn't know how to hold it securely. When it passed into my hands it began flapping its wings and going crazy. One of my father's nephews, who lived in thc house, came to the rescue and took the chicken outside for me.

I had no idea what a huge honor and special gift it was to receive a chicken.

"Come outside when you can," said my father. "People are waiting to meet you." It seemed the entire village woke with the roosters, as the house was devoid of people. Nevertheless, hot breakfast waited for John and me on the kitchen table. A white food cloth tented over the two plates kept the flies away.

Kona, a full-bodied, old, beautiful African woman, was hired by my father to cook Western food on the outdoor three-stone fire during my visit. Having cooked for American missionaries for years, Kona knew how to make pancakes, scrambled eggs and fried Spam, banana bread and hot butter cake.

I removed the food cloth just as John walked out of his room. With his camera charged, he was ready for whatever the day would bring.

Mary came inside to check on us.

"Is this coffee?" asked John.

"No, it is tea. Do you want coffee?"

"Oh, no, thank you. I was just asking," he said.

Little did we know that Mary sent someone to Bo later that day to retrieve bags of instant Sanka for John.

I spied through the front window onto the shaded veranda. Villagers wanted to say hello, see Joe Konia's daughter close-up, and view an American. Over thirty people sat along the benches waiting to meet me. I had not yet realized that village life was lived in public: people stopping over to tell stories and sing songs at all hours of the day. If one spent too much time alone, or in one's room, it was considered antisocial and bad manners.

Out the window I saw something that made me blink. In the midst of the African stained glass prints and vibrant tie-dyes, a young boy wore silky blue-and-white Duke University shorts; another wore a faded mesh Beckham soccer T-shirt.

It later was explained to me by my Uncle Tibbie Kposowa that bales of used clothing were shipped from the West and middlemen sold the clothes to Africans. Unloaded from the docks at Freetown, the world's third-largest natural harbor, these mammoth sacks and bales trickle into the street markets. Before the war these clothes came loaded with a stigma and sinister misinformation. Sierra Leoneans could not fathom the amount, the absurd quantity of used clothing pumping in from the West. How was it possible that so many clothes arrived every day in Freetown? Rumors spread that the beautiful shirts, shorts, pants, and shoes did not come from the West but from dead civilians murdered in Congo's ferocious civil war, giving the used Western clothing the ominous nickname "Congo." *Don't wear Congo!*

After the Sierra Leonean civil war, however, the stigma dropped because so many people needed clothes.

Desperate for a shower before I would meet some of the people, I ducked into the bathroom. Mary had one of the nephews set a bucket of hot water in the bathtub for me. Most everyone in the family and in the village bathed with palm oil soap in the Tabe River, but my father and the chief had "modern bathrooms" in their homes for guests. A modern toilet consisted of a bucket of water by the toilet which needed to be filled before and after use.

Standing in the bathtub, I poured warm water from the bucket all over me. Bathing with the river water was a risk, as the water could carry larvae from freshwater snails that could bore through a human host's skin. Even minute exposure could run the risk of schistosomiasis if the water was not heated above 122 degrees Fahrenheit.

But Mary promised me this water was boiled over the fire.

I did not find out until after my trip that a few years ago a black spitting cobra wound its way into my father's bathtub—the very same one I used—telescoping through the drain. Hindogbae spotted it in time and villagers killed it with a long stick.

I dressed in a short jean skirt and red tank top. I did not know I was showing too much leg; I did not know my skirt was a bit too short for village standards, but by the next day three gorgeous African dresses appeared on my bed for me to *please wear*. The dresses were also gifts that they had made in advance to make me feel welcome.

Outside on the veranda the group had doubled. Young people stood, children clowned on my father's grass, and three old African women in head wrap crowns and dazzling dresses—the colors of a ripened tangerine, a perfectly sweet yellow mango, and a frothy turquoise sea—lounged on palm frond chairs like queens.

John emerged on the front porch, camera poised, only to find his muddy sandals from the day before spotlessly clean—every drop of mud removed. Slipping into his shoes, he didn't know whom to thank.

A young woman with high cheekbones and kind, soft brown eyes turned to her side, revealing her baby, snug and secure on her back, wrapped into the folds of her *lappa*. Two little girls, with hair in perfect cornrows, huddled together following John's camera. A toddler still dressed in the emerald *ashobi* dress from last night wobbled around the porch. Chickens pecked at the ground and mangy dogs tried to cool themselves away from the relentless sun. Suddenly a mass of white, brown, and dapple-coated goats ran past the house in a herd of twenty.

"Are the goats going to run away?" I asked out loud on the porch.

"No, they come back every evening to their pens," a villager told me, smiling at my concern.

Four boys around eleven years old waited on the lawn to dance for me.

My father nodded to them—permission to begin.

A serious, diligent drum player beat on an empty, rusty World Food Program tin with two twigs. A second drummer joined in, thumping on a yellow plastic gasoline container. With the beat established, the two dancers created a step—a cross between the Electric Slide, a tap-dancing move, and the spring of a person dancing on hot coals. Everyone on the porch focused on the music and dance quartet.

"Can you teach me?" I asked when they stopped. I joined the boys on the front lawn as the crowd watched. *One, two, three* the boys moved in step. *One, two, and three*. I mimicked their moves with my feet.

Laughter erupted from the boys at the American girl who copied their moves.

"Sarah, please come here," my father called. He whispered to me and John that it was customary to pay the boys a nominal fee for their performance. We dashed back inside the house and grabbed a few leones to pay the four young performers.

As I danced with the children, the villagers spoke in whispers to each other and to my father. "Joe, she has an African body. She has our hair."

When I awoke one morning and sat down for breakfast with my hair in full spasms, even Mary smiled and said, "Yes! You are African." When my skin, compared to my father's seemed an impossibly light shade, my hair reassured Mary, reassured the village, that I was my father's daughter. My hair, my African hair, that once brought me embarrassment and shame, now was the visual link and connection for the people.

CHAPTER SEVENTY-ONE

Bumpe

"Sarah, John, this afternoon you will come meet my students. I will drive you to Bumpe High School," said my father after the morning's dance performance.

After the heat of the morning settled a bit, my father dropped John and me off in the schoolyard in front of a cluster of white, one-story cement buildings; a large group of well-groomed students hung out, their British-inspired blue-and-white uniforms crisp against the green mowed grass.

"Look around and then come to my office," said my father, who left us to talk with a circle of children who gathered around John and me.

Bumpe's students stared wanting to look at us close-up. Finally, after some handshakes and giggles, I asked a student, "Where is the principal's office?" A group of students became instant tour guides leading us to my father.

Inside his small cinder-block office, long tie-dye green drapes hung like banners behind his desk. Garbed in a black-and-white Hawaiian shirt, with the psychedelic tie-dye curtains behind him, my father looked like a very hip principal. Notebook paper reminders and loose bulletins fluttered on the wall.

"Can we look at the school?" I asked.

"Yes. Look anywhere you like. I will find you in twenty minutes after I finish some work," he said.

Everywhere John and I moved with the camera, students followed us, narrating each room's purpose. Every classroom built from painted cinder blocks had a high sloping roof with a wall of divided windows. No glass protected the students from flies or mosquitoes during the long school days. Window after window was smashed into glass confetti or shot out by the rebels for target practice. Wooden desks dotted the rooms, some with chairs, others with chairs missing a back. Some desks had only a metal arch where a seat back used to be screwed on.

After visiting the few functional classrooms, students brought us to the abandoned buildings unsuitable for use. Bullet holes, blackened from gunpowder, pocked the walls.

"This is heartbreaking," John said aloud, filming each classroom. "This isn't right."

"But it's exciting because it's like what's next. You know what I mean? That's how I see it," I said, wheels spinning in my head, spinning out a plan to help.

"What's next is right," said John.

My father found us in one of the classrooms with a tiny schoolboy dancing in the middle of the dirt floor.

John asked my father, "Joe, if you had a wish list for the school what would be on it?"

My father took a deep breath, then used his fingers to count.

"Windows to be replaced in the classrooms. Classroom buildings and staff quarters to have roofing." He pointed to a roofless white building in the distance, "We were using flush toilets over there. All that has been destroyed."

In the ten years since 1994, vegetation burst like a second rebel attack through the buildings. Roots and vines gunned through the walls and floors, sprouted straight through cement with the force of artillery. Each successive building we toured looked like abandoned Mayan ruins, consumed by vines.

The school kitchen, which once prepared meals for over six hundred students, was replaced by two cooking fires in the dirt surrounded by three corrugated zinc walls. A pot of rice and vegetables simmered on the primitive fires.

My grandfather, Francis Kposowa, must have been turning over in his grave at the state of the school. In 1963 he wrote about the school, "A basic curriculum and a sense of dedication are the unique heritage this school offers. Bumpe High School must continue to attract some of the best students in Sierra Leone and provide them with an education and orientation to fit them for living in the modern world."

There was nothing modern about the school except for the teachers' and students' dreams. Dedicated teachers and ambitious students wished to rebuild and modernize Sierra Leone.

Wilting from the noon heat, exhausted from the constant public attention, I returned to my father's house to rest. Inside, my sister Jeneba, finished with her chores, asked if I would like my hair braided.

Nothing sounded better than shaping my hair into manageable braids, twisting them into ropes free from the sweat and heat. Together we sat in our father's bedroom, the ochre-colored walls now golden in the sun, sunbeams sifting through the tie-dye curtains. With the mosquito netting gathered and tied up for the day, I sat in a chair facing a single mirror set in between shelves, a makeshift vanity. However, the top half of the long thin mirror was missing, broken in half like a sloping ski mountain. In this mirror I watched as Jeneba sectioned my hair with a big, pink plastic comb and began to sing, "How Great Thou Art."

Then sings my soul, My Saviour God, to Thee,
How great Thou art, How great Thou art.
Then sings my soul, My Saviour God, to Thee,
How great Thou art, How great Thou art!

I knew the song well from church. I jumped in and joined her, harmonizing as her high African voice and my classically trained voice surged and fell in unison. Looking in that jagged mirror in front of me, I wondered if it could have reflected a different future for me. What if my father had taken me back to Africa with him? Would I be alive? Without the medical care, the vaccinations, the eradication of childhood diseases in America, would chicken pox, measles, my allergies, or rebels have killed me?

Unlike Jeneba's hair, which consisted of a much tighter natural coil, my kinky hair was very soft, with huge natural spring. When my sister divided my hair into five pigtails all over my head to braid in an exact copy of her hairstyle, I did not know what to say. On her, the pigtail braids looked adorable with her youth and hair texture. On me, the pigtails looked like Pippi Longstocking stuck her finger in an electrical outlet. I did not want to offend her, so for the next two days I wore my hair in this matching style.

Together we sang "Amazing Grace," our voices filling the entire house.

Amazing grace, how sweet the sound
That saved a wretch like me!
I once was lost, but now am found,
Was blind, but now I see.

'Twas grace that taught my heart to fear,
And grace my fears relieved;
How precious did that grace appear,
The hour I first believed!

Through many dangers, toils and snares,
I have already come;
'Tis grace hath brought me safe thus far,
And grace will lead me home . . .

That evening I wrote in my leather-bound diary by candlelight:

> This world, my family, is a gift from God and I'm so thankful to you for your guidance for the next steps . . . as I sit here writing by candlelight I think about how wonderful life is and how my life is whatever I make it.

CHAPTER SEVENTY-TWO

Road to Bo

"Watch your feet," said my father. His shiny, powder blue, decade-old Mercedes sported a gaping hole in the floor of the backseat. A mat, placed over the cavity, attempted to keep debris from shooting up inside the car. An unaware passenger, if applying too much pressure, could lose her ankle if it slipped through the rusty fissure. As it was, the mat bubbled and dust inevitably billowed up, coating our feet. I slid into the backseat for the hour-long, sixteen-mile ride to Bo, gingerly placing my feet on either side of the mat, avoiding the hole.

Used Range Rovers and Mercedes shipped from Belgium to Sierra Leone were deeply coveted; they were some of the few car engines that could handle the roads. Hindogbae and my father's many nephews kept the exterior of the car in a constant sparkly gleam. His Mercedes looked like a bluebird streaking across the red dirt. But the car didn't have much more life in it.

Before my father started the engine he said a prayer, "Please, God, take care of us on our journey, we pray that we get there safely." Roads in Sierra Leone were wretched—just a few months back my father careened into a ditch. Still shaken from the near miss, he now said his driving prayers aloud.

Dangling from the rearview mirror, three air fresheners in the shape of Christmas trees, striped like an American flag, swung back and forth. Long past scenting the car, they shimmied as patriotic decorations. The dashboard acted as a traveling shelf, complete with a box of Kleenex, a round plastic drum filled with white Q-tips, and stuffed animals.

John and my father sat in the front. Jeneba and I sat on the backseat.

"Sarah, Jeneba will take you to an excellent tailor in Bo," said my father. He will take your measurements and make a dress for your mother's service."

Before my trip, my father and Bumpe's Reverend Morlai planned a memorial service to honor Penny. In Sierra Leone it was customary to wear white at funerals and memorial services. Again, to show solidarity my family picked out a white bolt of fabric to make the family's shirts and dresses.

As the car tackled each and every bump, John and I cracked endless bad jokes about Bumpe's bumpy road. Then my father, in his deep baritone, and Jeneba in her high sweet voice, began singing church hymns in rounds. I thought of my dad in West Virginia, how much we liked to sing during family road trips to my grandparents' farm in Illinois. How coincidental that both my black and white fathers, continents apart, sang songs with their daughters as they rolled across the countryside.

Our car rolled into the city of Bo—the second largest city in Sierra Leone.

Best compared to an African version of an Old West gold town, Bo's center consisted of long, dusty roads surrounded by two- and three-story buildings and zinc-roofed shacks housing peddlers with "city wares": aspirin, bouillon cubes, salt, used shoes, and cheap plastic sunglasses. People hung out on storefront porches, idled by outdated cars, and rode battered mopeds throughout town. Market women crisscrossed the streets with tires stacked so high on their heads, Dr. Seuss would go giddy. Diamond stores, with gems crudely painted on the wooden doors advertised their wares. Constant honking blasted along the streets. Driving was a free-for-all as people, bikes, mopeds, trucks, buses, and young children rushed the road.

"First, I want you to meet a friend of mine," said my father, stopping the car in front of a Lebanese grocery store. My father bounded across the store's dirt yard as Jeneba and I trailed behind.

"We showed the owner the picture you sent us," my father said proudly.

How different I looked from the picture I mailed. The pretty, long Caribbean-style hair in a weave was a far cry from my African hair in five sprouting pigtails.

Instead of a JanSport backpack that I brought, a raffia straw purse hung on my shoulder, another gift from my father. My name was even stitched on the side in purple raffia string. More than gifts, I think my father wanted to protect me. It was safer for me not to advertise a Western backpack to pickpockets. Using Jeneba's measurements, my father and Mary had dresses made for me.

For this trip to Bo, I wore an African top, a short-sleeved pullover in bright lime green, as colorful as a tropical parrot. My top hung mid-thigh; the long matching skirt reached my ankles.

I shook the Lebanese grocer's hand who smiled and offered greetings in English.

"Now, we must meet some more relatives," said my father, leading me to our next destination. Walking a few more blocks along the dusty main street, we ducked through an open door into a dark alley. Jeneba took my hand, led me down the dank hallway, which opened into a dirt courtyard behind the storefronts. Laundry hung from clotheslines like colorful flags across the yard. A round-roofed pavilion sat in the center of the yard, circled by strutting roosters. Three African women in fantastical fabrics called me over onto the pavilion. One woman wore a dress that mimicked a cobra skin. Another wore a lappa in the deepest purple, and the third woman wore a checkered-patterned dress.

"*Bu Waa* (Bo wah)," I said, trying to call out *Good morning* in Mende.

The three women smiled.

"*Gbevaa bi gahun* (beva be gahun)?" I asked how they all were.

They nodded.

"*Kaye ee Ngewoh ma* (Ki ya E gey wah ma)," I repeated, which means *God is without fault. I am fine.*

"I said it right?" I asked in English.

They laughed, hugged me, and said, "Ohhh, Serrah!"

"*Besia!* (Bee see a)" I said, thanking them.

"Ohhh, Bumpenya, Bumpenya!" (Boom-pen-ya) they said.

My Aunt Amy named me Bumpenya and everyone started using the nickname. "What does that mean?" I asked.

"The lady of Bumpe. Bumpenya," said one of the three women under the pavilion.

Everywhere I went, in whispers I heard, "Bumpenya. The lady of Bumpe."

"We need to leave for lunch," said my father, the whirlwind tour guide, just ten minutes after arriving at the pavilion. Down the street through another alley, we arrived at another family gathering in a courtyard, where my Aunt Amy was also a guest. I sat down to rest, speak English, and chat with my Aunt Amy while we waited for steaming rice platters to be served.

I asked my Aunt Amy, "Were you happy to come back?" I wondered if the adjustment back to village life was difficult for her after living in London for over thirty years.

Aunt Amy said, "You see, in England they don't make you forget . . . you are an outsider. You will not forget. They remind you in the shops. They remind you at work, anywhere you go they remind you."

Jeneba grabbed my hand. We needed to visit the tailor while we waited for lunch. We could not waste time. We had to drive back to Bumpe before dark.

"We will be right back," I said to my aunt.

"Follow me," Jeneba said, and we wove through the webs of dusty streets to a tailor's shop. Inside, two men—one, in his thirties, had his head bowed over a sewing machine, the other was the skinniest man I had ever seen—worked in silence. Patterns for African dresses plastered the walls.

The skeletal man took my measurements, then pointed his gnarled finger to the wall, gesturing for me to pick a pattern.

"I am not sure what I want yet," I said, in perfect English.

His eyes bulged. "She's American! She can pay more money!" he spat to Jeneba.

Jeneba said, "No, she is my sister. This is my sister. She is Mende."

I tried to bluff, uttering the few Mende phrases I knew, but the man asked a follow-up question. I stood in silence.

"She is not Mende. She is American, she can pay more money."

He tripled the original price. Instead of $2.50, I was charged $7.50 for each custom-made dress.

CHAPTER SEVENTY-THREE

Bumpe

News spread quickly. In the late afternoon, a group of high school girls and boys arrived at my father's house to perform a talent show for John and me.

The first act: glass eaters.

A crowd of villages pushed onto my father's back lawn. Even an amputee attended, traveling from the amputee colony on the outskirts of Bumpe. Two boys set a small money bowl and three sharp pieces of green glass on the seat of a wooden chair. The glass pieces, curved and thick, appeared to be from a broken soda bottle.

More people congregated, some even brought wicker stools to sit on.

Dancers from the first night's welcoming ceremony arrived in raffia skirts, white sleeveless tops, and blue berets. Drummers and rattlers accompanied the dancers who chanted and clapped, hypnotically hyping the audience for the glittering glass show.

Standing in the center of the lawn, both fourteen-year-old boys were dressed in Bumpe High School T-shirts printed with the school crest on the front and the slogan, "We Perform Wonders" on the back. "Wonders" referred to academics, not glass consumption, but I don't think anyone caught the double meaning.

Each boy picked up a few pieces of glass and began to slowly eat. Walking around as they ate, the boys amazed the crowd who cheered in a synchronous beat to the drums and the chewing. One of the boys stopped chewing, bent down, and wiped the piece of glass on the lawn.

John called out, "What are you doing?"

"Cleaning the bug off," the boy answered.

Apparently one could eat glass, but not bugs.

I couldn't believe my eyes. "Come here," I said to one of the boys. Still crunching, he left the center of the grass and stood in front of me. "What are you doing? You're eating glass?"

"Yes," he said through crunches.

"Oww! Doesn't it hurt?" I said.

"Yeah," he answered and chomped away as if working on a large sourball.

I did not know what to do. Was it culturally taboo to ask them to stop? Would it embarrass my father who taught the students at Bumpe High School?

The boys' jaws moved up and down with great effort.

John called to my father, "Joe, can't you get detention for that?"

The high school girls' voices pounded in a steady chant, matching the boys' appetite. Each boy devoured piece after piece of glass.

Two village men walked up to the single chair set in the middle of the yard and deposited money in the boys' money bowl. Any kind of performance: dancing, drumming, or glass eating was performed for money.

"I think they should stop eating glass," I said.

"I know," said John.

"Are they okay?" I said.

All eyes of the villagers gazed with pride at the boys. Soon all the pieces of broken bottle vanished inside the caverns of their teenage mouths. Looking back, I wish I had done something. I have since discovered that eating glass, called *hyalophagia,* can be fatal if the glass punctures the stomach, intestines, or throat.

CHAPTER SEVENTY-FOUR

Bo—Freetown

A goat bleated nonstop in the back compartment of my Aunt Amy's 4Runner. In the backseat, John and I sat inches away from its hungry mouth. My father and Amy sat up front. We bumped along the road to Bo, headed to a Muslim wedding.

Tribal beliefs compel Sierra Leoneans to set libations out for the ancestors, consult medicine men, and invoke thunder medicine if crossed; yet, Christianity and Islam practiced throughout the country exist in a harmonious balance with each other and with tribal tenets. Our truckload represented a Christian contingent, adhering to the Mende tradition of bringing a female goat to a wedding. Female goats are presented to the bride as a symbol of birth, the ability to multiply, and a future abundance of food.

Leaving Bumpe early in the morning, we readied ourselves for the bumps and potholes, mustering the stamina it required to travel anywhere in Sierra Leone. But the goat would not shut up.

Aunt Amy said, "It is expected to bring a goat as a present for a wedding."

"Sarah," added my father, "when you get married one day, I will wait to receive a goat from the man who wants to be your husband."

I laughed in the backseat.

"I'll have to remember that."

A whining sound, a cross between a neigh and a man with a stomachache kept belting out behind us.

John asked, "Are goats like Christmas fruitcakes in Sierra Leone, everyone keeps passing around the same one at weddings?"

Maybe it was the heat, or being tossed centimeters from the ceiling, or our stomachs sloshing every which way, or the absurdity of riding in the car with a goat in the backseat, but for some reason John and I found this incredibly funny. A goat and fruitcake. We laughed hysterically.

"I don't understand," said Aunt Amy. John and I explained the re-gifted Christmas fruitcake circulating for years in America. Aunt Amy laughed, delighted to learn a cultural nuance.

Mende words passed between my aunt and the driver. Suddenly the driver jolted the truck to a stop. The driver's door flung open and he hopped out into the bush. I assumed he needed a bathroom break, but he returned with a giant shrub resembling tumbleweed. Popping open the truck, he jammed the bush inside, covering the goat and eliminating all visibility. A few branches bloomed through the headrest.

"Huh?" I said, looking at John.

"Ennhhh, enhhhh, ennnhhh," cried the goat.

After an hour we rolled into Bo. The goat devoured not only the leaves on the branch, but the entire bush—not a leaf or twig remained.

"Hungry goat!" I said.

"Fruitcake," said Aunt Amy, laughing.

A week later we attended a second Muslim wedding back in Freetown. Our group planned to attend the wedding and then drop John off at the ferry. He decided to only stay a week so he could fly back to the States for Christmas with his family.

I did not know then that his stay in Sierra Leone had realigned cells inside him. Red clay dust, leafy cotton trees, and the sweet faces of children wrapped themselves around his soul. John asked himself what he could do for the people of Bumpe. A tireless desire to help the people of Sierra Leone stirred inside John.

Soon silence overtook the truck, and with the exception of the driver, we all slept or gazed at the scenery. As my head bobbed in sleep, I turned over some disturbing information John shared with me. Two hundred dollars had been stolen from his backpack, zipped in an inner pocket. He did not know how or when this happened. I did not want to share this news with anybody, especially my parents back home. John also knew another secret. Most every night when it was too dark to be witnessed, I sat with John under a willow tree in my father's backyard and cried.

My circuits, overloaded with emotion, needed an outlet and a good listener. The amount of attention I was receiving, the constant swirl of people, my inability to know what to do or say, the awkwardness of everybody serving me, my new feelings of closeness toward my new father competing with feelings of betrayal of my parents back home, my home sickness and my constant stomachaches, my anger at being called *poo-moi*, my feelings of responsibility toward the villagers, all ran in gushing torrents under the tree night after night. Both John and I needed to process the newness and poverty of the village, but a whole subtext of identity saturated my thoughts as well.

From a diary entry I wrote later:

> At night under the trees there was a slight breeze as I sat on the bench. I was feeling completely overwhelmed with emotion that I didn't know what to do with. I was angry with myself that I couldn't just relax and enjoy meeting everyone. I told John, "I'm so frustrated, I feel like I don't know what to say, I feel like this really isn't happening. Why can't I just talk and have fun like you? Why am I constantly in my head thinking, "What do I say?" "Is that my cousin?" "What do I call my father, Joe? Father?"
>
> What am I supposed to wear? If I wear something that African women don't wear—will I be an embarrassment to my family? What's expected of me? My father told me when I was dancing around the fire with everyone one evening that I should go and rest. Why? I wasn't tired. Was I embarrassing him? Are the daughters of the Kposowa Family not supposed to dance with everyone? I love to dance, why is he

telling me not to dance? I felt like a child. I'm 28 years old and he is telling me to go to bed?

John just listened. Even in that humid evening air I had chills as my body did not know what to do with all the emotion pouring through me. My thoughts and emotions felt like a never ending hundred-yard dash. John was wonderful and a fantastic listener. Then he gave me this advice: *try asking everyone questions.*

That was a great place to begin. So that's what I did and it began to help.

"Freetown," announced the driver after six hours passed.

After the long drive, we eagerly awaited our hotel in the city complete with modern bathrooms and showers. When we checked into our rooms, we were informed that the hotel had no running water. Staff scurried to bring buckets of water for bathing to our rooms. Since leaving Bumpe, I dreamt of a hot shower, my new great luxury. But it was bucket-style bathing only.

We washed with buckets and dressed for the ceremony.

On the drive to the event, something bizarre riveted my attention: a woman with blotches of white, brown, and black skin lurched through the streets of Freetown. Was this a form of leprosy?

I made a note to ask Mary about this when we returned to Bumpe.

Right before the wedding, Aunt Amy took me aside and said, "Sarah, I noticed you are struggling with what to call your father."

It was true. Calling him *Kay Kay* felt odd, but *Father* seemed too formal, and *Dad* unnatural—that word already had twenty-eight years of history attached to it.

"You can call him *Dad*, it's okay," she said taking my hand.

I hadn't been able to give myself permission to call my father *Dad*.

The Muslim ceremony was inside a large room, stifling hot with too many people packed inside on prayer mats. The oiled mahogany skin of the men rained buckets of sweat down their backs. The women sitting behind them fanned themselves to keep from fainting as prayers and speeches lasted deep into the night. After the prayers, my father's cousin, J. P. Genda, the commissioner of labor for the country, spoke about the war and what Sierra Leone needs.

"Do not forget us," he said to me and John facing the camera. "When you return to America do not forget our country. Our daughter has come home and I ask through her for America to help us! Many make promises and never keep the promises . . ."

CHAPTER SEVENTY-FIVE

Bumpe

Back in Bumpe, as the deep blues of evening fell, a woman came to the front door of my father's house carrying a plastic platter on her head with a large napkin covering a mound on top of it. Speaking first with my father in Mende, and receiving a nod from him, she removed the cloth. An animal's severed head lay on the platter. It was a creature I have never seen before, a cross between a groundhog and a guinea pig. Its tongue extended outside of its body frozen in a "slurp" position.

Reaching into his pocket, my father gathered a few leones for the woman.

"What is that?" I asked, staring at the grotesque head.

"It is a cutting grass. Delicious. Mary will boil it for me."

"You're going to eat that thing with the little tongue sticking out?" I said.

"Yes, it is very good," he chuckled.

"Look at its tongue!" and I slurped my own tongue to mimic the creature's petrified pose.

My father laughed so hard at my imitation.

The more I got to know my father the more I witnessed the intense pressure he bore as the principal of the school and as a community leader. He was one of the few educated Leoneans from his village who returned to Bumpe. My father returned as a teacher and as a leader for the people. He maintained a certain image, a serious demeanor, the walk of a "big man." My father's playful side was rarely revealed outside of his private walls. Sometimes I felt sorry for him having to maintain this propriety. I knew how exhausting keeping up images could be.

As dinner cooked outside on the pit, Mary took a moment to rest, sitting in a chair by the fire. In the eight days I had spent in Bumpe, I never saw Mary relax. Always cooking, cleaning, pruning, shelling, serving, she worked tirelessly to make the house run.

"Mary," I called. "Can I ask you something?"

"Yes," she said. Together we walked to the bench under the willow tree where John and I always sat.

"Mary," I said, "I saw the strangest woman in Freetown. It looked like she had a skin disease, or like she was . . . bleached?"

"Yes, people bleach their skin here. It makes your skin lighter. The bleach kits are expensive, but people ask for them for presents."

My mouth hung open. I traveled all the way to Africa, only to discover that bleaching kits were expensive, desired gifts. I can still see the pigmented islands, fragmented blotches of color all over her body. Was skin-bleaching a form of self-hatred, a form of racial shame? In a country where almost everyone was black, why would someone do this? I couldn't wait to return to my roots only to find some of my roots wanted to change color.

I later discovered these skin-bleaching kits were shipped in from Nigeria, Morocco, Saudi Arabia, and the United States. They burn off the skin, resulting in blemishes, blisters, puffiness, and pain.

Mary said, "Sarah, can I ask you something?"

"Sure," I said.

"Do you bleach *your* skin?"

Air rushed out of my lungs.

"No," I said weakly. I wondered if it was hard for her to believe that her ebony husband was my father, or if she fully understood that I was biracial. "Mary, my mother was white so that makes me a lighter shade."

"Oh," she said, "yes, I know. I was just wondering."

And in comparison to the deep black of the villagers skin tone, I did look fully white.

Maybe it was confusion or bad information about my birth mother, but Mary's question depressed me.

"Sarah, can I ask you something else?" she said.

"Yes."

"I would love to talk with you. You are always talking with your dad, asking him things, always sitting with the men. You can ask me things, too."

"Oh, my gosh, of course. I'd love to talk with you more." Almost every night my father sat on the edge of the bed in my room, shared tomorrow's plan, and answered my questions about Penny. I hadn't meant to leave Mary out of these conversations.

CHAPTER SEVENTY-SIX

Bumpe—Outskirts

An amputee colony clustered in a group of seven homes within walking distance from my father's home. Erected by the government in 2003, the homes were intended to shelter the amputee victims and channel resources to one location, making it easier for the disabled victims to obtain food and clothes. Except after the crude lodgings were constructed and the amputees moved in, nothing else was done.

On the parched clearing, the cement-block buildings drifted in limbo with the amputees and their families waiting for something to change and someone to help. Because promises of resources went unfulfilled, the amputees were actually worse off than before they moved to the colony. They now needed to walk ten, twelve, thirteen miles back to their villages, beg for food from relatives, and make the long trek home.

I wondered if I had walked into a scene from Dante's *Inferno,* a level of hell, as I met a group of amputees who sat on plastic chairs in a dirt yard.

When the amputees first saw me arrive with a camera, my brother, Hindogbae, and his friend Joseph Lahai (who John nicknamed "the Orator" because of the eloquence of his English), we were told to go away. The designated leader of the colony told Hindogbae in Mende that no one wanted to speak with me. "Is she going to take pictures and leave?" The amputee colony was sick of being a macabre tourist destination.

Hindogbae appealed to the man and said, "But she is Joseph Konia Kposowa's daughter."

Middle-aged with a long, gaunt face and one atrophied arm hacked below the elbow jutting the limb out like a wing, and the other hand severed at the wrist, the man searched my face, assessing the level of kindness or voyeurism. He wore a jersey knit polo shirt with the words "Hillcrest Christian" sewed on it.

"Okay," he said, and told everyone to answer my questions.

The five women and three men answered the same question: "Please tell me what you were doing when the rebels attacked and what happened?"

The gaunt-faced man, his skin stretched over his hollowed-out cheeks, recounted the rebel attack in a single paragraph with no emotion:

> I heard they were coming and I hid. I was caught, brought to town from the bush and told to sit down and put my hand on a stick. They cut this hand and they told me to put my other hand on the stick and cut it . . . my wife died and my mother and I now live with my sister who helps me.

After speaking, he got up and walked inside his house.

The second man, wearing a dirty kelly green oxford shirt, spoke in more detail. Unlike the double amputee victim, he had the use of one good hand:

> One fine day I go to wash beans with my wife and children. When the rebels came to town my wife was cooking and I was sitting in the chair with one child by my side, the other child on my lap. My wife went to fetch water and my son to fetch cassava. My wife came running back saying the rebels have come and are killing people. With my children by my side the rebels surrounded the town and began hacking the hands off the women. Everywhere I looked I saw soldiers with guns. Inside my home I hid with my child. When rebels searched my house, they heard my child crying.
>
> The rebels said, "Who is there?"

> "I am the only one," I said and walked outside to spare my child.
>
> They told me to sit with the other villagers. I watched as the town chief was stabbed in the head with a knife. After they killed him, punctured his head, they cut off his son's hands. The rebel said, "We are coming to kill you." Placing one of my hands down, they cut it off. Ready to cut off the other one, they held up the axe, but the rebel commander at that moment came by and said, "Leave him, we are finished here." My blood covered my children. My son, who left to fetch cassava, came back crying, as I bled all over the ground. My son carried me to another village where he set me down by the road to look for help. A woman ran up and said rebels are coming. I said to my son, "Let them kill me. I am unable to walk." But my son begged two people to help carry me in a hammock. "Please let my father not die," he begged. Two men said, "Let's take this man." They balanced me in a hammock.

He ended the interview by lifting up his green shirt sleeve. Dangling loose at his side, his shortened forearm was rounded like a dark shriveled plum.

One young woman spoke: "When they heard the voice of the gun" in her village she realized they were ambushed. Two of the four female amputees sat with toddlers on their laps.

One mother's hand was nearly gone; only her thumb remained. What was left of her hand curved in a long sinewy line from her thumb nail into her wrist. The way her hand healed was almost beautiful, as if her four other fingers never existed and instead she grew one great, elongated thumb with extraordinary length and flexibility that compensated for the missing digits. As her toddler sat in her lap eating a banana, she wrapped her extra long thumb around his tiny arm keeping him secure. Oblivious to his mother's deformity, the child's large eyes stared into the camera.

Finally the last woman spoke. Hiding between her legs, clinging to her knees, was her daughter. The woman relayed how she and her family sought safety in Bo, but hunger brought them back to the village.

When I arrived back in the village, with a pregnant belly, my mother, father, and my husband came, too. Back in the village I gave birth, and my mother cooked some soup and cassava for me as I nursed. Suddenly rebels banged on the door, forced us to come outside. First they killed my father, cut my mother's arm off, stabbed my husband several times with their knives, and cut off my hand. My family collapsed in a pool of blood and stayed there until night fell when relatives came and dragged us into the bush. A rumor circulated that white people came to Bo to treat people without paying, so we managed to get to Bo, where my husband died in the hospital.

"White people came to Bo to treat people without paying," she said.

White people were spoken of as saviors, relief in an unfair world.

The final amputee I interviewed, a fifty-year-old man with tight gray curls on his head, and a wide jolly face, had both an ear and a hand cut off. His arm looked like a long brown baguette: no hand, no fingers, just a long thin limb curved smooth at the end. He said, "If white people help them [amputees], they will be very happy."

Hindogbae, Joseph Lahai, and I all walked in silence back to the village.

CHAPTER SEVENTY-SEVEN

Bumpe

Late that night, back at my father's house, Hindogbae put a DVD of a Nigerian hip-hop group into the DVD player attached to my father's television. After spending the day with the amputees, we all needed a release, space to process the horrors we just heard; maybe subconsciously we needed to celebrate our limbs so easily taken for granted. Maybe Hindogbae needed to be a teenager and not a journalist-translator in a war-torn country.

Usually at night the house was lit with small kerosene lamps that cast small pools of light in our rooms and lined the hallway, a poetic mosaic of flickering flames. But tonight my father powered the generator and the Nigerian hip-hop stars Mad Melon and Mountain Black, who make up the group Danfo Drivers, crooned their reggae-hip-hop songs. Everyone in the house began to dance around the living room.

I don't know why we picked that night to dance. After the amputee colony it could be seen as disrespectful or sacrilegious. I don't know why my father decided to run the generator letting us watch the DVD my brother bought in Bo.

I do know, however, that after I spoke with the amputees, everyone begged me to bring a message to America to not forget them, that white people needed to know of their tragedies. For the villagers of Bumpe, I was fast becoming a savior, a light-skinned bridge between black and white worlds. How could I tell them that I hadn't come to save them, or build a school, fix a well, or bring medical supplies? How could I admit to anyone I had come for the most selfish reason of all—to be loved by my father.

That evening we danced until midnight. Mary shook her hips; Hindogbae taught me a dance move. The television blared as loud as a siren. Over forty children from the village heard the music and sprinted to my father's house. As quiet as mice, with eyes as large as owls, the village kids perched on the outside porch, looking into the living room as we danced. They knew if they made a peep my father would shoo them out, but if they peered in without disruption, they could view hip-hop on a twenty-inch television screen.

I closed my eyes and danced.

CHAPTER SEVENTY-EIGHT

Taninahun

Late Christmas Eve, my father, Hindogbae, and I drove to my grandmother's village of Taninahun. "Tell Sarah to come soon. I am getting very old," she said to my father months ago. Over a week had passed and I still had not met my grandmother.

Taninahun, more compact than Bumpe, was less developed and more pastoral. The sky, filled with tropical sounds, breathed liked a living entity. Calls of monkeys, gray parrots, rustling banana palms, all wove a wild soundtrack rising over huts hit hard by rebels.

As soon as we arrived, Hindogbae and my father began setting up a small generator to give us light for the evening. "Wait here," said Hindogbae, "we will be right back."

I waited on my grandmother's porch alone.

Suddenly people poured out of their homes and gathered around me. No one spoke English. *"Bu waa Besia,"* I said, smiling. Children and neighbors came out to stare.

Finally, Hindogbae pounced up the porch steps and said, "I will introduce you to our grandmother, Musu."

He led me into the dark house. Inside stood a woman in her late sixties. Anger set in every muscle of her face. With her lips pulled into a tight thin line, small darting eyes, gold earrings, and her hair in a head wrap, she looked like a stern pirate.

"Hello," I said holding out my hand. "It is so nice to meet you." Hindogbae translated my words. I stood there smiling.

My grandmother spoke a few swift sentences back in Mende.

"What did she say?" I asked.

"She asked if you have any money for her," translated Hindogbae.

My stomach tightened. I looked back at her unmoving face.

"Tell her I'll have to talk with our father about that," I said.

Again my grandmother spoke in rapid Mende. Hindo continued, "She is very angry with Daddi. He has not come to visit in a long time, nor has he sent money to her."

I wondered if some of the money spent on my celebration ceremony, or the journey to Bumpe from Freetown was siphoned from her allowance.

My father came inside. A storm was coming. With the darkness and poor roads, "It was best we stayed the night," he said. I wished we could drive back to Bumpe.

Anger between my father and his mother crawled on every surface of the house. After my grandfather died, my father took care of his mother. The house we stood in was built by my father. Although it had almost no furniture besides a few beds and a small kitchen table, it was large and the beds had sheets and pillows.

My grandmother, her sister, and her brother served us a meal filled with tension. We all went to bed early.

At two in the morning a storm hit. Rain split like rockets against the roof. Lightning—long wild javelins—fell outside my window, and thunder echoed so fiercely I clutched the side of my bed. Could a house this flimsy be lifted loose by the winds?

I curled up into a ball with a single sheet over me. Suddenly I realized I had no mosquito netting over me either. Every hair on my body stood like antennas. Was zinc a good conductor of electricity? I darted to my father's room and knocked on his door.

"Sarah?" he called, groggily.

"Is this a hurricane?" I asked, cowering with each coming crash.

My father chuckled through the noise. "No, it's just a rainstorm. Go back to sleep."

At twenty-eight I felt like a child scared of thunder, but this African tropical storm seemed to possess lightning bolts that could pierce deep trenches into the continent. Thunderstorms in West Virginia sounded like muffled hiccups in comparison. Then again, sleeping in a house with a flat zinc top roof and cinder-block walls twelve inches thick was not much protection against the elements, sound, lightning, snakes, or disease.

Christmas morning could not come fast enough. We packed up the generator and headed back to Bumpe. Before leaving my grandmother's house, I gave her, her brother, and her sister some money in the amount my father suggested. I also whipped out the camera with Hindogbae one last time to ask some final questions before leaving. Outside, in front of the car I asked my grandmother about the war and her village. My final question to her was, "What is your dream?"

"Nothing," she said.

"Nothing?" I repeated.

"Nothing, I am unable to do anything." She spoke in rapid-fire Mende to Hindogbae.

"She says she needs money to start a petty business," he said.

"Owww!" I yelled. A giant black driver ant bit me.

"Sarah, Hindo, we must go now," called our father.

"*Besia.* Thank you," I said to my grandmother who had smiled only once during my visit.

Two months later, after I'd was back America, my father wrote me a letter: my Grandmother Musu had died.

CHAPTER SEVENTY-NINE

Bumpe

Dipping up and down over the bumps, with the rising morning heat cloying, I could not believe it was Christmas Day. No bells, no Santa, no carolers, no snow, no church service with the family, only heat and sweat and humidity in a chugging car struggling to Bumpe.

"Kaay, Kaay?" I said. "Can we stop so I can call my parents to wish them a Merry Christmas?"

"Yes, the first hill right before the village sometimes gets reception. We will stop there."

The hill came into view. My father parked the car and told me to follow him. Hindogbae waited in the car. "This is where I have luck making calls."

Together we stood in the bush grasses in the middle of the hill. Besides this hill, or in Bo sixteen miles away, it was impossible to make a call. Instead of phones, villagers relied on children to run messages for a small fee.

My father stepped aside as I dialed my parents with my calling card. "Hello, Mom?" I said. "Merry Christmas!"

"Sarah!" she said. I pictured the family, gathered around the table, eating my sister's famous maple bacon rolls. Early every Christmas morning, my sister Lynne baked the maple rolls, the rising dough was the first thing we all smelled upon waking. I envisioned the fragrant pine tree in my sister's living room, and imagined my nephews throwing hugs around my parents for assembling a toy. When I was small, my parents helped me set out a plate of cookies for Santa. They also reminded me to leave a saucer of sugar for Santa's reindeer on Christmas Eve. "You can't forget the reindeer who work so hard," they said. During the night my mom would dribble tiny droplets of water on the sugar. This would look like a reindeer's wet nose had left an impression after bending down to lick the granuales.

"Everything's great," I said, loud enough for my father to hear. So much was great, and so much was overwhelming; but I did not want to make my father in Africa feel badly or worry my parents in America.

"Love you all," I said, swallowing the lump in my throat. Was it terrible to want to be back in America full of familiar smells: roasting turkey, hot baking bread, and fragrant pine trees?

The line cut out before I could talk to everybody.

"Huh?" I said and dialed again and again—but I lost reception. I slid back into the car.

"When we arrive home the carolers will come by," said my father.

"Carolers?" I said, perking up.

"Carolers come over on Christmas. Then we will go to the Paramount Chief's house for dinner. Mary and Amy have been cooking for the past two days," said my father.

Moments after we arrived home, a flock of fifteen boys, around twelve years old, rushed the front porch carrying small sticks. In a call-and-response beat the tallest boy in the group belted out a vocal African rhythm. The younger boys echoed back, beating their sticks. One of the boys dressed as a monster.

"That was great," I said to the Christmas carolers. Retrieving a bag of candy I saved for Christmas day, I gave each boy a handful of Jolly Ranchers wrapped in plastic and some money.

"We must go," said my father, and we locked the house and drove to the Paramount Chief's compound. Close to the Tabe River, on a large chunk of land, seven houses comprised the Kposowa compound.

A sacred round house graced the center of the Kposowa plot. Although this round house had only a thatched roof and consisted of painted mud bricks, my grandfather, the great Paramount Chief, his ancestors, and even my Uncle Thomas, the current Paramount Chief, all slept in the round house.

A large, eight-bedroom house, built from glass and cement, anchored the compound; however, the Paramount Chief still sleeps in the round, primitive hut. It was believed that an ancient medicine man scattered powerful medicine there, creating a sacred vortex for the Paramount Chiefs. In the round hut the chiefs were believed to be protected, renewed in sleep, and granted wisdom.

During the war, rebels torched this sacred round house. Neighbors who hid in the surrounding bush swear that when the blessed hut burned, the whole sky went black. Day flipped into night. Total darkness covered the sky as if nature itself became confused.

After the war, the Paramount Chief chose to rebuild the round hut on the same consecrated land. However, a rule or ritual must be adhered to when building a Paramount Chief's round house. It must be erected in one day only. First all the building materials must be gathered: the sticks for the beam structure, the mud bricks to place in between the sticks, the white clay plaster to cement and smooth the building, and the palm fronds to create the roof. Next the Paramount Chief called upon the Kposowa women. When the sun rose, the women would begin to cook for the men. With the first ray of sunlight, the men began working non-stop to complete the structure before sunset.

A smaller round house also sits on the property. Called a *toi,* or a mausoleum containing the bones of former chiefs, it is known as the House of Fame.

To my great surprise when I walked into the main modern house, cool from its cement walls and high ceilings, my Aunt Amy had erected a fake Christmas tree and decorated it with balloons. Pink, yellow, blue, and white balloons tied to the branches flopped in all directions. This confused Birthday-Christmas tree was most appropriate for Sierra Leone. When I asked village children if they were excited for Christmas they responded, "Yes, we are excited for Jesus's birthday."

No gifts were exchanged, only a large meal where the men all ate *fufu,* a gritlike food. The men ate with their hands from one platter. Aunt Amy, understanding how things were done in London, set out a separate plate for me. After dinner, a man dressed in a wooden mask, carved in the shape of a ram's head, barged into the house and danced for us.

Only later that evening, alone with my immediate family at the house, I passed out gifts to each family member. I shared with my father that my friends and family raised $2,500 for school desks but I did not want to carry that amount of money in cash with me. My uncle in America told me traveler's checks were not the best option in Sierra Leone. Together we decided wiring the money to a Sierra Leonean bank when I returned home was best.

I continued passing out the wrapped presents. Jeneba received the Western jeans she wanted. My father adored his new leather briefcase fit for a principal. Hindogbae opened a pristine soccer ball and a sports watch purchased by my sister. After spending time in Sierra Leone, I realized that Hindogbae really wanted a gold-plated, more formal watch. Many of Bumpe's teenage boys wanted to look like successful "big men."

CHAPTER EIGHTY

Bumpe

The morning after Christmas, Jeneba knocked on my bedroom door. "Do you need help with your head tie, Sarah?" she asked.

In front of my father's broken mirror, I stared at my reflection. My shimmery white memorial service dress could pass for a summer wedding dress. Delicate round flowers wove up and down the fabric. The skinny tailor in Bo included extra fabric to use as a matching head tie.

"Sure," I called to Jeneba, who came into my room. She fastened my head tie so it rested in the middle of my forehead, covered the top of my scalp, and tied in the back. My long braids trailed out.

She held my hand as we walked to our father's car. Outside in the sunshine, the fabric looked even more like a polished pearl against the deep tones of my family's skin. Although the church was walking distance away, and the service started at ten o'clock in the morning, my father feared that dust might coat our white finery. Instead we piled into the car and drove to the bright yellow church in the heart of the village.

Outside the church, my family posed for a family photo. Then we solemnly entered the modest, one-room, square building with its raised roof. With a Shaker simplicity amid the retro colors, the inside walls divided into a mustard yellow and a maroon band marking the bottom perimeter of the walls.

In the center of the church, was a makeshift stage with a large wooden crucifix raised up two steps on a platform. Up the center aisle, flanked on both sides with wooden benches, a procession of seven men and women in traditional mint green choir robes began the memorial service singing, "Joy to the World" in English. "Let heaven and nature sing," rang against the cement painted walls.

In the front row, my family stood in the pew: my father, me, Mary, Hindogbae, and Jeneba in our matching whites.

Ushers passed out a program my father photocopied earlier that week in Bo. When he asked to borrow a picture from the photo album of Penny's pictures, I did not know he was using a photo to grace the cover of the memorial leaflet he made for the congregation. On the front of the folded paper, it read:

MEMORIAL SERVICE

AT THE LANE MEMORIAL UNITED BRETHREN CHURCH

BUMPE

ON

SUNDAY 26TH DECEMBER 2004

AT 10:00 A.M.

FOR THE LATE

LILLIAN P. METHENY

Who Died on Monday March 9, 1987 in Morgantown W.A.[sic] USA

Age 45 Years

The program divided the two-hour ceremony into fifteen sections, which included hymns in both Mende and English, sermons, readings from Job 14:1-14 and Luke 2:1-7.

The Reverend Morlai first greeted the congregation. Then Hindogbae walked up to the pulpit to read from Job:

If a man dies, will he live again?
All the days of my hard service
I will wait for my renewal to come.

I did not know why they chose that scripture, but I interpreted this memorial service as a renewal for my birth mother, being honored in front of the large congregation. Maybe through one's children people can live again. I wanted to share and celebrate my birth mother's warmth and openness. Hearing Hindogbae speak, I realized that besides placing flowers on my mother's gravestone, I had never publicly honored her with songs or hymns in memory of her life.

Africans singing and clapping shook the church after the solemn reading.

Next my father slid out of the bench, approached the pulpit, and read a tribute speech about my mother:

> "I'm here to give a very short tribute to Lillian Metheny who was commonly known as Penny . . . Penny was never a stranger to anybody. She accepted everybody regardless of race and color. She was very close friends to the African students. She was very outgoing and always had a beautiful smile on her face . . . even when things went wrong she was always smiling . . . she never had a very good job and had very little, but she was always willing to share the little she had with friends and relatives. Indeed she was a very good woman, very kind and sincere. May her soul and all the souls of the departed rest in peace."

Listening to my father speak filled me with an even greater respect for him. I did not ask for him to organize this special service for my birth mother. After my father's eulogy, the Reverend Morlai spoke about my mother's "untimely death" at 45. For a citizen of Sierra Leone, where life expectancy is 37 for men and 42 for women, I thought this was a very interesting perspective. When the Reverend spoke again of the word "untimely," he shared how God will come for us and how we don't know when our time is, but it is okay whatever he chooses.

Maybe it was the heat inside the packed church, or thinking about my birth mother, or contemplating death, but my chest began to heave, inhale and exhale rapidly, until big tears rolled down my face. I thought again of God's plan, why I did not grow up in this village, why I was given up, why I was here now, why . . .

Mary leaned over to me, "Sarah, stop." She waved her hand in a "zip it" motion.

I blinked at her through my tears.

"Stop crying?"

Again she made a low hand motion, a quick jagged horizontal cut like, *That's enough.*

Mary, with her deep kindness, would never be cruel, so I assumed I had violated a taboo. Being strong in public was admired. Public tears were frowned upon. I sucked in my tears and willed myself to stop crying.

The service ended with three young men, a reggae troubadour ensemble singing "Praise Jesus, Hallelujah!"

I stood up and shook all the people's hands in the packed church who came to pay tribute to my birth mother.

CHAPTER EIGHTY-ONE

Bumpe

The night before my return to America, I rested on the long wooden benches lining my father's front porch. Chickens and roosters clucked all around me, as the slow purples of night descended. There was so much I would miss: the smell of fresh earth all around me; the crackling of fires on large flat stones smoking every hour of the day; the big fluid eyes of the children following me; the intense quiet without car alarms or washing machines competing with nature.

Just as day and night conducted their final exchange, five African women materialized on the road. I squinted my eyes to make sure I wasn't dreaming, tricked by the fading sky and dust as they moved along the red clay. But the beautiful older African women, graceful in their long *lappas* walked straight toward me.

"Mary?" I called.

Mary emerged on the porch. In the distance she, too, spotted the women. She wiped her hands on her apron. "Sarah, your aunts have come to take out your braids."

"My aunts?"

My first day in Bumpe, Jeneba sectioned my hair into the five pigtails, which I wore for a few days to not offend her. However, in the middle of the week I paid a local woman to braid my hair into long cornrows all over my head. It took hours, but was worth it; braids in Africa kept my head cool, my hair tight, and saved time every morning. Running my hand over my scalp, I felt my loose plaits. Mary was right, the braids needed to come out. My hair started puffing up, but unraveling a head full of braids would take a full day with my arms shaking from the effort.

"Hello, Serrah," called the women with their heavy Mende accents. "We are all your aunties. We cannot let you go back to America without new braids."

During my entire trip, I never met these aunts, but I realized because my grandfather, the Paramount Chief had over a *hundred* wives, I would probably never know all my relatives.

One of my aunts, who introduced herself as Mabel, positioned a plastic chair in the center of the driveway. A circle of women spun around me.

The rhythmic music of women's Mende voices sang, a dizzy orbit of laughter pealed as my braids unraveled. Braid after braid uncoiled in ten, strong, powerful hands. One of my aunts traveled all the way from Freetown; she had much catching up to do with the ladies. I drank in their sounds, breathed the rich smells of their skin rubbed with cocoa butter oil, and memorized my last African sky.

I would miss my father and our talks on the edge of the bed. I would miss the kerosene lamps and their soft shadows in my bedroom.

"We're finished!" they said. I had never had braids unspooled so quickly. When I stood up, my crazy Afro unleashed. My aunts nodded their heads approvingly, "She is definitely an African girl."

"Oh, Serrah," they said with their heavy accents. I hugged each aunt.

"Thank you," I said.

"This is our duty," they said.

Then the group streamed inside for more talking and for Mary's cooking.

"Serrah, wait here," said my Aunt Mabel who moved my plastic chair to the side of the porch where a light hung overheard. My father turned on the generator, so a single bulb illuminated my scalp for Aunt Mabel. For the next two-and-a-half hours, as that little light pushed against the darkness, Mabel carefully and precisely began rebraiding my hair.

Joseph Lahai, "the Orator," who accompanied me to the amputee colony, stopped over for a visit. Using an upside-down bucket beside me as a stool, he chatted with us as Mabel plaited each strand. Joseph shared his dreams of studying at a university. Then he asked me, "Do you know Snoop Dogg's songs?"

"Snoop Dogg, the rapper?"

"Yes," he said smiling. "My friend bought some of his music in Freetown. I know so many of his songs—every word."

I could not believe that in a village with no electricity, no plumbing, no phones, Joseph had memorized Snoop Dogg's lyrics. For these young black men, hearing a black man rap in English with such verbal fluidity inspired them. The boys repeated every word. I realized the power that rappers have in the Third World and how they need to take responsibility for their message.

"Serrah, I am very happy you come to Sierra Leone," said my aunt, finishing the braids. "I wished you had come to this country before the war. It was so beautiful. Peaceful. Freetown was not so crowded then. There wasn't all that garbage."

Midnight struck. I still needed to pack.

"Thank you so much," I said and hugged her.

"Can I give you some money?" I asked.

"No, Serrah. I am your aunt and I wanted to do this for you."

"Thank you."

Back in my room, a kerosene flame danced in the broken mirror. My hair looked beautiful.

Busy packing, I stuffed my bag with all my custom-made African dresses. A knock vibrated my door.

"Yes?"

Mary poked her head in. "Sarah, I baked some banana bread for your trip." She handed me a warm baked loaf, just risen from the embers at the edge of the fire.

"Mary, thank you for everything."

By now it was one o'clock in the morning. My father and I needed to leave for Bo at four thirty in the morning. From Bo we would park the car and catch a bus to Freetown. Out in the living room, I thanked everyone and shared how honored I felt to call them my family.

Exhausted and overwhelmed with good-byes, I slept until three thirty in the morning. After I quietly dressed, I tugged my suitcase into the living room, ready to meet my father. The generator had been switched back on and the kitchen and living room glowed with lights. Eggs, hot toast, and tea waited for me on the table. My father carried my suitcase to the trunk of the rusty Mercedes.

"Sarah, we must go," he said. I tiptoed out the door, careful not to wake anybody. To my surprise the entire household gathered in the front yard to say good-bye again. It was four in the morning. "*Malorhoi* (Mal-o-way)," they called. Jeneba, Hindogbae, my father's two nephews, Mary, and Joseph Lahai all stood in the yard. Hindogbae hovered close to the house, gaunt and thin. In the past two days he had contracted malaria. I gave him what was left of my malaria pills. Would Hindogbae be okay? Would I ever see anybody again? Thank goodness it was dark and no one in the group noticed my wet face.

CHAPTER EIGHTY-TWO

Bo—Freetown

My father's jaw tightened, teeth clenched. I had never seen him this upset. "Wait here," he said, and he dashed away.

Alone in Bo's "bus terminal," which consisted of a broken patch of cement off the side of a dirt road, I guarded our bags. We missed the large government bus to Freetown.

Ten minutes earlier when we arrived in Bo, we picked up one of my father's closest friends, Jonathan Daramy, who rode with us to the bus station. At the curb we unloaded our bags, jumped out, and Mr. Daramy drove my father's car back to his house for safekeeping. The jalopy Mercedes could never make it to Freetown.

No ticket booth, no orderly line, no posted schedule appeared at the "terminal," only a tall slender man dressed in gray pants and a gray shirt who sulked by the patch of gravel. "You have missed the bus," he repeated.

Although we traveled to Bumpe in a rented Land Rover, my father did not have enough money for a return trip. Only now did I realize how much money from different people pooled together made my trip possible; the car rental, hotel rooms, extra kerosene, extra food, and gas for the generator cost a fortune.

Ten minutes later my father returned very agitated. "I have found another bus, but it is going to be very crowded."

Instead of a bus, a battered, mini van, called a *poda-poda,* pulled up to the curb. A *poda-poda* is like an ancient Volkswagen van that should be rusting in a grassy field. *Poda-podas* are the cheapest form of public transportation and although dangerous, most Sierra Leoneans will risk the ride because they are the only affordable means of long-distance travel. The interior metal chamber of the van is gutted and long wooden benches with no seat belts are inserted; a driver will then pack as many paying customers as possible inside.

For luck and protection, inspirational or religious slogans are painted on the hood of the vehicle. Inscribed on the slanted hood of our *poda-poda,* a slogan shone out from under the red dust: IN GOD WE TRUST. Other *poda-poda* slogans included: LIVE ON HOPE, MOTHER'S BLESSING, FEAR JUDGMENT DAY, I AM COVERED IN THE BLOOD OF JESUS CHRIST, and TO BE A MAN IS NOT EASY.

Plastered on the rear doors of the van, old magazine photos of Madonna in her 1980s *Like-a-Virgin* stage, crusted in the sun.

Three African women ducked their heads inside the van and tucked their chickens in square, woven crates underneath the seats. Six more people forced their way inside, forcing bulging bundles under the benches; everyone sat knee-to-knee facing each other across the aisles. Oxygen evaporated in the van, air conditioning was only a cruel dream.

My father assessed the backseat and shook his head. He held his last leones in his hand. From my $2,000 travel money, I gave everything away, nothing left but lint in my pocket. The van swallowed more and more bags under the benches. Its roof groaned from piles of burlap bags, bundles of clothing, my three suitcases, bald tires, woven baskets, and yellow plastic gasoline containers. I wondered if the *poda-poda* would tip over. My father haggled with the driver, a smiley man with a giant grin. He styled his hair in a low-cut Afro. He wore a long-sleeved dress shirt in spite of the heat, and greasy pants. The driver's clothes could not have inspired less confidence; he looked like he had just crawled out from a long night of drinking. Finally my father said, "Sarah, I have paid the driver extra so we can sit up front."

On the pickup-style seat cushion, nicked with deep gashes, I smushed between the driver and my father, my knees contorted around the gearshift. At least we had access to the window, which my father rolled all the way down. At first, on the semi-paved roads of Bo, the drive, in spite of the outrageous heat, was manageable. But then a pothole-infested obstacle course spread before us; the van pounded up and down as if we hit severe airplane turbulence. My father seized the door handle, and I clutched my father's arm. My head skimmed inches from the van's roof when we hit a bump. If the bumps escalated any further, I could be knocked unconscious.

Red dust barreled into the van and my father and I covered our face with a rag to keep from gagging. The dustier it became, the faster the driver pressed the gas, sending the small, top-heavy van careening over craters. The chickens behind us squawked uncontrollably. My father began to wonder if the driver was on drugs or high.

"Slow down!" commanded my father.

But the driver ignored him, his face frozen in that dopey smile.

Three hours into the trip, everyone in the van was soaked in pools of sweat, which allowed red dust to adhere to every body part.

As we whizzed past the bush grasses, hitting every dirt mogul, I spotted a farmer standing in front of a stack of firewood for sale. On top of the firewood, a dead mangled animal stretched upside-down along a stick. Ropes around its arms and feet secured it.

Our driver continued another quarter mile when he slammed on his brakes. People and chickens sailed through the air. Pounding the gas and shifting roughly, the driver reversed the van down the center of the two-way road. No one knew what was happening. The driver backed up so fast that a piece of jutting wood from the farmer's woodpile scratched my father's arm, which was resting on the open windowsill.

The driver jumped out of the car, bought the dead animal, and carried it toward the front seat of the van.

"What is that animal?" I asked my father.

"A cutting grass," he said.

My throat started to pulse as the driver approached the passenger side door. "If he throws that rancid animal in the front seat . . ." Instead, the driver used the extra rope from the animal's legs and tied it to the front of the *poda-poda* like a Christmas wreath.

Jumping back into the van, the driver pressed the gas pedal to make up for lost time.

"What are you going to do with the animal?" I asked over the sound of the wind rushing the van.

"When we get to Freetown, I will put it in my soup," he said.

"Oh," I said. Did the driver not know that the heat of the engine and the sun would rot the meat into a gray paste?

Finally the green hills of Freetown rose before us. When my father and I stepped out of the van, my hair was coated in red dust along with the insides of my ears and nostrils.

"Sarah, I am so sorry we missed our bus," said my father. "I promise we will never do that again."

My father's friend Joe Bob and his son Emmanuel waved from the bus stop. We would rest at Joe Bob's house before my flight.

CHAPTER EIGHTY-THREE

Lungi Airport

My two suitcases and one carry-on rolled through Lungi Airport. Having distributed so many gifts, my suitcase flopped around with all its empty space. Instead, my carry-on bulged with precious African dresses, beaded necklaces, and woven cloth to give to my friends and family.

As I approached the airline counter, my father ran into his friend, the airport official. They chatted while I checked my bags, the only time during the entire trip that my father or a family member did not help me manage something. A very pretty woman began to tag my bags when she insisted on weighing my carry-on. "I'm sorry, you'll have to check that, it's too heavy."

"Oh, I can't check that, there are too many important things in there," I said aloud, too tired to keep my voice down, too exhausted to be savvy.

"I am sorry," and she smiled. "You need to check it."

It did not dawn on me that carry-ons are rarely weighed as long as they measure a certain size. I said, "Fine, I just need to take some stuff out." In full view of people swarming the airport I opened my suitcase and extracted my photo album of my birth mother, my camera, the video camera, my journal, and my wallet. Too tired from the *poda-poda* ride to Freetown, the ferry ride back to the airport, the seventeen-day emotional ride, I did not think to even dig out my beautiful emerald African dress or any of the handmade presents for my parents.

I checked all three bags, keeping only a backpack with the items I removed from the carry-on.

"My plane is ready to board," I said, returning to my father.

My father stared at me.

"Thank you," I said. "This trip has been a dream come true. The welcome celebration was one of the best moments of my life. I love you."

"I love you, Sarah," he said. "I will call to make sure you arrived safely."

An overwhelming sadness hit me. What would happen to my brother back in the village, sick with yellow eyes and malaria? I turned around and waved to my father. Would I ever see him again? The health issues in Sierra Leone are so severe, medicine so difficult to obtain, that two funerals occurred during my seventeen-day stay. When people die in Sierra Leone no one knows what they really die of unless it is an obvious drowning or snakebite.

I waved one final time.

As I walked across the tarmac, it hit me how easy it was to find my father, how simple to pick up the phone, buy a plane ticket, and visit. Was it so easy for a reason? I wondered if what I had witnessed—the bullet holes embedded in the school walls; the garish scars of the amputees—carried with it an ethical responsibility?

How could I listen to the amputees stories and do nothing?

I couldn't stop thinking about Hindogbae. Of all my relatives I felt a special bond with him. His shyness and elegance, his grace, and self-respect, made him a favorite friend. I was thrilled to have a brother for the first time.

I prayed my malaria pills worked for him.

Sinking into the airplane seat, physically exhausted and emotionally overwhelmed, I focused only on two things: a hot shower and my family waiting for me in Maryland.

I slept for the next twenty hours.

CHAPTER EIGHTY-FOUR

Washington, D.C.—Maryland

White-blond hair shone under the airport's fluorescent lights. Waiting by Dulles Airport's baggage carousel stood my tow-headed twin nephews, Austin and Spencer, their blue eyes aglow; my third nephew, Jonathan; my sister Lynne; and my mom and dad. A day ago, an entire continent ago, I left an ebony airport and flew across the world to a blond one.

My six-foot two-inch dad stood out in the crowd of Christmas travelers. Next to him my nephews shouted, "Aunt Sarah!"

I ran to my family.

I hugged my mom, breathing in the subtle scent of her "Poeme" perfume lingering on her sweater.

"I missed you so much!" she said squeezing me.

"Hey, Squirt," said my dad, calling me my childhood nickname, wrapping me in a giant hug, his gray beard scratching my cheek with his kiss.

"Hi, Dad! I'm so happy to see you," I said.

Holiday decorations decked the airport. Busy travelers lugging suitcases traversed the glossy floor. My dad hurried to the parking lot, retrieved the family van, and picked us up at the curb. When the glass doors of the airport slid open, a blast of frigid December air hit my face. I was thrilled to be cold!

Inside the family van, heated and plush, holiday music rang from the

CD player. Questions bombarded me from all sides, but all I could do was admire the roads—so smooth and well paved it seemed we were gliding. Even in the half-hour ride to Lynne's house, I couldn't believe how much I took for granted about life in America before my trip. I realized everyone in the car had fantastic health care and current immunizations; we drove along perfectly maintained roads where help for any emergency was only a cell phone call away; and bountiful food was available off any highway exit.

My sister jingled the keys to the front door of her house. An elegant nativity, bountiful red poinsettias, and three painted nutcrackers greeted us in the hallway. Her two dogs—Tasha, the black toy poodle, and Marley, the white Maltese—bounded down the stairs with Christmas bandanas tied around their necks that read: "Deck the halls with bones and holly!"

I thought of the mangy starving dogs in Bumpe. I rubbed Lynne's dogs' fluffy fur, both dogs well groomed and sweet smelling. My sister's dogs, with their routine checkups, inoculations, and grooming appointments had more physical care than most of the children I met in Sierra Leone.

The scent of fresh pine from the Christmas tree sent me straight to the kitchen foraging for leftover maple bacon rolls. After seventeen days in Sierra Leone, my sister's kitchen in Maryland had transformed into a palace. Christmas cookies and breads covered every counter, shiny appliances transformed food into hot or cold with the push of a button, and multiple cupboards burst with food. Her refrigerator was so densely packed it was difficult to close. Electric lights glowed all over the house. My sister walked past me. "Are you looking for these?"

She uncovered a plate of homemade rolls she saved. "I made this batch for you."

I hugged her and popped three rolls in the microwave to warm them. Each bite of the maple bacon roll released sensations of home, safety, warmth, and abundance. Everyone gathered in the kitchen around the table to hear about my trip.

"We want to hear everything!" said my mom.

"The entire village, hundreds and hundreds of people welcomed me. I wore this emerald dress . . . hold on," I said. "I want to show you . . ."

I ran to my suitcase to retrieve the green *ashobi* dress. I wanted to paint a picture of the villagers, the masked devils, the children running alongside the car, the singing, the swaying. "I have gifts for you! Jeneba and Moyitu sewed food covers. I helped pick out the cloth," I called from the foyer, kneeling before my carry-on.

I unzipped the bag, so excited to share my eight African dresses, the beaded necklaces, and all the gifts.

Nothing.

Two skirts and the one white dress from my mother's memorial service remained inside the nearly empty black-bottomed bag.

Everything else was stolen.

"I'm so sorry," I sobbed. "Everything is gone. I had all these beautiful gifts for all of you." Seventeen days of processing a continent, a new father, a village, poverty, and amputees boiled to a breaking point.

Thankfully my birth mother's photo album, the only pictures left of my mother, my camera with all my photos, and my journal were stashed in my backpack. I reached for my notebook inside the backpack and found my Aunt Doreen's telephone number in Maryland.

"Aunt Doreen," I said into the phone, my voice breaking, "everything's gone, stolen from my bag."

"What? Sarah, I'm so sorry."

I needed to tell someone who had traveled to Sierra Leone, who could relate to what I had just lost: the African clothes and the green dress, my visual connection and symbolic tie with the villagers. No single item cost much, but every gift was invested with great care. I lost my appetite for the piping hot rolls.

Deflated, I sat back down at the kitchen table with my family.

The phone rang again.

"Sarah, this is your Uncle Joe. I am so sorry. Doreen told me what happened and we will make sure you get everything back. I am sending money to Sierra Leone. We will have every single dress remade for you, every food cloth sewed again for your family."

"Uncle Joe, thank you, but that's not necessary."

"Sarah, this is what I am going to do," said Joe. As the eldest son of my grandfather, the Paramount Chief, he was in charge. If he said he would do something then that was what would happen.

I thought back to the airport, rewound the conversation with the airline representative. Was she in on the theft? Wasn't it odd to weigh a carry-on that looked normal size? Could it have been a baggage handler who stole my belongings, or was my carry-on intercepted by someone who witnessed me rifling through my bags on the floor of the airport? I knew every item was stolen in Sierra Leone because all the dresses were missing except the white memorial dress. In Sierra Leone, stealing a white funeral dress would bring very bad luck.

For a moment anger toward my father surfaced. Why did he let me go alone to the baggage check-in? Why didn't he warn me, tell me what to watch out for? Why didn't he protect me? Why wasn't he there when I needed him?

I shook my head. I wasn't being fair.

My family sat with me around the table again.

"Sarah, can I get you something to drink, some tea?" said my sister.

"Thank you," I said and took in the warmth of my family, the luck, and the blessings all around me. So much food surrounded me that I had to will myself not to overeat. Clean, disease-free water, running in hot and cold faucets all over the house was at my disposal. Electricity glowed up and down the street, lighting thousands of colorful Christmas bulbs that cascaded from neighbors' rooftops.

"You know whoever stole my stuff needs it a lot more than me," I said. "Whoever stole the gifts will sell them, make some money, and maybe feed their kids."

I called my aunt back. "Doreen, I'm really okay now. Sorry. I'm so tired. Whoever took the stuff needs it."

Instead I brought my digital camera to the table. We passed around the tiny screen as I pointed out Jeneba and Mary sewing, my father smiling, the villagers dancing, and the small boys eating glass.

CHAPTER EIGHTY-FIVE

Los Angeles

"Ladies and gentlemen, we will be landing in Los Angeles in approximately twenty minutes. Local time is 11:00 P.M. Please fasten your seat belts . . ." said the flight attendant over the loudspeaker.

A grid of lights floated below me. Nighttime Los Angeles waited. A city chock full of every kind of imaginable food. Wire after graceful electrical wire looped through the streets, illuminating the city. No wonder America sparkled like a distant dream to Third World villagers. In this metropolis of 8–9 million people, buses ran on schedule, paved roads flowed like magnificent river tributaries, medicine for stomachaches, earaches, coughs, and chest pains overflowed on shelves in pharmacies on every other street corner. Hospitals rose up into the sky, filled with doctors who delivered babies without blaming the mother and an evil witch spirit inside her if the baby struggled through a birth canal.

I could not wait to be alone in my one-bedroom apartment on North Martel Street. In the past twenty-one days, besides moments of grooming and sleep, I had not spent any alone time. I craved personal space. To think. To process what I had just experienced. Anyone who visited Sierra Leone, ventured to an amputee camp, witnessed the daily race for survival would be deeply affected by the trip, but for me, the people I left behind were family.

But before a single night alone passed in my apartment, my phone rang at three o'clock in the morning. I bolted upright in bed. Was it news about Hindogbae? Did he die?

"Hello?" I whispered.

"Hello, Serreh?" said an unfamiliar male voice.

"Yes?" I said.

"I am Jeneba's friend. Can you send me money to pay for my school fees?"

I never gave him my telephone number.

A half hour later the phone rang again.

"Hello, Serrah?" said a male voice. "I am a friend of your family. Can you send me money? My daughter is sick."

A pile of mail and bills needed to be tackled Sunday morning. Monday morning I had to teach dance. My empty refrigerator needed stocking.

My phone rang off the hook, alternating between desperate pleas from Sierra Leone and from my friends eager to hear about the trip. "Sarah! How was your trip? Was it amazing?" Everyone wanted details about the masked devils, what my father looked liked, and the ceremonies. Inside I bottled the overwhelming guilt and responsibility. I feared I would never see my father or family again.

I did not know how to speak about the young amputee woman with her baby clinging to her elongated thumb. I was embarrassed to tell friends how my number was circulating in Sierra Leone and that adults and children called at three and four o'clock in the morning. Each new plea more desperate than the last: please send money for medicine for a teenager's ulcer, for a sick baby whose stomach had distended, for a casket for a toddler who fell into an open well.

Letters began to pour in. A twelve-year-old begged for a bicycle. He had so many chores to do before school that unless he made up the time with a fast bike ride he could not attend school.

Dear Serai,

I hope you are in good health and condition is going with well in

> America mainn God centian to help you . . . I just want you to help me to have a cicyle we use to go to school because at the morning hour there are many work in the house. So at the time we fist doing my time has be lost. So if I have get the we not always last going to school. Many greeting at home. Thank.

"Let's meet for dinner," said a group of my friends and I knew the split bill would be around twenty dollars per person. Twenty dollars! Twenty dollars was half a month's pay in Sierra Leone. I could pay for a child's school fees if I didn't eat out with my friends.

Walking down Melrose Avenue, a few blocks from my apartment, store windows glittered with one-hundred-and-fifty-dollar shoes and eight-hundred-dollar cashmere dresses. The entire city burst with beautiful objects. I looked closer at a pair of shoes, a slingback sandal three inches high, dazzling with rhinestones, perfect for salsa dancing in a short dress. Could I ever buy shoes again?

As a part-time teacher and struggling actress, I wished I were more successful so that I could say yes to every single request for help. Why did I struggle to pay my own rent, cover my own health insurance, manage my own life as a single woman?

A few months passed and one of my Sierra Leonean aunts in America called asking if I would marry a Sierra Leonean friend of hers so he could become an American citizen. I stood with the phone dangling on my shoulder, mouth agape. Is this what family members do for each other?

I said, "I can't do that." Rage consumed me, but then for some idiotic reason, maybe fear she would report that I was a selfish African family member, I added, "But thank you for asking."

I set the phone down. My entire body shook.

Struggling in Los Angeles, pursuing a dream of acting, I wondered if this desire was okay when a country needed so much help? So afraid my friends and family would think badly of my African family—not understanding their poverty and desperation—I tried to protect everyone. In silence, I plastered on a smile.

My father let me know that Hindogbae was okay. Then he sent a thank you note to my parents in West Virginia.

Dear Mr. & Mrs. Culberson,

Greetings from Bumpe, Sierra Leone in West Africa.

Let me hasten to thank you for bringing up Sarah and educating her to master's level. You are indeed wonderful parents . . . God will surely bless you for making it possible for us to see Sarah after over twenty-eight years . . . Too bad they stole the gifts Sarah brought for you guys but we will try and replace them when Uncle Alie is returning to America in February. I better end here and get this to you. Good luck and may the Lord continue to bless and to supply your needs. Once again I say thanks.

With Love, Joe Konia Kposowa

I called John. "Are you getting calls in the middle of the night?" John had received letters from children asking for him to adopt them, bring them to America. They would leave their own parents to live with him. Could he please pay for their school, too?

I needed an escape, a night of forgetting so I headed to the King King in Hollywood. Red strobe lights hit the cement dance floor. A live salsa band, on a raised stage, complete with trumpets and congas boomed a rhythm. Sweating bodies packed tightly on the square of space moved, grooved to the pulsing salsa music. Every nationality seemed to be represented on that grid of electrified space. Cubans, Haitians, Salvadorians, Israelis, Guatemalans, and Mexicans mingled in the salsa rhythm.

In fact it was here at the King King that a woman approached me on the dance floor. Ana Maria Alvarez asked, "Would you mind dancing with my friend?"

"Sure," I said and danced with Fernando who led me in salsa moves as if we were gliding on ice. When we finished the dance, Ana Maria came over to me and said, "Congratulations! That was your audition. I've been watching you these last few weeks and you're an incredible dancer. I have a professional dance company called Contra-Tiempo and I'd love for you to join us."

I couldn't believe it! I'd always dreamt of being part of a professional dance company.

In a diary entry I once wrote about dance:

> When I dance I feel like I'm in a zone. My legs and my body are free, moving back and forth in my heels. I feel sexy, confidant, stunning, free, and powerful. I can kick my leg over my dance partner's head, go down in a split and then pull right back up to continue dancing. I get to be an athlete moving to music and it is sooo much fun! When I salsa dance all the stress of the day melts away. I just feel the melodic beat of music. Dancing is my outlet, my sense of freedom, and my full self-expression. Some people like to paint, others like to read, play sports, or watch TV. I am passionate about dancing. When I go dancing I love meeting new people, talking and laughing. I love to be part of a dancing community. When I let go and dance, nothing in that moment matters and I feel at peace and present. Movement connects me to the world. If I get too busy and don't have an opportunity to dance for a long period of time, I feel as if a part of me is dying.

Having recovered some energy and hope I left the King King and headed back to my tiny apartment.

I would never regret my trip to Sierra Leone, but now I had to reckon with the huge expectations placed upon me. After I contacted my birth mother's family, they sent cards on my birthday and Christmas with angels and small checks tucked inside the envelopes. What did I expect from my father's family who suffered through an eleven-year civil war? A country where malaria, typhoid fever, and cholera were still daily realities? Of course they held me accountable to help.

CHAPTER EIGHTY-SIX

Brentwood

Brentwood School asked me to write an article for the school newspaper about my trip. At first I politely declined. There was too much I wasn't ready to tell. Part of me longed to share the beautiful parts of my trip, which sustained me through the daily phone calls for money. But I was afraid if I started to talk, I would reveal the underbelly of things.

So many students wanted to hear about my trip, especially my students who were adopted. Everyone asked to see photos. I began to write in my journal and talk with one of my closest friends, Fatima, an El Salvadorian who understood the needs of relatives from a Third World country. Finally I wrote the article and included the amputees, the poverty, and how my father still needed even more money for desks. In the concluding paragraph of the article I wrote:

> "This trip to Africa has changed my life and I have learned a great deal from my journey. The most important things I've learned are to be unstoppable even in the face of fear, to know that the unknown doesn't have to be scary, to let go of the result, to always resolve relationships, and to take risks. I have a whole new family, an extraordinary addition to my life . . ."

Priorities in my life began to drastically shift. More than anything I wanted to help the children of Bumpe. But I could not do it alone. I was overwhelmed. After several meetings over the next year, John and I decided that it would take a village to save a village.

We decided to form a nonprofit organization dedicated to rebuilding Bumpe, and called it The Kposowa Foundation, after my African family. Thankfully, while I dealt with processing my two new families and coming to terms with the new expectations heaped upon me, John went into leadership gear. He did all the research, paperwork, and footwork to complete a 33-page application to obtain nonprofit tax status 501(c)(3) from the Internal Revenue Service.

We asked my father to help us coordinate efforts in Sierra Leone and my mom, Judy, became one of our first board members. John and I also invited Jerry McGonigle, my former WVU acting professor and Associate Professor, Division of Theatre, at WVU, to be a board member. We hoped The Kposowa Foundation would one day be synonymous with the words *change, hope,* and *possibility.* The application queued in the long application line at the IRS.

Our primary goal was the reconstruction of Bumpe High Boarding School so that it could regain its prominence as a "shining star of academic excellence in West Africa." Before the war, the school had more than six hundred students enrolled and was highly regarded by families in and near Bumpe, as well as those from as far away as Nigeria. We wanted to recreate what the rebels had so viciously destroyed, and help provide a place for young people to learn, thrive, and dream.

I thought about all the things I had wanted to be as a young girl: a dancer, a singer, and actress. All of those things seemed possible. In contrast, most of the young students of Bumpe High knew only a life of war and its aftermath of broken buildings, broken people, exhausted teachers, and little hope.

The one thing that everyone in Sierra Leone knows for certain is that few dreams can come true without an education. My father knew that when he went to the United States for his master's degree. He knew that when he and other teachers taught students in Bo throughout the war. He also knew that Sierra Leone would never recover from the war unless its children were able to go to school.

And that included the girls. Many families chose to send their sons to school instead of their daughters. The girls who attended school often dropped out because they were unable to manage their menstrual cycles with no bathroom facilities. Shame and embarrassment forced them to stay home once a month. Falling behind in school from the missed lessons often led to dropping out entirely.

While school was important for everyone, it helped save girls lives in a way that was different from the boys. Sierra Leone has the highest maternal mortality rate in the world: one in eight women dies from pregnancy or childbirth. But the more education a girl receives, the fewer children she has, which increases her chances of living.

I decided that if the children of Bumpe could persevere after what they had been through, nothing could stop me from trying to give back to these children.

I organized a friends and family fund-raiser carnival at Brentwood School, "Bounce for Bumpe." My dance class made the posters and came up with the name of the event. A Brentwood family donated bouncy machines, popcorn, hot dogs, and water slides. A group of seniors helped run the event. I know the Bumpe High School students would have liked to be there. They would be blown away by these gigantic bouncy machines!

We raised our first $820 for Bumpe's children. On February 3, 2006, the state of California granted us nonprofit status, allowing people to make tax-deductible contributions to further the organization's mission.

The following week, on February 15, 2006, my father contracted typhoid fever.

CHAPTER EIGHTY-SEVEN

Los Angeles

My father needed immediate medical care and not from a medicine man. With my savings, I raced to wire him money to pay a doctor in Bo. My father drank contaminated water—he did not boil it—and now he needed a Cipro intravenous drip and a series of chloramphenicol pills three times a day to keep him alive.

How many villagers who contracted typhoid were able to call a relative in the United States to send money that same day? How many children died from malaria when all they needed was a cheap mosquito net? How many women died in childbirth when they needed medical care—not a beating on the abdomen to chase away a witch?

As I dashed to transfer money to Bo, John gulped a grande black coffee in Starbucks in Studio City, California. His laptop open, he worked on the foundation Web site. We decided on Bumpenya.com after the name my Aunt Amy bestowed on me.

A few tables away from John, a pretty young woman with long, wavy brown hair, and a dusting of freckles across her face, typed with incredible focus on her white Mac laptop.

"What are you writing?" he asked.

"Oh, an article," she said.

"That sounds like the newspaper," said John.

"Well, I'm a writer for *The Los Angeles Times*."

"Really. What kind of stories?" he asked.

"Human interest," she said.

"Boy, do I have a story for you," said John, with a huge smile.

"I have to go to the bathroom, can you watch my computer?" she asked. "Then I'll hear about your story."

"Absolutely," he said.

When Kelly-Anne Suarez, a reporter at *The Los Angeles Times,* came back to the round table, John shared my story with her. He happened to have the six-minute video trailer he made about the foundation on DVD, which he gave to Kelly.

After watching the video the next day, Kelly did a background check and called the Sierra Leonean embassy to confirm the Kposowa family was a ruling family. When they confirmed all the facts, Kelly called me for an interview. With twenty-six inches allotted in the newspaper for a human interest story, she was ready to listen.

Over the next few months I met with Kelly and shared my story. First I shared the good news that my father recovered from typhoid fever thanks to the Western medicine he took. When Kelly finished the article and sent it to her editor's inbox, instead of a standard 26-inch column, she forwarded a 90-inch feature. Her copy editor titled it: "Princess Finds the Shoe Fits."

Back at Brentwood School, many of my dance students, also enrolled in an American Studies class, learned that stories placed above the fold of the newspaper's front page crease garnered the most attention and were often the most compelling.

On Friday, September 15, 2006, the story of my journey to Bumpe landed on the front page, column one of *The Los Angeles Times*. At seven thirty that Friday morning, I had not yet seen the paper, but my sixteen students brought one to class. "She's coming! She's coming!" I heard one of my students call in the doorway. The kids always said they knew when I was coming down the hallway when they heard my thunderous laugh from a mile away. When I walked into my classroom, in unison, the girls started cheering, "Above the fold! Above the fold! Ms. Culberson's above the fold!"

From that one article, picked up on the AP Wire and printed in newspapers throughout America, calls came flooding in from all over the world. "Sierra Leone?" "A rebel war?" "How can we help?" "Rebuilding a school?"

E-mail messages jammed my parents' inbox:

> "What a wonderful surprise and inspiration to read about Sarah Culberson in our local newspaper this Sunday morning . . . please provide us with information about your foundation to provide financial help for the people of Bumpe, as we wish to add it to our annual donations list . . . Jim and Jackie

> "Jim, it was nice to talk with you and learn about the project in Africa. I am most willing to put time and effort in raising money for a Rotary project as well as for the newly formed foundation . . . fill me in on your and Sarah's progress. I am looking forward to joining you and Sarah to help make their dreams come true.
>
> Kindest Regards,
>
> Sandy Burkart

John's sister, Louise Woehrle, shared the story with a contact at *Good Morning America*. Thirteen days later I flew to New York City and appeared on *Good Morning America* with Robin Roberts, *CNN* with Soledad O'Brien, and *Inside Edition* with Deborah Norville. By the time I returned to Los Angeles, $30,000 in donations had been raised to help rebuild Bumpe High School.

A sixth-grade class at Suncrest Middle School in Morgantown, West Virginia raised $700 for the rebuilding effort. The students raised the money by raking leaves, babysitting, cleaning their rooms, sweeping the kitchen, or sweeping their neighbors' steps. Along with the money they earned, they brought a note from an adult stating the work performed. The kids were so excited and proud of themselves!

Letter after letter flowed in from people who wanted to share their own adoption stories with me. Some letters requested the name of the private detective who helped find my father, some contained donations. A few checks came in for amounts as small as $5.00 with a note stating this was all that person could afford, but that he or she wanted to contribute.

Inspired, encouraged, and amazed by the outpouring of people who offered help, I could not wait for an upcoming event in Morgantown that my parents were organizing. News of my trip to Africa and my reunion with my birth father spread throughout the local community. Coming full circle with my journey, beginning as a foster child in Morgantown and now speaking to the community about my search, the father I found, and the village in Africa I hoped to help rebuild was better than my wildest dream. Although I did have another secret dream: I planned to ask my parents if they would travel with me to Sierra Leone and meet my father. After his typhoid fever scare, and the reality that 37 was the average life expectancy for a Sierra Leonean male, I wanted my two dads to meet before it was too late.

CHAPTER EIGHTY-EIGHT

Morgantown

Asking my parents to fly to Sierra Leone, endure endless hours over dangerous, almost impassable roads, and sleep in a village without running water or electricity was asking a lot. Not to mention my mom becomes horribly carsick. I needed to wait for the right moment.

John, Jerry, my mom, and I all began to brainstorm a Morgantown fund-raiser. I hoped that maybe during the planning or even at the event they would be so inspired that they would want to meet my father in Africa.

Jerry offered to produce an event, titled "Journey to Bumpe," showcasing African and Appalachian music. Jerry juxtaposed the best of percussive African music, which honored my birth father, with Appalachian music that paid tribute to my birth mother's roots in West Virginia. The fusion of these two musical forms, birthed continents apart, came together in an incredible synthesis.

Jerry also galvanized WVU's internationally recognized African Ensemble, which included percussion and dancers, to perform. He contacted musician Keith McManus, who invited four other professional Morgantown musicians to play Appalachian songs on a hammered dulcimer, a banjo, a fiddle, a guitar, and fiddle sticks.

My parents offered to coordinate all event publicity, which included contacting the local and WVU newspapers, local television stations and radio stations. All around town my parents and friends distributed specially designed posters for the event. My mom handwrote individual addresses on five hundred postcard invitations featuring pictures of my birth father and me as well as some children of Bumpe. She sent the invitations to personal friends and family, church groups, medical center faculty, Rotary Club members, WVU's theatre department, my friends and former classmates, her sister members of the Philanthropic Educational Organization that promotes women's education initiatives, and anyone else she thought might have an interest in the evening.

My parents put up their own money to rent, for just under $1,000, the historic Metropolitan Theatre, a beautiful neoclassical revival building first opened in 1924. Bob Hope, Bing Crosby, and Helen Hayes all once graced the stage of the old-fashioned theater, now registered on the National Register of Historic Places.

Jerry's wife, Teresa, contacted local groups to prepare African food at the event. My mom contacted the women in her P.E.O. Group, Chapter P, who offered to bake cookies to give away.

Admission was donation-based.

The week of the event I spoke at my elementary school and Cheat Lake Middle School, where American Homes of Morgantown and Clear Mountain Bank sponsored a Read Aloud fund-raiser at the school donating 25¢ for every book a student read. Two thousand books later, the young students raised $500 for Bumpe High School. I also spoke at Suncrest Middle School and at my dad's Rotary Club.

At the schools, adopted children came up to me and shared how they wanted to find their parents. I always tell adopted children to wait until they are older to search in case the person he or she longs to connect with is not ready, and may never be ready, to have him or her in their life. Parents are human and may come with deep flaws as well as wonderful surprises.

I warned them they might not get a warm welcome. Some people's pasts are very painful. Just because a child is ready to search does not mean a parent or relative is ready to welcome that child into his or her life.

It is painful to accept rejection at any age, but as a younger child I am sure any rebuff would have been devastating. As it was, only as an adult was I able to process the new information I learned about both my birth parents and about myself. If I had discovered either parent at an earlier age, or as a teenager, it may have caused a great deal of confusion at a time that was already complicated enough.

When the kids asked me about being from a royal family, I showed them pictures of the poverty in Sierra Leone and the destroyed buildings still rotting from the rebels' rage. I shared that for me, the word "princess" means a responsibility to help others.

The night of the event, Wednesday, November 15, 2006, a steady rain made the night even cooler. The board deliberately chose a weeknight, hoping to attract more people who might already have weekend commitments. My mom thought, "If only a hundred people come it will be good."

Edith Vehse, the choir director at my church, loaned her late husband's collection of African flags to adorn the theater. Multicolored flags hung high from the balcony added gorgeous rainbows to the event. Exotic African woven cloths—capulanas and java prints—angled over the tables created a backdrop for donated platters of African food. Fried plantains with roasted peanuts; a *nhopi* dip made with squash, cream, and brown sugar; coconut cakes called *bolinhos de coco;* and puff puff with coconut all graced the table.

Nine platters of seventy-five dozen homemade cookies, including snickerdoodles, molasses crinkles, bourbon balls, petite pecan tarts, thumbprint jam cookies, and seven-layer bars, anchored another table. Fifteen of my mom's friends baked the cookies from scratch.

I arrived a few hours early, wearing my emerald *ashobi* dress. Just as my Uncle Joe promised, a duplicate was sent from Bumpe to replace the stolen one. Inside the theater, Jerry's team of professionals checked lights and sound. A stage manager spoke with the musicians tuning their eclectic instruments backstage. A huge movie screen descended from the top of the theater to showcase John's six-minute documentary trailer about Bumpe. West Virginia University student volunteers readied themselves as ushers. The cover of the programs my parents made featured the outline of the state of West Virginia connected by an undulating wave to Sierra Leone on the African continent.

Down in the dressing rooms, I applied makeup for the stage. I looked at myself in the mirrors with giant light bulbs surrounding me; the mirror was a far cry from my birth father's jagged mirror in his Bumpe bedroom. And yet I was here, ready to share with the community what I witnessed and learned in Sierra Leone . . .

. . . if anyone showed up.

The theater opened at seven o'clock at night for the seven-thirty performance. When I came back upstairs so many familiar faces from my childhood walked through the door: my elementary school teachers; my high school teachers; a former high school principal; my classmates from school as far back as kindergarten; basketball teammates from high school; my childhood hairdresser's sister-in-law; my childhood dentist; choir members from church; my parents' friends; Aunt Fran and Uncle Paul; my sisters' friends; and my father's friends in the Rotary Club. My sister Laura and her daughter Mackenzie flew in from Illinois; my sister, Lynne drove three-and-a-half hours in the rain; John flew in from Los Angeles.

Over seven hundred and fifty people attended in spite of the rain.

My parents welcomed the crowd. My mom spoke first,

> "Good evening! Thank you for being here. Thank you for sharing this journey. It's wonderful to look around and see our community. We've lived here for thirty-eight years. We've loved living here, and we've loved watching our children grow up in this community. We've watched many of your children grow up, too. We're very grateful for all of the special people and special opportunities they've all had to grow and be all that they can be . . . Thanks so much for being here to share Sarah's journey."

My dad also spoke:

> "Good evening. As soon as Judy and I learned about this remarkable journey Sarah is on, especially The Kposowa Foundation for rebuilding the school, we immediately wanted to get Morgantown in

on the fun—for two reasons. First, it all started here and second, because you are all the players in this drama! Many of you out there have played a big role in Sarah becoming who and what and where she is. Judy and I really do believe that it takes a village to raise a child, and we have always felt really good about the village that helped us with ours [Morgantown!].

Whatever you may have heard before, we actually have three princesses, our three daughters, who have spent the majority of their lives here in Morgantown and who got off to a great start as a result of those early years. I want you to meet them now, seated down in front. They are gone from Morgantown now, scattered from coast-to-coast, but each one of them—in her own way—is building community where she is, and is helping to raise the village kids. So Sarah's experience is slightly different as an adopted child, it now develops that she has two whole 'extra' villages to look to, and when she did that—well—one of them turned out to be a real village! But I am getting ahead—You all have come here tonight to hear her tell her story, not to listen to me. We are very proud to introduce our daughter, Sarah Culberson."

Right before I spoke the Appalachian musicians took center stage. Bob Shank played the hammered dulcimer; of Celtic origin, this incredible instrument resembles the inside strings of a piano played with two small hammers. A banjo and fiddle accompanied him.

Suddenly one of the Appalachian musicians walked off the stage and put down his fiddle sticks. He returned tapping a *jembe*, a large African drum hung around his neck. Shaped like a wooden goblet with goat skin stretched over the hollowed-out lenke hardwood, it vibrates high-pitched, defined, sharp sounds. A flat, flush hand on the goat skin, stretched to a high tension, produces a longer sound. A slap across the skin produces a quicker snapping tone. Slowly the musician tapped an African beat—slaps and tones—with his hands, harmonizing with the Appalachian songs.

A second percussionist, Gordon Nunn, the director of the ensemble, joined the jam with a *dundun*, a type of bass drum from the Mende region played with a stick. Gordon, on his four trips to Mali and Guinea, hand-selected all the drums used on stage for the performance.

Appalachian fiddlers jammed with African drummers and created a new rhythm, a harmonious blend singing the odyssey of a Sierra Leonean man who created a child with a West Virginian woman.

Back in Bumpe, music connected me to the chorus of African women welcoming me. Again, music now brought together two worlds into one beat, electrifying the theater.

The entire WVU African Ensemble dancers thrilled the audience by performing four African dances: the *Yankadi*, *BoBoobo*, *Didadi*, and *Kpanlongo*. Barefeet shook the wooden floorboards.

When the stage cleared I walked into the spotlight. I spoke to the village that raised me. I thanked my parents who gave me the safety net and love to begin the search. In my journal I wrote about that moment so I would never forget:

> As I stood on the Met stage I could feel the warmth and love surrounding me. There was a sea of people in the seats, on the floor, and in the balcony above me. The stage was brightly lit and the faces in the crowd became dim and my throat tightened with emotion. Tears gushed from my eyes as I began to speak, "It is such an honor to be with all of you this evening . . . you have no idea the gift you have given me being here tonight and you have no idea, the difference just by being here, that you are making for the lives of the people in Sierra Leone."
>
> I shared that when I came home to my new family, the Culbersons, I was wearing a green dress with a butterfly on it. I spoke about meeting my birth father, who gave me this beautiful green dress to wear while entering the village. In that moment I said to everyone, "I just realized that I had on a green dress when I was first adopted and then I was wearing a green dress when I was welcomed to Bumpe." I couldn't believe it.
>
> As I stood up there sharing with everyone, we laughed

> together and we cried together. We became one. I was completely humbled by the honor of having the village that I knew so well in front of me. All of my fears of being rejected, left out, overlooked, not good enough, left in that moment.
>
> I didn't need to prove anything or be the best. I just allowed myself to be vulnerable and share myself and share about the work that we are doing in Sierra Leone, and that was enough.

For the finale, dancers with bodies as limber as puppets slammed the stage. I jumped into the dance, performing the African dance moves I had studied. The Appalachian musicians circled back on stage, joining all of us. The entire stage surged with the beats of Appalachian and African music into one mass of rhythm, laughter, and joy.

That evening we raised $20,418 to help rebuild Bumpe High School. My mom wrote handwritten thank you notes to every single person who donated. But with all the excitement and chaos of my last few days in Morgantown, I still hadn't found the right moment to propose the most important question. I flew back to Los Angeles without asking my parents if they would meet my father in Africa.

CHAPTER EIGHTY-NINE

Los Angeles

"Mom, I need to talk to you. Can you get Dad on the phone, too?" I said, sitting alone in my kitchen.

"Okay, I'll go get him. Hang on a minute," said my mom.

Sitting straight in the wooden dining chair, I stared at the half-melted candle pillar on the table. The rust-colored candle still smelled of spices. I fiddled with the hard wax, breaking off chunks, waiting for both my parents to pick up the phone.

Traveling to Sierra Leone to meet my father was a lot to ask my parents. Even at twenty-eight years old, I came home exhausted from Bumpe with a messed-up digestive tract. My parents were in their mid-sixties. Although my parents had traveled extensively, worked on service projects in several developing countries, and had taken the entire family around the world to eight countries during my dad's 1978 sabbatical, Sierra Leone was not an easy destination. The twenty-five-hour flight to Sierra Leone was the most luxurious part of the journey compared to traveling within the country. Once we landed, the dangerous roads, with no ambulance, paramedics, police, or firefighters to aid in a calamity presented a huge problem. When it came to car accidents in Sierra Leone, a traveler was either lucky or dead. No toilets, no running water, and no electricity for over two weeks would not be easy on anyone. However, if my first dream was meeting my father, my second dream was for my parents to meet him, too.

I began pacing the tan-carpeted apartment. Not only did I need to ask them if they would go, but I also needed to tell them I was leaving.

"Hi, Squirt," said my dad. "I'm here."

I sank down onto the black leather sofa. "Mom and Dad, I need to share a few things with you. First, I'm going back to Sierra Leone this April, in three-and-a-half weeks."

"Oh," said my parents.

"We need to check on the high school's construction. Plus, John has done all the research and work to set up an NGO [a nongovernmental organization] in Freetown for the foundation. If we set up an NGO under the Sierra Leonean Ministry of Education, bank transfer fees drop and more money goes to the rebuilding of the school."

"Okay," said my parents, surprised.

"I'm only going for ten days, but the NGO is really important."

"Are you going alone?" asked my dad with a tremor of concern in his voice.

"No, John and an American cameraman, Bill Carlson, will come, too. John wants to oversee the NGO, and he wants to film the Kono diamond-mining district. One of the areas of most intense fighting during the war."

"Wow," said my parents, processing this sudden information.

"We're also dropping off medical supplies to an American doctor who founded a medical clinic." In Kono, John and I planned to meet a young American medical student, Dan Kelly, from Albert Einstein College of Medicine who, at only twenty-five years old, had founded Global Action Foundation. Working with a Sierra Leonean doctor, Mohamed Bailor Barrie, in Kono while on a Global Health Fellowship, he was raising funds to build a medical facility, and worked in a medical clinic treating countless people a day.

"Besides April, there is one other time to travel to Sierra Leone. In December the rainy season ends. Would you both come with me then to meet my father and family? It would mean so much to me if you could meet," I asked, and held my breath.

Silence hung on the phone lines.

"I don't want you to miss Christmas or anything," I said. "We could all go mid-December and be back in time for Christmas Eve with everyone."

"Well, Sarah . . . ," said my dad.

". . . I know it's a lot to ask. I don't want it to be too much for you, but . . ."

My mom chimed in. "We would love to go with you, Sarah. We know how much this means to you. Give us some time to think about this and go over our schedules, okay?"

"Really?" I said.

"Really," said my mom.

"I've always wanted to go to Sierra Leone," said my dad.

"So it's a possibility?" I said.

"Absolutely," said my mom.

"You guys are amazing! You know there are some great hotels in Freetown to rest up before the journey to Bumpe."

A friend told me the Barmoi Hotel just west of the city was like an oasis. He reminded me that Europeans used to flock to Sierra Leone before the war to enjoy the wide beaches. White sand stretched for miles as crystal water lapped its shores. Exquisite food served at the upscale hotels included barracuda marinated in sweet sauces with mango, banana fritters and red snapper, and giant lobsters—as long as a man's torso.

"We could all see the progress of the school. Dad, you could check out the wells for the Rotary Club, too."

"We will strongly consider this. Give us some time to see if we can work out the details," said my dad.

CHAPTER NINETY

Sierra Leone

Three weeks later I left for Sierra Leone with John and Bill. After successfully setting up the NGO in Freetown, we wanted to document what changes occurred in Bumpe. Almost a year and a half earlier, my father said habitable classrooms were the most immediate needs for Bumpe High School. Gratefully he gushed over the phone lines how wired funds fixed the bullet-shattered windows, added zinc roofs to the open-air buildings, hung doors in the jambs that rebels had burned for firewood, hired local carpenters to build desks and chairs, which all simultaneously stimulated the local economy and helped reduce the area's 70 percent unemployment rate. The foundation's annual report required before-and-after documenting where funds had made the greatest difference.

When we arrived back in Bumpe, gleaming blue and white school buildings, matching the students' blue-and-white uniforms, stood before us. Five classrooms, completely rebuilt, boasted shiny coats of paint, smooth cement floors, working windows, stable desks, and solid chairs for the students. Walking into the new library, I could not believe my eyes. Rows and rows of books, textbooks, encyclopedias, and novels were stacked from the floor to the ceiling on newly constructed shelves. Long tables grouped in the middle of the room provided a place for the students to study. Vinyl tiles placed over the cement floor lent the library a Byzantine flair, sanctifying it as one of the most important buildings on campus.

"Sarah, your friend gave us the books," said my father.

"Excuse me?" I said. No one I knew donated books.

A woman named Dr. Nancy Peddle from Chicago, who worked in Sierra Leone and who was evacuated out of Sierra Leone during intense rebel fighting, founded the LemonAid Fund for people who manifest "indomitable spirit" and "turn the lemons of life into lemonade." When my father was in Freetown, he heard an American lady had books for schools; he visited Nancy and she gave him over 300 books for Bumpe High School. LemonAid Fund then gathered and shipped 28,000 pounds of books to Freetown for Sierra Leone's children. Oprah's Global Fund for Children's Books also donated to the effort. LemonAid Fund has since given sports equipment, school furniture, and mattresses to Bumpe High School.

A diary entry I wrote during that trip:

> After we finished the NGO we traveled to meet Dr. Kelly and Dr. Barrie. They were holding an open clinic at the home of an amputee. There were people lined up around the house eager to be seen by the two doctors. When we arrived they put me to work. They taught me how to take the blood pressures and the temperatures of all the patients. There were many older people with high blood pressure and children who were sick and malnourished. It was incredible what Dan and Dr. Barrie were providing for the community.
>
> After the clinic we went to the mining area where workers were panning for diamonds in deep muddy chocolate milk–like water up to their waists. I couldn't believe how hard they were working in the hot Africa sun in the hope of finding a dream diamond.
>
> After spending a couple of days in Kono we went to Bumpe to see everyone. When we arrived at the school we were met by the students. Bright, newly painted buildings rose behind the students. Bumpe High school is a pillar of hope. As I stood there in the library with tears in my eyes, I saw

that it takes a team to make a difference. I thought of people who donated from all over the world. But there was much more work to do: the home economics building, the dining hall, the bathrooms with the septic tank still needed to be built. I could feel my head spinning. I had to stop myself and remind myself of the miracle that was occurring right in front of me. I just met my father and now we all get to work with him to rebuild a school that will impact the future of this country. After all of these years filled with fear about finding my father, I never dreamed it could end up like this.

A little girl about the age of four came up and took my hand as we looked at the school. She had dark skin and little cornrows braided in her hair. I asked her name and she didn't speak English. Her mother was close by and I asked, "What's your beautiful little girl's name?"

"Blessing."

I gave the little girl a hug.

When I returned after my ten-day whirlwind trip, I called my parents.

"Mom and Dad, you will not believe what is happening in Bumpe! Entire buildings are being rebuilt! You guys have to see this!"

"Sarah, we've made our final decision. As long as we all buy travelers' medical evacuation insurance and can be airlifted to medical help . . . our answer is YES!"

CHAPTER NINETY-ONE

Los Angeles

I sent the first list of items to pack. At the top of my list (learning from my airport experience) *padlocks*.

1. Padlocks
2. Snacks you would like, Cheez-It, granola bars, snacks that won't melt etc.
3. Tight-to-the-body money pouch that you can strap on underneath your clothes
4. Bug repellent
5. Lots of wet wipes (antibacterial)
6. Imodium AD
7. Malaria pills
8. Towels/washcloths
9. Comfortable shoes
10. Sunscreen

My mom, a former elementary school teacher, believed our trip was also an opportunity to bring school supplies to the children whose bare cinder-block classrooms did not sport a toy, book, game, or even a poster.

My mom and dad brought two fifty-pound bags each, plus two carry-ons of supplies they purchased themselves. One of my mom's fifty-pound bags contained:

pencils

spiral notebooks (paper)

coloring books

colored pencils

pencil sharpeners

A set of fourth-grade reading books from the elementary school where my mom taught (Woodburn Elementary School).

A complete collection of Curious George stories, an (eighteen-inch) Curious George doll, a Curious George game, and a Curious George calendar (to be presented to Mary for her class of three-, four-, and five-year-olds).

Family, friends, and neighbors also asked to contribute to the gifts being brought over. My sister Laura's daughter, ten-year-old Mackenzie, wanted to give her extra Halloween candy to the children of Bumpe. She called me about this. I said sending over hard candy would be fine, but chocolate would melt. I shared that anything delivered had to be safe for the children and easy enough for my parents to carry. She wrote a letter by herself, which she printed on lavender paper with an African-style border. Mackenzie passed the letter to fifteen neighbors.

My name is Mackenzie and my aunt is . . . going back to Africa with my grandparents in December. I recently talked to her and she can bring candy, toys, or even just clothes to the kids in Africa. Now these items to these kids bring so much joy in their hearts. We would appreciate it if you could donate some items but you don't have to. But since Halloween is coming up this week if you have any extra candy or any leftover from giving out (and no chocolate please, it melts) Aunt Sarah could deliver it to the children. Also, the toys must be small, something that could fit in a suitcase like McDonald's toys in Happy Meals or card games things like that would be so amazingly wonderful if you could and nothing with batteries either. She can take clothes from something special your child has grown out of or even you yourself. We do not need shoes. Please do not send anything with glass, anything that will frighten the children, anything that is broken, can't be used, or can harm them. If you have any questions, comments or donations please do not hesitate to call or e-mail. We would like to have all the donations by Thanksgiving. Thank you for reading my paper and thank you if you are giving donations. These items bring many smiles to these children's faces.

From Mackenzie

Mackenzie collected candy, stuffed animals, and little blue jeans to add to my parent's already bursting suitcases.

With my parents preparing for the trip in mid-December 2007 and my entire family contributing in some way, I thought of how far the word forgiveness had carried me. In a later diary entry I wrote:

> I have a whole new life now. My purpose has become clear to me after letting go of my anger. I let go of a twenty-eight-year-old story of hating my father. Inside of letting that go I have the honor and the privilege to share my families and share about the people of Sierra Leone. I have the opportunity to get over my petty fears and think about how to contribute to the people of Bumpe and all of Sierra Leone. Wars start with people being angry and right and unwilling to forgive. We want leaders in our world to

stop war and yet we are unwilling to stop our own wars in our heads.

Inside of forgiveness, no matter what the other person does or doesn't do, there is freedom. I've learned not to be attached to the results because we never know what can happen. The results can often be more magnificent than anything we can imagine. Our minds only go so far. We have no idea the possibilities that can open up!

CHAPTER NINETY-TWO

Freetown

Flying from Los Angeles, I arrived in Sierra Leone two hours earlier than my parents. Already I worried that the airport would be difficult for them. Lungi Airport's baggage claim resembled nothing close to American airports, where orderly, albeit slightly annoyed passengers wait for their suitcases. At worst, in the States, an occasional line-cutter or interloping carriage snuck to the front of the baggage belt, but it rarely, if ever, degenerated into a free-for-all. I prayed my parents would arrive on time and we would soon be snug in the waiting cars, removed from the baggage melee, safe across the waters on the overcrowded ferry, and tucked into our hotel rooms.

Outside the airport, my father's friend, Joe Bob, waited for our group with two SUVs. My father did not meet us at Lungi. We had insisted that he stay and meet us in Bumpe since we planned to stay in Freetown for a few days. He arranged for a driver to take an SUV from Bumpe to pick us up. We planned to meet in the village, where he prepared his home for seven overnight visitors. My mom, dad, my boyfriend, Von, and I planned this journey together.

Von, of Persian descent, sported a shaved head and a little soul patch under his lip. Many people mistook him for someone of Indian descent. Von would need to return from Sierra Leone a few days before me to get back to his child and work. Hana, Von's eight-year-old daughter, wanted to give the children in Sierra Leone something special just from her. She picked out a few of her favorite summer dresses to give away, one a beautiful rich mango color with thin delicate straps and bows on the shoulders. Two of her cherished, colorful sun hats, one the color of a ripe strawberry, another with red hibiscus flowers in bloom, were hand-selected to give away.

Von flew to Sierra Leone with my parents after meeting them in London. Von's sister, Taraneh Salke, Executive Director of the Family Health Alliance (FHA), also traveled with us. Taraneh was assessing the medical services in Sierra Leone and considering implementing new health programs through FHA, which focuses on practitioner education to decrease maternal and neonatal mortality and morbidity.

Another friend I knew from Los Angeles, Yeniva Sisay, planned to meet us in Freetown. Originally born in Sierra Leone, she recently moved back to Sierra Leone to teach and help combat the country's "brain drain." With such high unemployment rates, many of the best and brightest young students moved away to London and the United States. Also in our group, an American filmmaker, Adisa, accompanied us to capture the moment my parents met my father. We all planned to rest in Freetown for three days before attempting the six-hour caravan over the roads to Bumpe.

Our first morning in Freetown, the news buzzed on the streets and in our hotel. *The Amistad*, a replica of the infamous slave ship from 1839, just sailed into Freetown having traveled across the Atlantic from New Haven, Connecticut on *The Atlantic Freedom Tour.* Commemorating the 200th anniversary of the British abolishment of the Atlantic slave trade in 1807, and in the United States in 1808, this replica—with two diesel engines added—sailed into Freetown's harbor, representing the mid-point of a 14,000-mile journey celebrating freedom. The ship served as a traveling classroom with its theme titled "Confronting the Past, Transforming the Future." We decided to visit the ship after breakfast.

Our entourage moved closer to the cement wharf where the vessel docked. Large crowds massed in rows twenty people deep, all standing in line, waiting to tour the reconstructed ship. The original *La Amistad,* once held fifty-three slaves—forty-nine men, and four children (three little girls and one small boy)—all captured from Sierra Leonean villages.

Standing before the ship, its hull bumpered with rubber tires along the wharf, I marveled at the tall masts and rigging. Its significance hit me with great force. In 1839 the slave Sengbe Pieh led a rebellion against a life of slavery. As a Mende rice farmer, he was wrested from his wife and three children in his village by slave traders. When Sengbe and the fifty-two other Africans were being transferred between Cuban ports, he led a rebellion that killed *The Amistad*'s captain and forced the two Spanish plantation owners onboard to navigate the ship back to Africa. Instead a violent storm swept the vessel up the American shoreline as far as Long Island, New York. The U.S. Navy took the ship into custody, imprisoned the Africans, and an explosive national trial ensued.

Abolitionists declared the Africans, captured illegally, were free men who deserved to be returned home. Opposing groups, including United States President Martin Van Buren, asserted the ship fell under Spanish jurisdiction and the Africans should be returned to Cuba where slavery or death waited.

American abolitionists called upon former president and lawyer John Quincy Adams to join their freedom cause. The national case soon became known as "The trial of one president by another." John Quincy Adams spoke for four and a half hours in defense of the Africans to the United States Supreme Court. His impassioned and noble defense of the Africans and of the rights of men earned him the nickname "Old Man Eloquent." The verdict on March 9, 1841 declared unequivocal freedom for the Mende captives. Mid-January 1842, the thirty-five surviving Africans, along with five American missionaries, after a long voyage, arrived back in Freetown to create a mission.

The two masts on the hundred-and-twenty-nine-foot-long schooner, piloted by a black American captain for this leg of the trip's tour, rose high in the air waving the Sierra Leonean flag. Bright green, white, and periwinkle blue flapped in the gorgeous December sky. On the second mast the American flag waved its stars and stripes. The masts were made from Leonean timber, hauled to Mystic Harbor in Connecticut for construction.

The Amistad's American captain, William Pinkney, came over to say hello to our group on the wharf. Not only did Bill sail the replica ship into Freetown, but in 1992 he became the first black man to sail solo around the world. At seventy-one years old he radiated incredible energy and charisma. With his white beard, red shirt, baseball cap, and small gold hoop earring, he looked every inch an old salt.

We peppered the captain with questions about the replica ship. Meanwhile the crowds, frustrated with the lines, impatient from the slow pace of the tours, started breaking the lines. With such a high rate of unemployment and so little public amusements, the ship attracted great crowds. Guards began hitting the crowd with sticks to control the forward rush. Elementary school children in green polo shirts started streaming off the boat. Their teachers protectively guided them off to the side until the crowds ebbed behind the guards' rope.

Walking alongside the boat, we did not set foot on its decks; too many people stood in line before us. Already the boat hosted a second group of schoolchildren. We were grateful to meet the impressive captain and salute the symbolic ship.

In a strange way my own life was influenced by *The Amistad*. The missionaries who came to Sierra Leone with the returning Africans began the first mission post. These missions, later appropriated by the United Brethren in Christ, were the forerunners of the schools all over the country. My father was educated in mission schools. Without graduating from a mission school he never could have come to America where he met my mother.

CHAPTER NINETY-THREE

Road to Bumpe—December 2007

Seven o'clock the next morning my mom slid her elastic, motion sickness bands on both wrists. Half an inch of gray material promised to help my mom endure the six hours of rugged roads ahead. She nibbled on snippets of bread to fill her stomach instead of eating anything that might exacerbate nausea. Even though my five foot one mom was the tiniest of the SUV's passengers, my dad, Adisa, and Taraneh all insisted she sit up front in the passenger seat where some of the bouncing might be lessened. Our caravan set off to Bumpe. Following behind my parents' SUV, I sat with Von, my friend Yeniva, and a Leonean cameraman, George.

We first snaked through Freetown's bumper-to-bumper city traffic, past the blasting music from market stalls, past the woman walking with (we counted) six stacked fruit baskets on top of her tiny head, past the sidewalk vendor selling sneakers—a parked car his makeshift display, each athletic shoe part of a neat line traveling across the hood of the dirty vehicle, up the windshield, and on the roof.

Just as we hit the outskirts of the city, a honking entourage forced us to the side of the road as they zoomed past. The newly elected president of Sierra Leone, Ernest Bai Koroma and his bodyguards, ministers, and soldiers whizzed past us in procession toward Bo for a conference. Our drivers in both cars pulled over immediately to let the government caravan pass. For the next five hours we thought nothing more of the president's cavalcade.

Instead we all leaned into the hills, learned not to fight the bumps. However, when the SUV slammed down from a rogue mogul, nothing could be done. If my family even for a split second wondered if I had exaggerated the size of the potholes or the bumps—no one doubted me now.

Only a few miles outside of Bo, I breathed a sigh of relief. The dirt roads now interlaced with more and more friendly patches of pavement. We planned to fill the cars with gas and then continue on the final leg of the trip to Bumpe. Prematurely, I called my father from my cell phone outside of Bo and said we would arrive within an hour and a half, now that we were minutes from Bo.

As we rolled closer to Bo, our caravan hit traffic. Our two SUVs descended into a massive presidential parade with twenty thousand demonstrators cheering for the newly elected president. Endless rows of people lined the two-way streets. Groups of people marched down the roads, flowing in and out of cars. They carried banners and shouted for the president. Women in matching *ashobi* dresses, clad in fiery red *lappas* with tie-dye yellow suns in the middle of the fabric, pushed through the crowd. Banner after banner filled the air. One banner read:

> "Members of the Staff of the Ministry
> of Mineral Resources, Southern Region,
> Welcome his Excellency, Ernest Koroma,
> Long Live the President."

Blaring horns ricocheted through the packed *poda-poda* buses; passengers adhered to every surface. Fifteen people squatted on top of a van, while other men held tight to a bar on the back of the moving vehicle. Young boys hung out car windows. Flatbed trucks crammed with people sputtered along the road. Men jumped up and down trying to glimpse the president through the rows of people. Vehicles parked in the grass alongside of the road sunk into the dirt from the weight of the people standing on the roofs. A group of women, all dressed in peacock-colored dresses waved their hands in the air toward the government cars. Another group wore matching white T-shirts with the president's face emblazoned on them. A single masked devil twirled through the marchers. Musicians blew into long, hollowed wooden logs creating low Indian flute sounds that contrasted with the beating drums. For the next few miles, the only way out of the parade was through it. Although a celebration, there was no way to remove ourselves from the melee. Thousands of people swarmed in every direction.

Traffic came to a complete stop when the president's bodyguards ran back into a long, green flatbed army truck covered with army canvas. Forty-five fully armed soldiers in camouflage with AK-47s ran up the truck ramp.

Just as we spotted the running soldiers, the SUV carrying my parents jolted to a halt. The back, left, Goodyear tire hit a sharp object and deflated into a rubbery mess. The driver exited the car to assess the damage. Our car pulled behind them in the middle of the densest part of the parade.

Suddenly one of the armed government soldiers ran up to our car with his AK-47 thumping into his chest.

"MOVE! MOVE! GET OUT THE ROAD!" he shouted.

The Sierra Leonean driver tried to explain our situation. He pointed to the deflated tire.

"MOVE! MOVE!" the soldier shouted. Another soldier walked over and stood beside the first soldier.

The soldiers did not like us blocking the flow of traffic. Our driver backed our car off the road onto the grass behind my parents' SUV.

Now that both vehicles were as far off the road as possible, the soldiers left us alone. Unfortunately my parents' SUV, packed with over three-hundred pounds of luggage, made changing the tire even more difficult. The driver, with his hand jack, slid under the overheated car and cranked the impossibly heavy load. He unbound a single spare tire strapped to the roof of the car.

A flat-bed truck wobbled past us carrying men and women in yellow-and-black zebra-striped matching clothes. Attached to the truck, a banner read: Agricultural and Food Security.

My dad waved at the people in the open truck. Then he looked up at the sky and said, "Look, Sarah, a Black Kite!"

In the middle of this crazy fray, my dad, an avid bird-watcher, noticed a single beautiful fork-tailed bird of prey.

Taking advantage of the forty-five-minute delay, Von and the Sierra Leonean video cameraman, George, began filming the parade. Suddenly, from behind us, a scream reeled toward our group. Thirty men with machetes, sticks, and axes marched in a pack. Their leader, waving a stick, ran up to our moored, defenseless cars. His bloodshot eyes bulged as he screamed to George and Von, "HEY, YOU! STOP IT THERE! I TELL YOU THIS ONE TIME! DO NOT FILM US! PUT THE CAMERA AWAY RIGHT NOW! DO NOT TAKE OUR PICTURE!"

George put the video camera away and warned Von that these people were dangerous.

"DON'T TAKE OUR PICTURES!" the man screamed again in accented English.

Von put away his camera. George explained to our group that these men were part of a secret society rumored to inhale cocaine, alcohol, and marijuana before a march. If threatened they were known to throw itching power, "magical powder," over a victim's skin causing welts, bleeding, burns, and lacerations.

With warning enough for all of us, we stopped filming until the tire was fixed, then we loaded back into the two cars. We continued down the road to a gas station, the last one before the final leg to Bumpe. At the gas station I marveled at the strangest old-fashioned gas pump I had ever seen.

"Look, Von, that pump is so cool. Can you take a picture of it?"

Just as I said that, my cell phone dropped on the ground. Out of nowhere a boy whizzed passed, nabbed it, and dashed down the road.

Both Sierra Leonean drivers darted off on foot running after the thief. They took the SUV keys with them. We were left alone in the two parked SUVs at the gas station. All the van windows were stuck wide-open with no way to roll them up without the keys.

With Von's back turned away from the crowds, he shot pictures of the pump. Adisa and my dad stood by the gas station waiting for the drivers and for the old-fashioned crank to fill the tanks. The pump consisted of a single, long lever attached in the middle of a circle that needed to be cranked back and forth in a continuous motion to release gas.

Being distracted, Von did not realize that the end of the parade had caught up with us, now only a few feet behind our two helpless SUVs. The marching male secret society spotted Von's camera and believed their image was being captured again. The leader, swinging his stick, eyes possessed, ran up to Von. Inches from his face, spitting and infuriated he yelled, "I TOLD YOU LAST TIME . . . !"

Adisa and George ran over to lend support against the enraged leader. Some of the Sierra Leonean gas station attendants also came over.

"Dad! Get in the car," I called to my dad who was standing off to the side. My dad and I slid inside the second car with Yeniva.

"Okay, okay," said Von to the leader, slowly lowering the camera. The man continued to scream in his face.

"YOU TAKE ONE MORE PICTURE AND WE WILL TAKE AGGRESSIVE ACTION AT YOU!" Veins throbbed in the leader's temples.

Adisa said, "We understand, brother. We got it. All respect due."

The leader kept yelling, "YOU CANNOT DO THIS. THIS IS AN ABOMINATION!"

While the situation exploded by the pumps, a second member of the secret society, carrying a very sharp decorated axe with ribbons hanging off the handle, approached the parked SUV. My mom sat in the front passenger seat and Von's sister, Taraneh, sat behind her. All the power windows in the car were rolled down.

With his gleaming, sharp axe, the glazed-eyed man approached Taraneh in the backseat. His hands reached inside the vehicle.

Taraneh, who has lived with nomads in the Kurdistan Region of Iran, spent five years in rural Afghanistan helping women, and worked extensively in other Third World countries, stayed cool. "Hello," she said. "What a wonderful event for the president. This music is great, everything is so beautiful."

"I am your brother," said the axe man with his hand still hovering inside the car.

"Yes, and I am your sister," she said.

Suddenly our driver ran back to the car (without the cell phone) and shouted at the ax man, "Move away from the car! Move away!"

The axe man next darted up to Von, Adisa, and George, still standing by the pumps. His incensed leader finally left them alone after spitting obscenities in Von's face.

The axe man said to Von, "Hey, brother. It's okay. I bless you!" Then he knelt down and placed the blade of the axe flat on Von's foot. Then he kissed the axe. "I bless you," said the axe man. He repeated the laying of the axe on Adisa's foot. Then he said, "Give me money."

Von reached into his pocket, took out 5000 leones (US$1.66) and handed it to the man.

"Thank you, sir," said the man. He rejoined his secret society, which had continued marching down the street.

"George, what was that about?" asked Adisa.

"The axe man cleared the evil spirits," said George.

With everyone safely back in the two SUVs, we continued through the parade.

CHAPTER NINETY-FOUR

Bumpe

I never thought I would be eager to drive along the road from Bo to Bumpe, a path so poorly maintained that my father prayed every time we traveled it. But after two hours stuck in a presidential parade, relief embraced me when we bumped along the dragway inching closer and closer to seeing my father.

Finally around four thirty in the afternoon, three-and-a-half hours late, we crossed the metal bridge over the Tabe River into Bumpe. Hot, hungry, and emotionally spent, we perked up when we heard the sound of drums. It seemed we rolled once again into a presidential parade, except this time the cheering, the drums, the rattles, and the applause were for us.

Lining the sides of the road into Bumpe, villagers of all ages cheered as our car came to a stop. A masked devil with a vibrant crown in purples and pinks swirled in a dervish's frenzy. Women danced, palms upward, waving round gourds inside a long net, throwing rhythm in all directions. At the head of the crowd, at the end of the bridge, my father waited in a regal emerald green African shirt. His collar, outlined in glittering light green beadwork gave his attire a ceremonial air. My father deliberately wore the emerald green shirt as a reminder of my first trip in 2004 when the entire village wore matching emerald fabric.

My sister Jeneba stood at the foot of the bridge. She rushed the car, reached her hand in the open window and grabbed my hand.

"Hello! Jeneba! Good to see you!" I said. "Sorry it took us so long!" I sat with my mom and dad in the backseat. Von took the passenger seat up front. The rest of the group traveled in the second car ahead of us. "Look at the masked devils!" I said, pointing to the dusty, swirling figures.

"Bu Waa Besia!" I called out the window to the crowd. When the driver stopped the car, we slid out of the backseat to join the parade. My father, smiling and nervous, walked up to greet us the moment we exited the car. With the SUV's doors still open I jumped into the introductions.

"Hi!" I called to my father, smiling. "Taken us awhile to get here!"

My mom exited the car.

"This is my father," I said to my mom, introducing them. "Joe, this is my mom."

"Joooe! Hello!" she sang and reached out to give my father a big hug.

"Good to see you," he said, smiling from ear to ear.

"So good to see you," said my mom.

Jeneba stood right in front of my dad, Jim. "This is my sister, Jeneba," I said, introducing my dad to my half-sister.

"Jeneba!" said my dad, while shaking her hand in a traditional handshake that I taught him. In Sierra Leone a person shakes hands, links fingers, shakes again, and touches a palm to one's heart to pledge honor. "Nice to meet you."

When my dad, Jim, looked up he stood facing my father. "Hello, Joe," said my dad, smiling. He extended his hand, "It's been a long time!"

Everybody laughed. Then my dad Jim leaned in and hugged my father.

"Good to see you!" said my father Joe.

"This is wonderful, thank you," said my dad Jim.

My mom walked next to my father Joe. "I feel like I know you," she said smiling.

"Thank you, yeah," said my father Joe.

Together we walked toward the village—all of us part of the welcome parade. Three masked devils swooshed over the roads. Drummers pounded their instruments in hypnotizing beats. For a half mile we all walked in the parade with the people until my father asked us to get back into the car and drive to the village field where a ceremony awaited us. Like my first welcome in 2004, hundreds of people from the village and the neighboring villagers filled the bleachers.

A row of tables shaded under palm fronds anchored the clearing. At the center table sat my Aunt Amy, the Paramount Chief's wife, my mom, my dad, me, Von, Taraneh, and Yeniva. My father sat under the palm fronds, but off to the side to direct the night's program. My sister Jeneba glowed with happiness in the audience. One of the amputees whom I interviewed in 2004 sat in the circle with the villagers. Reverend Morlai, who welcomed me on my first trip and who spoke at my mother's memorial service, welcomed the crowd in both English and Mende. Two teenage boys played a Casio electric keyboard as five girls in blue dresses and three boys in their crisp school uniforms commenced the ceremony with a song: "Welcome in Jesus's name. You are welcome in Jesus's name."

The Reverend Morlai passed the microphone to me. I introduced my parents to the village, "This is my dad. This is my wonderful father Dr. Jim Culberson, my love and my dear father, my dad. The next person is my mother, my mom Judy, Judy Culberson." Then the Reverend Morlai pointed to me and reminded me to introduce myself. "Oh," I laughed, "And I'm Sarah!"

"Sarah Bumpenya Kposowa," the Reverend repeated.

My father then introduced most of the school staff and asked forgiveness if he forgot anyone. Before my parents took center stage, a traveling African student acting troupe trudged to the middle of the green to draw attention to a very serious problem in Sierra Leone: *Brain Drain.*

A tall man, dressed as an old man, sported a painted white beard and dressed in traditional clothing. He hobbled into the clearing. A beautiful young woman, in a long African skirt and bikini top walked slowly next to him. On top of her head rested a wooden bowl full of sand. Markings in white clay painted on her skin made her even more exotic. The male actor called out to the audience in long mellifluous sentences, as enunciated and dramatic as an ancient poem:

"Oh, Africa
Land of sunlight
And beautiful golden beaches

People of many languages
Living side by side
Oh, Africa
May God bless you
Oh, Africa
Land full of beauty of Creation.
Land of vegetation
Land full of rivers, lakes, and beaches
Land full of sunlight . . .

Oh, Africa, our motherland, land of origin. When people are giving birth to African children, these children are clothed in African dirt. These children run for the rest of their days under African sun and they never feel sick. These children, when it showers, they move under the shower and washed clearly with African pure rain. When night comes, at night she lights out a lamp called Moon. Many children come out in numbers. Some gather around their grandparents while others drew lines on the ground to play with Mama Africa.

When early in the morning, we are woked up by sweet melodious sounds by African birds and other creatures, but despite all this encouragement when we grow up we considered Africa, we look at Africa different . . . we look at Africa as a land full of poverty. A land full of people under the hands of the punishment of God.

Is that so, Africa is?

Thousands of people every day are planning to leave this land.

Another actor called out to young children walking across the green as part of the performance. "My daughters, where are you going?"

"I am going to London," a child called back.

"I am going to England," said another.

"Can't you come to Africa?" he said.

A group of girls strolled across the green. "Gentle ladies, where are you going?" he asked.

"We are going to America," they answered.

"Only, we, the old are in Africa. We are sorry," said the actor.

"Yet African friends and brothers. Do not look at Africa this way," said the first actor. Many people consider Africa the land of honor. Land full of people with creativity, talented people. Africa is a land of promise."

The simple performance proved as riveting, eloquent, and well-performed as Shakespeare in Central Park. The audience cheered as the three actors, Sylvester G. Karimu from Bo, William Coker from Kenema, and Margret George from Barta Taninahun, with a slow dignified gait left the green. We later found out the actors were all high school graduates who joined the volunteer group Student Partnership Worldwide. Together they traveled all over Sierra Leone giving performances. The actors wrote the "Oh, Africa" poem themselves.

Reverend Morlai took the microphone after the performance and said, "Our sister, our daughter is coming back to her home, to her village, to her country."

Then against all traditions, the microphone was passed to my Aunt Amy. My uncle, the Paramount Chief, needed to stay in Bo for the president's visit and could not be part of the celebration. Instead Aunt Amy addressed the crowd. Seated next to my mom, she stood up, bedecked in a silky dress and matching headscarf. The gorgeous silk resembled the color of the red dust roads, reinforcing Aunt Amy's image as an earth mother and a maternal force in Bumpe village. Dotted across her head tie and around her neckline was a repeated pattern of ivory-shaped cowrie shells.

She spoke to the people:

> "I am extremely happy. Two things I'm happy about. One that I have been asked to represent my husband to give a talk. Normally this shouldn't have happened ten years ago or more. We are always at the background. But the men have come a long way to meet the demands of society. Now we share fifty-fifty and the men are encouraging us to do so. So I say thank you to Joe Konia for giving me the chance to stand here and talk on behalf of his brother. He should have done it

normally, or another brother, but now I am so happy that you know I am worth something.

The second thing I am happy about is our guests, the Culberson family. I cannot tell you how happy I am to see these people. I have been dreaming of them, thinking of them and now eventually I've seen them I am bursting with happiness. When Bumpenya came, I looked at her, I lived with her, I talked with her, I knew exactly which type of people you were . . . you have really done a good job with this woman. I don't think if Sarah has come to Africa at that time, I don't think we would have done better than what you did with her. So it was a very, very lucky chance she had. So I thank you for all the good things you put in her. We are very very happy and according to our traditions, now Sarah has got two families. I don't think a lot of people are that lucky to have two fathers and two mothers . . . we love her very much.

According to African tradition you [Jim and Judy] are now our brother and you are now our sister. So on behalf of my husband and the whole family I welcome the Culberson family. You are always welcome here. Make here your home. I know you won't have time to visit us often, but please do whenever you can. And most of all, I thank you ever so much for the difference you've made in our lives. We will never forget. We promise that the Kposowa family, especially Joe Konia, will live up to your expectations. May God grant you and give you all you wish and may he provide for us so he can continue to help us. Thank you very much and I welcome you to the family."

I clapped heartily for my Aunt Amy whose strength and spirit was making a huge statement to every little girl in the village. To represent her husband in a welcome speech for important visitors was unheard-of; however, I knew that my father had to renegotiate traditional female roles every time he spoke with me. I completed a master's of fine arts in theater. My father also earned a master's degree. Most every time he introduced me to the village he mentioned my master's degree.

When I spoke with my sister Jeneba I asked her, "Do you ever want to get married sometime?"

She said, "Daddi said I have to get my education first so no man will ever take advantage of me."

After two additional speakers my father again took the microphone. I realized as he stood up that all three of my parents wore green. This coincidence was not consciously planned. My dad, Jim, wore a silky green button-down shirt and my mom wore an olive green top.

Now my father Joe spoke:

> "What has happened today is like a dream and I want to tell the entire people here that Sarah coming into my life has changed me completely. And praise goes to the Culberson family. I appreciate it a whole lot. What you have done for Sarah, you have done it also for me. And the only reward you can get is from the Almighty God.
>
> I want to again tell you, the Culberson family, that you are now part of the Kposowa family and I want you to ever remain to be members of the Kposowa family. I also want to tell you that the Kposowa family are also members of the Culberson family. I want it to be a very strong tie. And I know God is going to make it possible. Like I said, I said it is all a dream . . . I never thought I would ever see Sarah. It was like a dream when she came into my life . . . I saw her only when she was a baby and the other time I saw her was when she was twenty-eight years old and she has a master's degree.
>
> You have made Sarah for what she is today and I want to tell you that the Kposowa family is very grateful and will ever remain to be grateful to you. Since Sarah came into my life she has helped this school a whole lot. She has formed an organization that is greatly assisting this school. All the beautiful chairs you are seated on here are provided by her organization. Most of the books you see in the library are all provided by her organization. The furniture, her organization has helped even to put up a home economic building here and we are working on constructing that now. Her organization is also assisting some students who are walking five, ten miles to stay at the boarding house.
>
> I know the Culberson family from Morgantown, West Virginia. You have also helped. You people from Morgantown have helped us

rehabilitate the boarding house so our children can stay there. I want you to know it's from the people of West Virginia. I will never forget West Virginia because that is where I went to college . . . I want to tell you that you are all welcome."

Tears filled my eyes. I may have been the catalyst for these changes but without so many people jumping aboard, working tirelessly, giving so much, none of this would have happened. Without Morgantown, without my friends, without strangers who wanted to help, there would be nothing to connect. Because of the Morgantown fund-raiser, student dorms were rebuilt and many students who missed school when the rainy season started now had an education.

Another large fund-raiser in Los Angeles involved the help of an extraordinary thirteen-year-old girl, Jade Iovine, who started her own charity, Totes for Teens. Wanting to help African teenagers, Jade partnered with The Kposowa Foundation to raise money so teenagers in Bumpe could have bags full of soap, shampoo, toothbrushes, pencils, papers, jump ropes, puzzles, and books.

Now it was my turn to speak. It might have been easier to sing or dance to express my joy. With my parents sitting by my side, both being honored by my father, I could not ask for anything more. Though my parents did not come to be honored. They came because I asked them, and they came because they, too, wanted to help. My dad planned to assess the current water-well system in Bumpe, sketch out a plan to develop a clean-water system to help eradicate waterborne diseases, and submit a grant application that would unite the Rotary Club in Bo with the American Rotary Clubs in service.

My mom brought suitcases of school supplies. Fastened inside her bags, beautiful squares of origami paper in paisleys, checks, foils, and vivid colors waited to be distributed to the students. She planned an origami lesson so the children could make paper cranes for their dorms.

Would I ever stop dreaming? So many people showed up on this journey. I spoke into the wireless microphone:

"I have tears of joy coming up because this is, like my father said, a dream come true. To have my parents from West Virginia who raised

> me, here, in Sierra Leone in the Bumpe Chiefdom, to be here with so many loving friends and family and to be experiencing this moment of complete bliss and honor. Everyone here is so beautiful and so incredible and so powerful. This is beautiful for what you all arranged for my parents and my boyfriend and my friends to all be here. What you have done has brought us so much joy, and the tears coming from my eyes are tears of joy and tears of thanks and honor . . . it takes a village to build a village and we are all one. Coming from America we are all one with you. I honor you. I thank you. I love you all. Thank you."

The program my father made and distributed to the villagers highlighted a slot for my dad to speak. I handed the microphone to him. My dad stood up—the lone, tall, blue-eyed, white man in the crowd. First he repeated my name. The villagers called me, "Sarah Bumpenya Kposowa," but my dad repeated my other name.

"Sarah Culberson is a hard act to follow," he said.

I smiled and wanted to wink at him. I could not be Sarah Bumpenya Kposowa without being Sarah Culberson first. Without the strength and love from my family I would never have had the courage to reach out to a village. Next time I introduced myself I needed to string all the words together that created me: Sarah Jane Esther Elizabeth Metheny Culberson Bumpenya Kposowa. All the words and their cadences rounding out all that I have been and all that I am becoming.

Then my dad did something that probably elevated the status of women in Sierra Leone more than twenty years of education ever could. He said, "I hope you will allow me to ask my wife, Judy, to join me . . ."

When my dad, a highly respected doctor stood up to address the village, he included my mother. The village witnessed my parents standing together as equals. My dad continued:

> "I hope you will allow me to ask my wife, Judy, to join me for two reasons because we want to thank you all so much for your extraordinary welcome. We have lived for a long time, I'll just say more than sixty years—and we have never had an experience like the one we en-

joyed this afternoon when we entered Bumpe. The second reason that Judy is joining me is because I'm a professor and she is the only one here who will tell me that my allotted five minutes are gone.

"Several years ago when Sarah had her first conversation with Joseph Konia, I thought then, and I've been thinking ever since, what should I say when I finally have a chance to meet him. I thought of many things, so this may be a long speech, but when we got to Sierra Leone something happened.

"We've had only two days here. We walked the streets in the incredibly colorful and exciting and very, very energetic city of Freetown and today we drove for a very long time from Freetown and then we encountered the greeting for the President [of Sierra Leone] in Bo and then we came along and encountered the greeting for us in Bumpe. I think the celebration was bigger here in Bumpe. So I think, but I'm not sure, that what we want to say from the bottom of our heart is *Bi See Ka* [thank you] Bumpe.

"The reason that we are here is Sarah, and we found out a long time ago that Sarah has a gift for making people happy wherever she goes. So we think that it must be God's plan as Amy Kposowa already said, that Sarah should have two families instead of one so that she can make us all happy both here in Bumpe, in Sierra Leone, and back home in West Virginia and wherever she goes."

My dad passed the microphone to my mom. Allotted five minutes for a speech in the program, he gave up the last few minutes to her.

With no speech prepared my mother addressed the people of Bumpe. She wore an elegant scarf over her olive top, looking refined in spite of the previous nine hours of travel. To honor my father she wore an African beaded necklace I gave her as a gift from my first trip in 2004. True to my mom's character, even while giving an impromptu speech she never forgot my sisters who helped raise me as much as my parents.

"I'm standing in this beautiful spot that Sarah described after her first visit. She described her welcome and we could only imagine what that was for her then. And now we **know** what her welcome was—we experienced it! I want to just add special greetings from our two daughters who are in the United States, Lynne and Laura. They would love to be here. They, Lynne and Laura, and Jim and I have loved Sarah from the first moment we held her and from that moment we were connected with all of you."

The moon rose higher and higher in the sky. The same moon I gazed at back in Morgantown, the same moon I wished under long ago to find my birth parents. Like the African children who sing to the full moon, "*Ngawu nini la*—the moon has appeared, we are standing in appreciation," I wanted to sing, too. Sing to the full moon. Sing of families and bridges and rhythm. Sing of adoption and gratitude. Sing a song for my mother Penny who carried me pregnant and alone; whisper to my mother that her bravery and sacrifice is helping to change a village. Sing to the social worker who took my case and said to my parents, "This child is for you." Sing to my father Joe who accepted me into his family and let us move forward. In his youth when he did not have the means or the maturity to support me, he now supports a village. Sing to my sisters Lynne and Laura who embraced me as a blood sister and nothing less. Sing to my parents Jim and Judy who constantly see the best in others and ask how we can dig wells for all the children. Sing to my friends and family who keep stepping forward to make clean water, education, and health care a basic right for all babies born in America and Africa. That evening under the African moon, the American moon, and the world's lamp we all sang our collective story.

Index

YOUR VOICE CONNECTS THE WORLD AND MAKES A DIFFERENCE...

To learn more about the Kposowa Foundation please visit www.bumpefund.org